BATTLEFIELDS

The brave men, living and dead, who struggled here, have consecrated it, above our poor power to add or detract. The world will little note, nor long remember, what we say here, but it can never forget what they did here.

ABRAHAM LINCOLN (1809–1865) – GETTYSBURG ADDRESS

BATTLEFIELDS

Exploring the Arenas of War, 1805~1945

NH
NEW HOLLAND

CONSULTANT EDITOR MICHAEL RAYNER

First published in 2006 by New Holland Publishers
London • Cape Town • Sydney • Auckland
www.newhollandpublishers.com

86 Edgware Rd	14 Aquatic Drive	80 McKenzie St	218 Lake Road
London	Frenchs Forest	Cape Town	Northcote
W2 2EA	NSW 2086	8001	Auckland
United Kingdom	Australia	South Africa	New Zealand

ISBN 1 84537 175 5

Consultant editor   Michael Rayner
Publishing managers   Claudia dos Santos & Simon Pooley
Commissioning editor   Simon Pooley
Concept design   Geraldine Cupido
Designer   Nathalie Scott
Production editor   Anna Tanneberger
Illustrator   Steven Felmore
Cartographer   John Loubser
Picture researcher   Karla Kik
Production   Myrna Collins

Reproduction by Resolution, Cape Town
Printed and bound in Singapore by Tien Wah Press (Pte) Ltd
1 3 5 7 9 10 8 6 4 2

PAGE ONE *This tribute to an unidentified American soldier who died in the D-Day assault was placed on the shell-blasted shore of Normandy after the invasion.*

PREVIOUS SPREAD *Although vulnerable to artillery fire, tanks helped the infantry to cross otherwise impenetrable barbed wire, and provided cover and close supporting fire to an advance on foot. Photograph taken in Flanders.*

ABOVE Sari Bair *by Terence Cuneo. Major Allanson leads a battalion of the 6th Gurkha Rifles against the Turkish-held Sari Bair ridge in support of ANZAC units.*

OVERLEAF Waterloo *(oil on canvas) by George Jones, shows a typically over-dramatized version of the landscape, with Wellington in a blue cape on his chestnut, Copenhagen.*

Contents

INTRODUCTION

By Michael Rayner

Battlefields have long held a fascination for those who survived the conflicts and for those of later generations. Motives for visiting these sites, rather than merely reading about them, are many and varied, which remains the case for the modern battlefield tourist. For many in the past and present the main reason is for commemoration and remembrance, which helps to account for the large number of memorials and other monuments on battlefields. These can range from ancient trophies dedicated to the gods to a modern plaque put up by a regimental association. For many, the overriding reason to visit is the desire to improve understanding of the events which took place on the 'haunted acres' of the battlefield. Generals and military theorists have always understood the importance of the ground upon which a battle is fought, with the Roman writer Vegetius informing his audience that 'a large part of a victory depends on the actual place in which the battle is fought'. A visit to this ground is therefore essential for the military historian, so much so that many would hesitate if not always refrain from writing about a battle without visiting its site. This is because the battlefield is a historical source demanding attention, interpretation and understanding like any written or other account. To understand a battle, one has to understand the battlefield. To do this, the nature of the historic landscape first needs comprehension, by stripping away the post-battle layers of development and land-use to return to the battlefield as it was at the time of the action. Naturally, much of this work must be carried out through consulting historic maps and other records as well as through landscape archaeology and geology. However, a site visit will help to support or refute ideas from the written and pictorial record.

Misconceptions about a battlefield, and therefore the battle, often occur, with a good example being the nature of 'Wellington's' ridge at Waterloo. This is depicted in numerous paintings of the battle and described in many accounts, but when these are compared with one's own observations it soon becomes clear whether the writer or artist has actually visited the site. The ridge is often shown as too high or too steep, whereas it is a relatively gentle incline of no great height, which in many ways makes it such an outstanding choice as the main feature of Wellington's position. A visit will make this clear, but much more must be factored in: understanding how the construction of the Lion Mound has altered the ground; knowing which buildings were there at the time; how the field boundaries have changed; and how the roads and tracks have changed in their course and nature. The visit will also help with improving knowledge of the soil type and conditions, which had such an impact on 18 June 1815, as well as seeing where hedges, trees and woods had stood, which in turn help with understanding lines of sight and dead ground. Such features can influence any visit of any battlefield

ABOVE *Gettysburg National Military Park – view looking west across the northern face of Cemetery Hill, with the equestrian statue of Major General Winfield Scott Hancock, who helped to secure this hill on the evening of Day 1. Cemetery Hill was a potential hinge in the Union lines, and was grimly clung to by Meade's army throughout the fighting.*

and, when coupled with other natural factors such as the time of year at which the battle was fought and the weather conditions that prevailed at the time, can add further to one's appreciation of the battle and the commanders' and armies' actions.

This book focuses on a number of battles dating from the last two centuries that are worth a visit today. Although mainly featuring fighting on land, Pearl Harbor is included, while Arnhem also has an airborne dimension. Visits and tours can be of a personal nature, but all the battlefields featured here are also serviced by commercial tour operators. Therefore, all are safe to visit and have some facilities in terms of interpretation, presentation and comfort for the modern visitor. Battlefield tourism is a growth industry, which has encouraged the development of facilities and better on-site interpretation at many of these and other battlefields. Comparative visits to the Somme battlefield in 1980 and in 2005 would have revealed substantial progress in improving the experience for those visiting. At the earlier date even basic visitor facilities were hard to find, while in 2005 sensitively planned, modern facilities and interpretation have been provided at Newfoundland Memorial Park and Thiepval, while others such as at Delville Wood have been upgraded. The increase in visitor numbers has helped lead to these improvements, but there is a cost in terms of pressure on the often narrow roads and the sites themselves. For example, at Newfoundland Memorial Park, visitors may no longer roam across 'no-man's-land' at will, since the resulting erosion would destroy the very site the visitors wish to see. However, it is surely through the increasing popularity of battlefield sites as tourist and school party destinations that will help to ensure their preservation. In an ideal world these sites would be preserved for their historic significance, but sadly economic pressures frequently gain the upper hand, with the result that many battlefields have been lost or damaged. However, by proving the commercial value of battlefields, local and national authorities are more likely to uphold the preservation of the battlefield, instead allowing it to disappear under tarmac or housing. It is to be hoped that governments will acknowledge the historic importance of these sites, and do more to preserve battlefields and their archaeology.

ABOVE *The impressively massive Thiepval Memorial to the missing of the Somme, designed by Lutyens and listing over 73,000 British and South African soldiers who have no known grave. The adjacent cemetery has 300 French and 300 British graves.*

The reader will be pleased to know that the authors assembled to write each chapter are experts in and on their fields. All have in-depth personal knowledge of the sites, gained through research and personal visits to the sites. Many of the writers have also conducted tours of the battlefields they cover, with the result that the entries contain helpful visitor hints and insights of the terrain. With the good quality and range of mapping and illustrations the volume has much that can be enjoyed at home, with the book being a likely companion through the gloomier winter months, perhaps inspiring the reader to sally forth in the spring or summer to visit at least some of these fascinating and significant sites of what Winston Churchill termed the 'punctuation marks of history'.

Napoleonic Wars

1805 – 1815

By Michael Rayner

The Napoleonic Wars is the name given to the period of warfare primarily between France, Great Britain, Prussia, Russia and Austria from 1804 – when Napoleon Bonaparte became emperor of France – to 1815 when the war finished at the end of the Campaign of the Hundred Days. Some writers would start the period with Napoleon becoming First Consul of France in 1799. In addition, the Napoleonic Wars were an extension of the French Revolutionary Wars, begun in 1792 and continuing throughout the remainder of the 1790s. In many ways this period of virtually unrelenting warfare can be seen as a world war, 100 years before the start of the more widely recognized World War I. Fighting against France and her sister republics, satellite states and allies was widespread, not only across the entire continent of Europe, but into the Middle East and the Indian subcontinent. The war of 1812 between Britain and the USA is also directly related to the conflict with Napoleon, while naval warfare took place around the globe.

The wars follow a pattern of rise and fall, with Napoleon scoring a string of brilliant victories against the armies of the opposing coalition powers, before experiencing a general decline and defeats for his armies until his final downfall at Waterloo. Throughout the period Napoleon was unable to make headway against British naval power, especially after the battle of Trafalgar (1805). On land his early successes were due in large part to the superiority of his armies, fighting in a more flexible way to that of his enemies and with greater vigour, thanks to changes in warfare during the 1790s. Napoleon's generalship also played a part in this success, although writers disagree as to the extent of this as a key factor, some preferring to single out the weaknesses of the allied generals and their armies – or even Napoleon's good luck. Whatever the causes, his armies won a series of stunning victories: at Austerlitz against the Austrians and Russians in 1805; at Jena and Auerstädt against Prussia in 1806; versus Russia at Friedland in 1807; against Austria at Wagram in 1809.

The armies of the coalition had started to reorganize their forces and tactics on the French model by 1809, leading to harder won victories for Napoleon. He overreached himself after deciding to invade Portugal in 1807 and then imposing French rule on Spain in 1808, events which led to the Peninsular War. Part of the reason for this was to impose his Continental System of trade embargoes against Britain, which later led to his disastrous invasion of Russia in 1812. In the Peninsular War, Britain was able to gain a foothold for her army in Europe, fighting alongside Portuguese and Spanish forces, leading to a string of victories in the field for General Arthur Wellesley (the Duke of Wellington), including those at Talavera, Salamanca and Vittoria.

Despite these setbacks for his forces, Napoleon invaded Russia in 1812, leading to the hard-fought battle of Borodino and the capture of Moscow, before a catastrophic retreat. Following this disaster, the coalition opposing him strengthened, acting in a more coordinated way than before, leading to the Battle of Leipzig, or the Battle of the Nations, in 1813. A defensive campaign in France could not prevent defeat and abdication for Napoleon. Exiled to Elba in the Mediterranean in May 1814, he escaped in February 1815 to become emperor once more. This led to the Campaign of the Hundred Days and his ultimate defeat at Waterloo, bringing to an end not only his rule, but an era.

AUSTERLITZ 1805

By Michael Hannon

The Peace of Amiens was no more than a temporary truce, and resumption of the war was inevitable. Following the coronation of Napoleon as Emperor of the French on 2 December 1804, the British Prime Minister, William Pitt, successfully organized the third allied coalition (see panel opposite for background).

Austria and Russia began another attempt to restore the situation to that of 1789 and Napoleon realized that the invasion plan would have to be shelved for the time being. Striking camp at Boulogne on 23 August, the Grande Armée was on the Rhine a month later. Never before had such a force been assembled and moved with such speed and precision. French organization and staff work was impeccable, and the standard of training of the rank and file was far superior to that of any enemy. It was organized in seven army corps, totalling nearly 220,000 men, including 30,000 cavalry and nearly 400 guns.

As so often among allies, the enemy suffered from confusion, not least because Russia was still using the Julian calendar, so a difference of ten days between dates went unnoticed until vital deadlines were missed. The Russian army of General Kutuzov arrived on the River Inn ten days after it was expected by the Austrians. Furthermore, they were not entirely agreed on priorities; the Austrians wanted the main effort in Northern Italy; the British urged for it to be in central Germany, with a view to involving Prussia; Russia was mistrusted by both for its designs on Poland and preoccupation with the Turks, and was anyway very slow to mobilize.

Austria and Russia were each to provide three armies, none of them in a very high state of training. The nominal Austrian commanders were three of the brothers of the Emperor Francis II, who himself was commander in chief. The Archduke Charles had the army in Italy, John was in the Tyrol and Ferdinand (with General Karl Mack at his elbow) in Bavaria. The Russian commanders were Kutuzov, Buxhöwden and Bennigsen. Kutuzov was advancing slowly through Moravia. Duke Feodor Feodorovich (Friedrich Wilhelm) Buxhöwden and Bennigsen, both waited for permission from Prussia to move across Silesia.

The Grande Armée crossed the Rhine on 25 September, and, by mid-October, most of Archduke Ferdinand's army was surrounded at Ulm. Ferdinand himself deserted General Mack, who was thus obliged to surrender on 20 October. The French took between 50,000 and

ABOVE *Mack, the most effective of the Austrian generals, offers his sword to Napoleon in surrender. Returning the sword, Napoleon sought to console him with the words 'All empires come to an end.'*

PREVIOUS PAGE *Colour lithograph by Sullivan. The symbolic fall of Napoleon at the Battle of Waterloo, as the Eagle of the French 45th Line Infantry is taken by Sergeant Ewart of the Scots Greys.*

THE TIGER AND THE SHARK

During the first few years of the French Revolution, 1789–92, the other four powers were more or less content with events in France. Great Britain foresaw an opportunity to enlarge her empire at the expense of her long-standing enemy, and the others (Austria, Russia and Prussia) were more concerned with acquiring as large a share as possible of Poland. But it soon became apparent that the French were determined to export their revolutionary principles to all of Europe, if not the world; so war was inevitable.

Between 1792 and 1799 France established control of most of the European mainland, but surrendered control of the seas to Britain's Royal Navy. The destruction of the French fleet at the Battle of the Nile in August 1798 was the thin end of the wedge that would eventually crush Napoleon's Empire. By the time the Peace of Amiens was signed in March 1802, the situation was that of 'the Tiger and the Shark': Britain had a navy but no available army due to operations in India; France had a vastly superior army. Neither was capable of inflicting much damage on the other. Britain therefore needed to hire some help to maintain the balance of power and had resorted to subsidizing the armies of Austria and Russia.

Napoleon, established as First Consul of France in February 1800, appreciated that to achieve his objective of European hegemony he must, sooner or later, eliminate England from the equation. He planned an invasion, and the Grande Armée of some 220,000 men was concentrated at Boulogne. Training was rigorous, discipline strict, and morale high. Furthermore, the army was now organized into corps of two or more divisions, each having its own dedicated staff officers, and its own infantry regiments, cavalry, artillery and wagon trains. It was this combination of training, morale, mutually supporting arms and organization which was to win the Battle of Austerlitz.

60,000 prisoners, who marched out of the town the following day. As they did so, Lord Nelson was destroying the combined fleets of France and Spain off Cape Trafalgar. The Shark was now supreme on the oceans; the Tiger was about to demonstrate invincibility on land.

Learning of the disaster at Ulm, Kutuzov, whose army had at last reached the River Inn, decided to withdraw eastward along the Danube. He was fortunate to cross unopposed to the north bank on 10 November, and then was narrowly denied an opportunity to destroy the French VIII Corps at Dürnstein. The French entered Vienna on 13 November, and successfully bluffed their way across the one remaining bridge to the north bank. A rearguard action by General Bagration ensured the smooth withdrawal of Kutuzov's force and concentration of the allied armies in the area of Olmutz.

Napoleon spent a few days at the Palace of Schönbrunn, just outside Vienna, where his quartermasters were helping themselves to the contents of the enormous arsenal, before heading north to join the advance guard on 17 November. Yet another arsenal

LEFT *Following his successful counterattack against the Russian Imperial Guard, General Rapp, one of Napoleon's aides-de-camp, presents his prisoners, among whom is the commander of the Tsar's personal guard, Prince Repnin.*

fell into his hands when Brünn, or Brnõ, was captured on the 18th. The next few days were spent resting and re-organizing. Napoleon certainly realized the risk he was taking with a long line of communication requiring substantial detachments. Away to the northwest, the few of Archduke Ferdinand's forces to escape from Ulm were being watched by the Corps of Marshal Bernadotte; and the city of Vienna was secured by the III Corps of Marshal Davout.

MAIN CHARACTERS FEATURED

OPPOSING NAPOLEON
Alexander I, Tsar of Russia
Francis II, Holy Roman
    Emperor and Emperor of
    Austria
General Mikhail Illarionovitch
    Kutuzov
General Mack, Baron Karl
    Mack von Leiberich
General Peter Bagration
Prince Repnin (Tsar's personal
    guard)
General Feodor Buxhöwden
General Levin August
    Bennigsen

GRANDE ARMÉE
Marshal Jean Lannes (V Corps)
Marshal Jean-Baptiste Jules

Bernadotte (I Corps)
Marshal Louis Nicolas Davout
    (III Corps)
General Anne Jean Marie
    René Savary
Marshal Nicolas-Jean de Dieu
    Soult (IV Corps)
Marshal Joachim Murat
    (reserve cavalry)
General Dominique Joseph
    René Vandamme
General Louis Vincent St
    Hilaire
General Nicolas Charles
    Oudinot (Grenadiers)
General Legrand
Marshal Jean-Baptiste
    Bessières (Imperial Guard)
General Jean Rapp

Tsar Alexander I | *Marshal Jean-Baptiste Bessières*

ALLIED MISJUDGEMENT

The allied staff had also noted the risk Napoleon was running, concluding, wrongly, that the French were in an increasingly weak position. In fact, of course, Napoleon was planning the concentration necessary for the coming battle. To help assess the enemy strength he sent General Savary to the allied camp with the offer of negotiations. This reinforced the belief of the younger staff in French weakness, although the experienced Kutuzov advised further withdrawal, suggesting that Napoleon would not dare to extend his line of communication even more.

The weather was foul and, unlike the French, whose men were well fed and enthusiastic, the Allies were suffering from the cold and lack of supplies. Having overruled Kutuzov's advice, Alexander and Francis had no alternative but to advance, with a view to cutting Napoleon's communication with Vienna. On 28 November Marshal Soult's advance guard was attacked just east of the village of Austerlitz and, following Napoleon's orders, fell back to a position west of the Goldbach (golden brook). This withdrawal finally convinced the inexperienced allied staff that the French were trying to avoid a battle, and the Tsar ordered the occupation of the high ground around the village of Pratzen. In fact, Napoleon's preparations were going smoothly. The Santon hill was fortified with trenches and a battery of eight guns, and orders had been despatched to Bernadotte and Davout to join the rest of the army by forced marching. Appreciating the allied intention, Napoleon relied on Davout's III Corps to hold the right at all costs.

Allied staff work was very poor, resulting in a chaotic attempt to deploy during the night of 1 December. It is said that the allied commanders took a very casual attitude to the situation, only a few of them bothering to review the plan on the map. Written orders were despatched very late, some not arriving until after the battle began shortly before dawn on 2 December.

NAPOLEON'S PLAN

Napoleon's initial appreciation was that the Allies would attack at Kobelnitz, but during the night the sounds of movements convinced him that they would actually go further south towards Telnitz and Sokolnitz. This suited him well for, provided Davout could frustrate their attempt to cut him off from Vienna, they would be encouraged to reinforce their left wing by withdrawing troops from the centre. The allied right, under General Bagration, would be held by the Santon position and the V Corps of Marshal Lannes, supported by Murat's reserve cavalry and Bernadotte's corps. Once the enemy centre was weakened, his main counterattack would be made by IV Corps in the centre, under Marshal Soult, with the divisions of St Hilaire and Vandamme. The Imperial Guard and Oudinot's Grenadiers would form a strong reserve.

RIGHT *Napoleon met Emperor Francis II of Austria on 4 December and agreed an armistice, embodied in the harsh terms of the Treaty of Pressburg, which was signed on 26 December 1805.*

At first the allied attacks were successful at both Telnitz and Sokolnitz, but staff and command failures denied them consolidation and General Legrand's division was able to hold the situation. A thick mist hid Soult's other two divisions behind the Goldbach from allied observation. It was cold, but there was a slight thaw. Hail and rain had made the night miserable for everyone, further undermining allied morale. Sunrise, at 08:00, revealed large numbers of Russian troops moving southward across the centre of the battlefield. Napoleon asked Soult for his estimate of the time it would take for his men to reach the Pratzen feature. 'Twenty minutes, Sire', said the Marshal, 'for my troops are hidden by the mist and smoke'.

'Very well', said the Emperor 'we shall wait fifteen minutes'. About 09:00, 'The Sun of Austerlitz' at last burned through the mist. Half an hour later the French central attack was going well, with St Hilaire's division on the Pratzen hill and Vandamme's on the Vinohrady feature. The Russian Imperial Guard made a spirited cavalry counterattack, which might well have resulted in a major crisis for Napoleon – had they not advanced at the trot over much too great a distance, arriving winded when joining the battle. Marshal Bessières restored the position by sending General Rapp with two squadrons of Chasseurs and the Mamelukes of Napoleon's guard. This famous engagement was later immortalized in the painting by Gerard, depicting Rapp, his sabre broken, reporting to the Emperor with his prisoners, including Prince Repnin, commander of the Tsar's personal guard, together with its colour.

FINAL STAGES OF THE BATTLE

By 14:00 French army headquarters had moved to the Chapel of St Anthony, where Napoleon issued fresh orders for the final stages of the battle. Bernadotte was ordered to hold the Pratzen feature, and the Guard, Oudinot and Soult were to envelop the enemy left (Bux-höwden's force), defeat of which was nothing less than a rout. Many eminent historians claim that Napoleon ordered the frozen 'ponds' near the village of Satchen to be shelled, thus drowning many of the fleeing Allies. However, when drained on Napoleon's orders

between 8 and 12 December 1805, the bodies of only two Russians were found. Nevertheless the Allies suffered casualties amounting to about 15,000 killed and wounded and 12,000 prisoners, as well as 180 guns and 50 colours. French losses were reported as 1305 killed, 6940 wounded and 573 captured.

TOURING THE BATTLEFIELD TODAY

Today, the battlefield of Austerlitz is relatively unspoiled. The recommended map is the 1:30,000 *SLAVKOV – Austerlitz, bitva tri cisarú* ISBN 80-85302-03-9 published by Geodézie Brnõ, 1991. On the site of Napoleon's tactical headquarters stands a memorial installed in 1930 and bearing an engraved sketch map of the battle. It is, of course, the ideal viewpoint from which to view the area, and is easy to find, just off the old Olmutz road (Route 403, Olomoucke

BATTLE NAME

The battle of Austerlitz took place short of the village of that name. It is said that on the eve of the battle the emperors of Austria and Russia had slept at the chateau of Austerlitz, and when Napoleon drove them from this, he wished to heighten his triumph by giving that name to the battle.

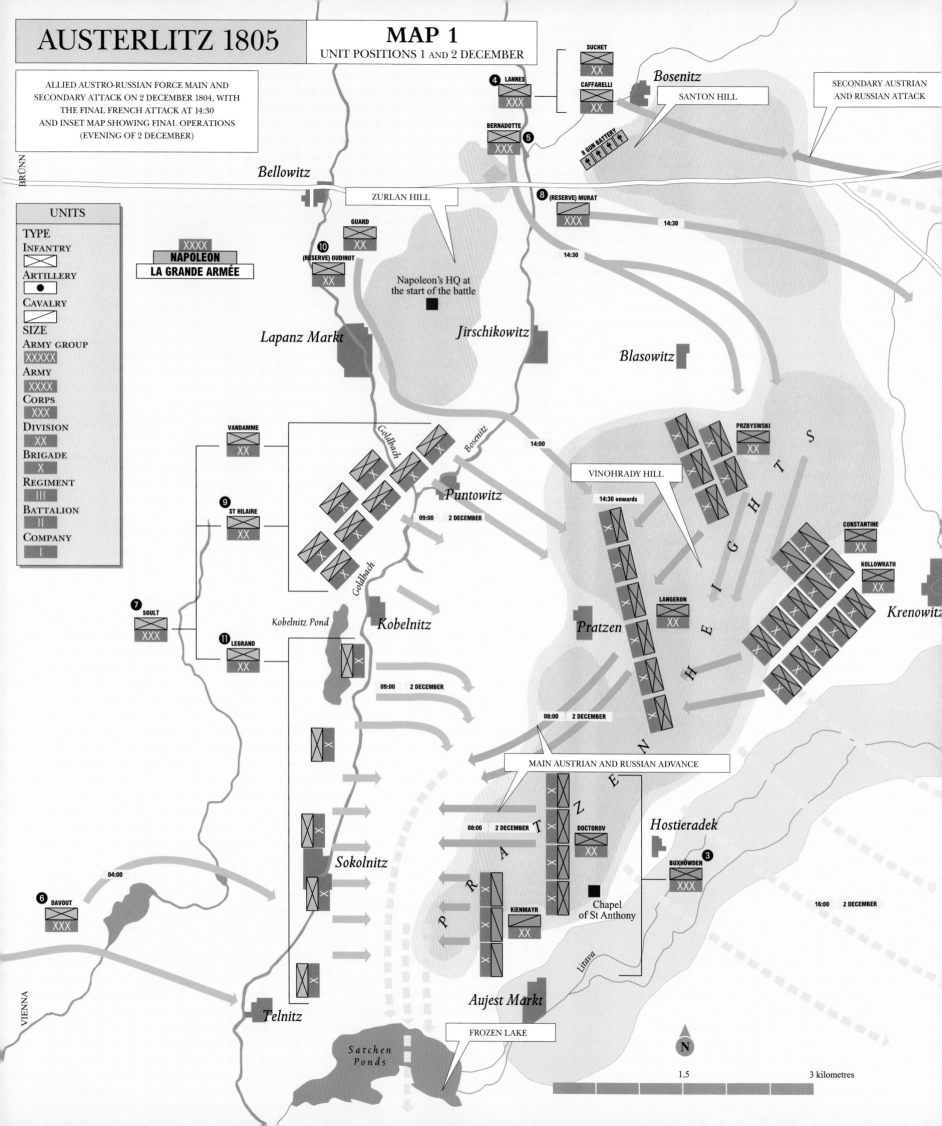

AUSTERLITZ 1805

MAP 1
UNIT POSITIONS 1 AND 2 DECEMBER

ALLIED AUSTRO-RUSSIAN FORCE MAIN AND
SECONDARY ATTACK ON 2 DECEMBER 1804, WITH
THE FINAL FRENCH ATTACK AT 14:30
AND INSET MAP SHOWING FINAL OPERATIONS
(EVENING OF 2 DECEMBER)

SECONDARY AUSTRIAN
AND RUSSIAN ATTACK

BRÜNN

SUCHET

4 LANNES

CAFFARELLI

Bosenitz

SANTON HILL

BERNADOTTE 5

8 GUN BATTERY

Bellowitz

ZURLAN HILL

8 (RESERVE) MURAT

14:30

GUARD

14:30

10 (RESERVE) OUDINOT

UNITS

TYPE
INFANTRY

ARTILLERY ●

CAVALRY

SIZE
ARMY GROUP XXXX

ARMY XXXX

CORPS XXX

DIVISION XX

BRIGADE X

REGIMENT III

BATTALION II

COMPANY I

NAPOLEON
LA GRANDE ARMÉE

Napoleon's HQ at
the start of the battle

Lapanz Markt

Jirschikowitz

Blasowitz

Goldbach

Bosenitz

VANDAMME

14:00

PRZBYSWSKI

VINOHRADY HILL

Puntowitz

14:30 onwards

09:00   2 DECEMBER

9 ST HILAIRE

CONSTANTINE

Goldbach

KOLLOWRATH

Krenowitz

7 SOULT

Goldbach

LANGERON

Kobelnitz Pond

Kobelnitz

Pratzen

11 LEGRAND

09:00   2 DECEMBER

08:00   2 DECEMBER

MAIN AUSTRIAN AND RUSSIAN ADVANCE

Hostieradek

08:00   2 DECEMBER

DOCTOROV

VIENNA

04:00

Sokolnitz

BUXHÖWDEN 3

16:00   2 DECEMBER

6 DAVOUT

KIENMAYR

Chapel
of St Anthony

Litava

Telnitz

Aujest Markt

FROZEN LAKE

Satchen
Ponds

N

1.5   3 kilometres

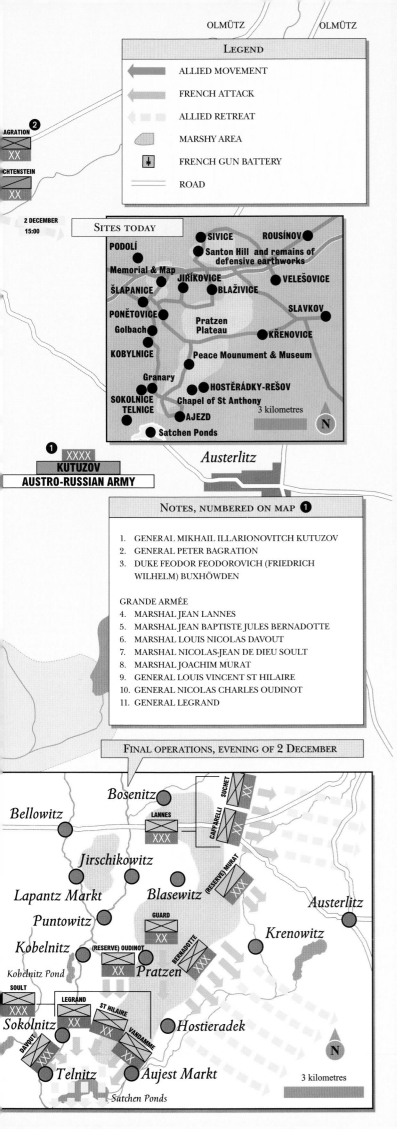

Strasse) about 9km (6 miles) east of Brnõ (Brünn). One can appreciate how the low mist hid Soult's troops along the Goldbach in the early hours, while allowing observation of the enemy on the Pratzen plateau beyond. One can walk up the Santon hill and see the remains of the defensive earthworks. On the hill south of the village of Pratzen is the Peace Monument and a small museum.

At Sokolnitz, the castle mentioned in many accounts was no more than a large country house, which was destroyed at an early stage of the battle. The present house was built some years afterwards. Nearby, however, is a huge granary similar to the one which formed the defensive bastion at Essling during the battle of 1809.

Near the village of Zatcany (Satchen) the flat fields around the Litava river (now controlled) were once the famous Satchen Ponds.

No tour of the site would be complete without a visit to Schloss Kaunitz, where Napoleon's headquarters moved after the battle.

AUSTERLITZ TIMELINE

25 September Grande Armée crosses the Rhine.
Mid-October Most of Archduke Ferdinand's army surrounded at Ulm.
20 October General Mack obliged to surrender.
10 November Kutuzov's army crosses the Danube unopposed to the north bank after reaching the River Inn and withdrawing eastward along the Danube.
13 November The French enter Vienna and bluff their way across the one remaining bridge to the north bank.
17 November Napoleon heads north to join the advance guard.
18 November Arsenal at Brünn (Brnõ) captured by Napoleon
28 November Marshal Soult's advance guard is attacked just east of the village of Austerlitz and, following Napoleon's orders, falls back to a position west of the Goldbach.
1 December Chaotic attempt by allied staff to deploy during the night.
2 December Shortly before dawn, battle begins.
    08:00 Sunrise reveals large numbers of Russian troops moving southward across the centre of the battlefield. Soult estimates it would take his men 20 minutes to reach the Pratzen feature.
    09:00 'The Sun of Austerlitz' burns through the mist.
    09:30 The French central attack going well, with St Hilaire's division on the Pratzen hill and Vandamme's on the Vinhorady feature. The Russian Imperial Guard makes a spirited cavalry counterattack, but arrive winded. General Rapp restores the position, with two squadrons of Chasseurs and the Mamelukes of Napoleon's guard.
    14:00 French army headquarters has moved to the Chapel of St Anthony. Napoleon issues fresh orders for the final stages of the battle. Bernadotte is ordered to hold the Pratzen feature, and the guard, Oudinot and Soult to envelop the enemy left (Buxhöwden's force), resulting in a rout.

JENA AND AUERSTÄDT 1806

By Michael Hannon

The events of Tuesday 14 October 1806 are among the most memorable and extraordinary in all the annals of military history: 'Napoleon won a battle he could not lose, while Davout won a battle he could not win,' to quote military historian Major General J.F.C. Fuller. The story of these battles really begins in 1805, when the French I Corps of Marshal Bernadotte had marched without permission through the Prussian province of Ansbach, on its way to take part in the Battle of Ulm, which resulted in the surrender of most of the Austrian army under General Mack. The Prussian Foreign Minister, Karl von Haugwitz, (who believed Prussia should remain neutral, and was thus not a particularly good choice of messenger with an ultimatum), was dispatched to find Napoleon and threaten retaliation. At Brnõ (Brünn) the Emperor had given him an audience, but declined to negotiate, being too busy with preparations for the crushing French victory at Austerlitz on 2 December. Von Haugwitz was invited to go on to Vienna, where he would meet his French opposite number, Talleyrand. By the time Napoleon returned to Vienna in December, all von Haugwitz could do was to offer

congratulations on the victory. However, one of the terms of the Treaty of Schönbrunn, which established peace between Austria and France, was that Prussia would be mollified by the acquisition of the state of Hannover.

The bulk of the French army (except for the Imperial Guard, which had returned to Paris) remained east of the Rhine, acting as an incentive to the German princes to sign up as members of the new Confederation of the Rhine – Napoleon's enforced replacement for the old Holy Roman Empire. But Saxony vacillated, despite warnings from France, eventually deciding to ally herself with Prussia, where the continued presence in Germany of French troops was seen by the high command as an affront. Furthermore, Napoleon was having second thoughts about the allocation of Hannover to Prussia, offering to return it to England in exchange for lasting peace. The news of this proposition infuriated the war party, led by the beautiful Queen Louise (colonel in chief of the 'Queen's Hussars') and Prince Louis Ferdinand, who persuaded the King, Frederick William III, to attack Napoleon.

On 10 August 1806, Prussia began to mobilize. King Frederick William was the nominal commander in chief, but had no military experience, and thus appointed Field Marshal von Mollendorf (aged 81) as his advisor. His immediate military subordinates, the Duke of Brunswick, Prince von Hohenlohe and

ABOVE The Battle of Jena, *watercolour on paper by Jean Antoine Simeon Fort, showing the large scale of Napoleonic battles, with massed formations of infantry in the middle distance.*

General Rüchel, were all sure of their own ability, and each had personal access to the King – the result was that planning for the forthcoming campaign was confused, and there was no clear and firm chain of command. Decisions were, more often than not, taken at 'councils of war', where everyone present thought his ideas the best. Furthermore, the Prussian generals were quite convinced of their superiority over the French. Several had served under the 'Old Fritz', Frederick the Great. One or two of them had actually been present, as young captains, at the Battle of Rossbach, on 5 November 1757. Only Prince Louis Ferdinand, at 34, was of comparable age to his French counterparts. The Duke of Brunswick was 71, his chief of staff, General von Scharnhorst, was 61, Field Marshal Hohenlohe was 60 and General Blücher 61. On the other hand, Napoleon was 37, and several of his Marshals about the same age.

The Prussians, and their less-than-enthusiastic Saxon allies, were organized in three army groups. The main army, with which both the King and the Queen travelled, was about 50,000 strong, and commanded by the Duke of Brunswick. The second army group was initially of similar strength, with Prince von Hohenlohe at its head, and the third was a reserve force of about 25,000 men under General Rüchel. The latter included the cavalry division of General Blücher. The Prussian plan for the campaign was confused, but eventually the armies moved to the area of Erfurt, Weimar and Jena, with a view to cutting off the French from the Rhine. After one of the many councils of war, Von Scharnhorst, one of the few Prussian officers who properly appreciated the capabilities of the French army, remarked, 'I know very well what we should do. What we shall do only the gods know.' What he knew they should do was to remain east of the Elbe, there to await Russian support, for Russia was still technically at war with France.

Napoleon promptly sent orders to Marshal Berthier to prepare a plan for concentration around Bamberg. Hundreds of German-speaking officers were now despatched to reconnoitre the routes to Berlin, the bridges and fortifications, especially those at Magdeburg, Wittenberg, Torgau and Dresden. On 12 September, Napoleon wrote to the Prussian King, 'If I am forced to take up arms to defend myself it will be with great regret. The interests of our two countries are so close.' That same day the Prussians marched into Dresden.

On 15 September, the Emperor ordered the Imperial Guard back to Germany. The operation was a complicated one, organized by the Director General of Posts, Lavalette. The *postes* in France were every two leagues (four leagues in Germany). 13,000 horses and 3259 vehicles were needed; each horse was paid for at the rate of 5 francs per day. In the event, only about 4000 infantry of the Guard, together with 40 guns, arrived in time for the Battle of Jena. The advance to war continued, with the French pushing northeastward

MAIN CHARACTERS FEATURED

FRANCE
Marshal Berthier
Marshal Bernadotte, I Corps
Lavalette, Director General
  of Posts,
Marshal Augereau (VII Corps)
Sergeant Major Guindet
  (French 10th Hussars)

Auerstädt
Marshal Davout (III Corps)
General Gudin
General Friant
General Morand

Jena
Emperor Napoleon Bonaparte
Marshal Ney (VI Corps)
Marshal Lannes (V Corps)
Marshal Soult (IV Corps)
Marshal Murat (cavalry)
General St Hilaire

PRUSSIA/SAXONY
Field Marshal von Mollendorf
General Blücher (cavalry)
Prince Louis Ferdinand
General von Wartensleben

Auerstädt
King Frederick William
  commander in chief
Duke of Brunswick
General von Schmettau
General von Scharnhorst
  (Prussian chief of staff)

Jena
Prince von Hohenlohe
General von Tauentzien
General von Holtzendorf
General Grawert
General Rüchel

Marshal Davout   *Duke of Brunswick*

towards Leipzig in three columns. The central column was preceded by the light cavalry of Marshal Murat's reserve force, and led by I Corps (Marshal Bernadotte) with III Corps (Marshal Davout) following. On the right were IV Corps (Marshal Soult) and VI Corps

(Marshal Ney). On the left were V Corps (Marshal Lannes) and VII Corps (Marshal Augereau). The whole totalled about 170,000 men and over 300 guns. Napoleon's orders were that the advance should proceed so that the entire army could concentrate on any one of its components within 48 hours. He likened the movement to that of a battalion square – and his nickname for this army formation was his *Bataillon Carré*.

A skirmish at Schleiz, on 8 October, resulted in the Prussians falling back towards Jena, but the first major engagement came at Saalfeld, on 10 October, where the advance guard of Hohenlohe's army under Prince Louis Ferdinand was routed by Marshal Lannes' V Corps, and the prince himself was killed by Sergeant-Major Guindet of the French 10th Hussars. This event had a serious effect on Prussian morale, and also reduced Hohenlohe's effective strength for the coming battle of Jena to around 40,000 men.

By 12 October, the Prussians were trying to concentrate between Jena and Weimar. From intelligence reports, Napoleon appreciated there was an opportunity to cut them off from Leipzig and ordered Davout to advance to Naumburg, while Bernadotte was to clear the main road to Leipzig. The remainder of the Bataillon Carré would swing westwards to engulf the enemy. Unknown to him, however, the Prussian high command held a council of war that evening, at which it was decided that Brunswick's main army, reinforced by Blücher's cavalry, would withdraw northward, covered by Hohenlohe at Jena and by Rüchel (now only 15,000 strong) at Weimar.

THE BATTLE OF JENA

During 13 October, Marshal Lannes' V Corps entered the town of Jena, and his advance guard clambered up the steep slope of the Landgrafenberg. The countryside north of Jena forms a large rolling plateau of farms and villages, with very steep wooded slopes on the south (the valley of the Muhlbach) and east (the valley of the River Saale). Roads, or rather tracks, to the high ground were few and tortuous; the only one immediately accessible is nowadays called 'Am Steiger'. French engineers set to work to improve it. Late in the afternoon, Napoleon himself, together with the 4000 infantry of the Guard, arrived on the Landgrafenberg and, as night fell, he could see the campfires of Hohenlohe's force, and somehow convinced himself that the whole Prussian army of over 100,000 men lay before him.

Although arguably the greatest commander in modern history, Napoleon shared with others, both before and since, a serious shortcoming, namely the temptation to believe that intelligence reports endorsed his own suppositions. As night fell, observation of the relatively few campfires of Hohenlohe's force firmly convinced him that he now faced the main body of the Prussians. Orders were given for the corps of Augereau, Ney and Soult to close up without delay. Davout, with III Corps, now at Naumburg, was ordered to advance on Apolda to threaten what Napoleon fondly believed would be the Prussian left rear. Berthier's postscript to Davout's orders suggested that I Corps should act in support of III Corps, and Davout immediately sent a written copy to Bernadotte.

During the night of 13 October, Napoleon, noting an apparent delay in the arrival of V Corps artillery, went personally to find out where it was. The column had mistaken the route up the hill and the leading gun had somehow become hopelessly stuck in a ravine. The Emperor immediately took charge, as if he were once again the battery commander, and the column soon moved on again.

Concentration of the Bataillon Carré now proceeded apace. Augereau's VII Corps was ordered to secure the road from Jena to Weimar, along the Muhltal, with one division, while the remainder were to form on the left of V Corps. In view of the steep wooded slope it is not too surprising that the

LEFT *Joachim Murat, the Emperor's flamboyant, brave and foolhardy brother-in-law, and one of the great cavalry officers of history, leads from the front as thousands of Napoleon's cavalry reserve pursue the Prussians.*

junction was not established until about 09:30. VI Corps (Marshal Ney) was ordered to form on the right of V Corps and Soult's IV Corps was to form on the extreme right flank. At dawn on the 14th, despite the best efforts of all concerned, the French position was relatively weak, with only V Corps and the Guard properly deployed, perhaps 25,000 men in all. The Prussians thus had a golden opportunity to sweep them off the plateau and into the Saale, but it seems that Hohenlohe had received an order from the King that no serious engagement was to be undertaken. In any case, Napoleon intended to be the first to strike. At 06:30, in a thick fog, Lannes launched two divisions in an attack on the village of Closewitz.

The main body of Hohenlohe's army, now only about 40,000 strong altogether, had camped for the night along the general line Isserstadt, Lützeroda, Closewitz, with outposts in Cospeda. Commanding this main force was General von Tauentzien. The left flank was guarded by a detachment of about 5000 men under General von Holtzendorf. The reserves, including General Grawert's division, were posted on the Dornberg, overlooking the villages of Vierzehnheiligen and Krippendorf, where the windmill provided a useful reference point for both sides.

In the fog, Lannes' leading troops somewhat lost their way, but broke the Prussian line between Closewitz and Lützeroda. However, St Hilaire's division, part of Soult's IV Corps, and with the Marshal himself at its head, cleared the enemy from Closewitz, and then advanced to Rodigen. Thus, when Ney arrived with his small advance guard, he found Lannes' right in touch with St Hilaire's division, but his left apparently open to counterattack. Meanwhile, Lannes himself had at first taken the village of Vierzehnheiligen, but then been forced to withdraw to the lower slopes of the Dornberg. The fiery Ney, despite having only his small advance guard to hand, immediately attacked to retake the village, but, carried away with his own excitement, quite overlooked the need for support and was soon isolated. Fortunately for him, the Emperor, from his vantage point on the hill overlooking the village, noticed what had happened. Furious with Ney, who received a severe reprimand later in the day, he despatched some cavalry to rescue his impetuous Marshal.

Hohenlohe (who appears to have thought the French operations were merely those of the advance guard) at last realized he needed to make a serious counterattack on Vierzehnheiligen. What followed was one of the most pitiful and extraordinary events in all military history. The Prussian infantry of General Grawert's division, magnificently drilled as they were, advanced as if on a parade ground, halting to fire volleys from time to time. The French infantry, on the other hand, supported by artillery, were firing as individuals from the cover provided by the shattered village. For the French it was like target practice; for the brave Prussians it was a terrible disaster. For two hours or so, they were shot down, standing in the ranks, exposed to the merciless fire of grapeshot and musketry.

Meanwhile, as the remainder of IV, VI and VII Corps arrived, together with most of Murat's cavalry reserve, Napoleon's strength had risen to nearly 140,000 men.

Hohenlohe decided to wait for reinforcements, either from Rüchel's army, on the way from Weimar, or from Holtzendorf's division, which was now running away towards Apolda, with Soult in hot pursuit. The gallant Prussian infantry, inspired by the bravery of their officers, managed to keep a front line together until about 14:30, but repeated cavalry attacks, led personally by Marshal Murat with a whip in his hand rather than a sabre, eventually reduced them to a rabble. Rüchel had at last arrived, (having taken four hours to march six miles!), and gallantly attempted a stand between Kapellendorf and Gross Romstadt. But again, Prussian parade ground tactics succumbed to the French cavalry and horse artillery, and Rüchel's men joined the others in a desperate rout, pursued by Murat.

JENA TIMELINE

10 August	Prussia begins mobilization.
13 September	The Prussians occupy Dresden, thus confirming their alliance with Saxony.
15 September	The Imperial Guard leaves Paris to rejoin the army in Germany.
8 October	The first engagement at Schleiz.
10 October	Battle of Saalfeld; death of Prince Louis Ferdinand.
13 October	French V Corps takes Jena; deploys on the Landgrafenberg. Napoleon issues orders for the remainder of the army to close up.
14 October	Thick fog at dawn.
06:30	Initial attack by V Corps between Closewitz and Lützeroda.
07:30	Imperial Guard artillery deploys 25 guns in support of V Corps.
08:00	Closewitz is taken by St Hilaire's division (IV Corps). V Corps advances to Vierzehnheiligen and the Dornberg.
09:30	VII Corps at last reaches the battlefield near Lützeroda. Ney's advance guard retakes Vierzehnheiligen but then has to be rescued.
10:00	The Prussians mount a major counterattack on Vierzehnheiligen but fail to carry it through, deciding to await reinforcement (which never comes).
12:00	Napoleon orders a general attack, all along the line.
14:30	Hohenlohe's army runs in almost complete disorder. Rüchel's small army arrives, attempts to restore some order, but fails.
18:00	The French pursuit reaches Weimar.
27 October	The standard of 'The Queen's Dragoons', who had sharpened their sabres on the steps of the French Embassy, is captured by French cavalry.
27 November	III Corps enters Berlin. Napoleon takes up residence at the palace, occupying the suite of rooms used by Frederick the Great.

THE BATTLE OF AUERSTÄDT

During the evening of 13 October, a minor cavalry skirmish took place near the village of Taugwitz. Reports of this alarmed Marshal Davout, now at Naumburg with the French III Corps. He immediately went forward personally, at the same time ordering a battalion to secure the defile formed by the hills and the bridge over the Saale at Kösen. His cavalry took several prisoners, from whom he learned enough to realize that the main body of the enemy, (Brunswick's army, now reinforced by a cavalry division under General Blücher) with the King and Queen at its head, was approaching the defile, evidently en route for Naumburg. Why Brunswick had not made arrangements to secure that defile remains a mystery to this day. Davout's immediate reaction was to order his three divisions forward by forced marching. He also sent word to Marshal Bernadotte, whose headquarters were also at Naumburg, but whose orders from Napoleon he chose to interpret as meaning he was to go to Dornburg. He thus failed to support Davout throughout the coming battle, and, in fact, I Corps took no part in either of the battles on 14th.

At about the same time as the attack of V Corps was launched on Closewitz, Davout's men were marching through the fog from Naumburg to Hassenhausen, with a view to advancing to Apolda in accordance with Napoleon's orders, and also to engage the enemy now known to be approaching. Brunswick's advance guard ran into that of Davout near the village. Davout's leading division, that of General Gudin, seized Hassenhausen, and prepared to meet the Prussian attack of Schmettau's division, which was supported by Blücher's cavalry. By about 08:30 a second Prussian division, that of Wartensleben, came into action on Schmettau's right. Gudin was now in serious trouble, but Friant's division arrived in the nick of time to take post on the French right, taking the village of Spielberg. For a while the situation was critical for Davout, but both Schmettau and Brunswick were mortally wounded, so the Prussian command structure faltered, giving the French time to reorganize. Furthermore, Davout's third division, that of General Morand, now came up to reinforce his colleagues on the left flank. King Frederick William, now actually as opposed to nominally in command, was bravely but inexpertly trying to encourage his right flank. He appears to have been under the impression that Napoleon himself was directing French operations. The Prussian chief of staff, Von Scharnhorst, was presently with the left wing and, it seems, was not informed of Brunswick's fatal wound for some time. The consequence was that, by about 13:00, Prussian morale completely collapsed and the will to fight evaporated. French artillery was now engaging the enemy in enfilade from both flanks. By 14:30 the Prussians were in full flight. During the afternoon, Davout advanced to the general line Eckartsberga–Auerstädt, where his exhausted infantry halted for the night.

Davout's report reached Napoleon, who had spent the night in Jena, at about 09:00 on 15 October. At first he could not believe what had happened. He said to the courier, 'Your Marshal must be seeing double!', a reference to the fact that Marshal Davout was extremely short-sighted. However, he soon realized the truth of the matter, and his praise for Davout and III Corps was more than generous. Davout, probably the most loyal and effective of Napoleon's marshals, was subsequently made 'Duke of Auerstädt'.

ABOVE *The injured supreme commander of the Prussian army, the Duke of Brunswick, is led away from the battle on horseback.*

AUERSTÄDT TIMELINE

13 October	III Corps (Marshal Davout) reaches Naumburg and secures the bridge at Kösen.
	Davout receives Napoleon's orders to advance on Apolda, begins crossing the Saale at Kösen.
	Bernadotte (I Corps) receives a copy of Davout's orders and decides he should return to Dornburg; takes no further part in the battles.
14 October	Thick fog at dawn.
06:30	Davout's advance guard clashes with Prussian advance guard at Hassenhausen.
	Davout orders his three divisions forward.
08:00	Schmettau's division attacks Gudin's at Hassenhausen, supported by Blücher's cavalry; attack fails.
08:30	Friant's division arrives on Gudin's right; captures Spielberg.
09:00	III Corps cavalry arrives at Hassenhausen.
10:00	Prussians attack Hassenhausen with two divisions, temporarily carry the village; Brunswick is mortally wounded; Prussian command now in the hands of King Frederick William.
	Gudin's division wavers, but Morand's division arrives at the double to cover his left; the Prussian attack falters; the French begin a general advance.
13:00	Prussians fall back on Auerstädt in disorder.

THE AFTERMATH

Early on 15 October the French began to follow up their success. One by one the great fortresses along the Elbe surrendered. By early November Prussia and Saxony had lost 25,000 men, killed or wounded, some 4000 guns and 20,000 horses. More than 100,000 men were prisoners of the French. The military might of both countries had been destroyed. In recognition of Marshal Davout's victory at Auerstädt, III Corps was accorded the honour of leading the army into Berlin.

From the point of view of strategy and tactics there have been few victories so decisive. However, Napoleon himself knew better than most at the time that, from the political point of view, he still had much to do. For the destruction of British credit was essential for his dream of a Europe united under France. This he hoped to achieve with his Continental System, which both Prussia and Saxony were obliged to accept.

VISITING THE BATTLEFIELDS TODAY

Both battlefields are easily accessible and relatively unspoiled. Recommended maps are the German Topographische Karte series 1:25 000 numbers 4835 Eckartsberga, 4935 Apolda and 5035 Jena (plus 5034 Weimar to cover the final stages of the Jena battle). The street map of Jena (*Stadtplan Jena mit Umgebungskarte*) published by Falk-Verlag is also very useful for the Jena battle, particularly the Umgebungskarte side at 1:100 000 which covers the whole area from Jena to Weimar to Apolda to Eckartsberga and Naumberg.

At Jena, the route taken by V Corps to ascend the Landgrafenberg begins at a turning off the Humboldt Strasse called 'Am Steiger'. At first a pleasant residential street, this road eventually becomes a forest track (closed to private vehicles) which leads up to the Windknölle, the highest point of the Landgrafenberg. It was here that French Army HQ was established on the evening of 13 October. The sadly graffiti-disfigured *Napoleonstein* is alleged to be the site of Napoleon's tent, but this seems unlikely – a better campsite would surely be in the hollow below the stone. Furthermore, the site does not offer a view of the Prussian front line, for which one needs to walk about 200m to the northern edge of the Windknölle.

In the village of Cospeda is the excellent small museum (Gedenkstätte 1806), with good models of phases of the battle. The whole of the Jena battlefield is marked with standing stones marking the positions of units at various times. A sketch map is displayed at numerous points to help visitors who wish to 'walk the battlefield'.

For the Auerstädt battlefield (modern spelling Auerstedt), the visitor is recommended to follow Davout's route from Naumburg, across the bridge at Kösen and up the steep hill to the plateau and the village of Hassenhausen. The site of Davout's tactical headquarters is about 600m (650 yards) north of the village, and is marked with a stone similar to those at Jena. This spot offers a splendid viewpoint.

At Eckartsberga there is a fine model diorama at the Schloss, with a commentary in German. At the Schloss Auerstädt, which was the Prussian HQ at the start of the battle (and Davout's after), there is another small museum with interesting exhibits.

The memorial to the Duke of Brunswick, on the spot where he was mortally wounded, can be found at grid reference 751656, midway between Hassenhausen and Taugwitz.

RIGHT *Memorial to the Duke of Brunswick. As a result of his death Brunswick units adopted black uniforms, which would prove to be doubly appropriate in 1815 when the then Duke of Brunswick fell mortally wounded at the battle of Quatre Bras, two days before Waterloo.*

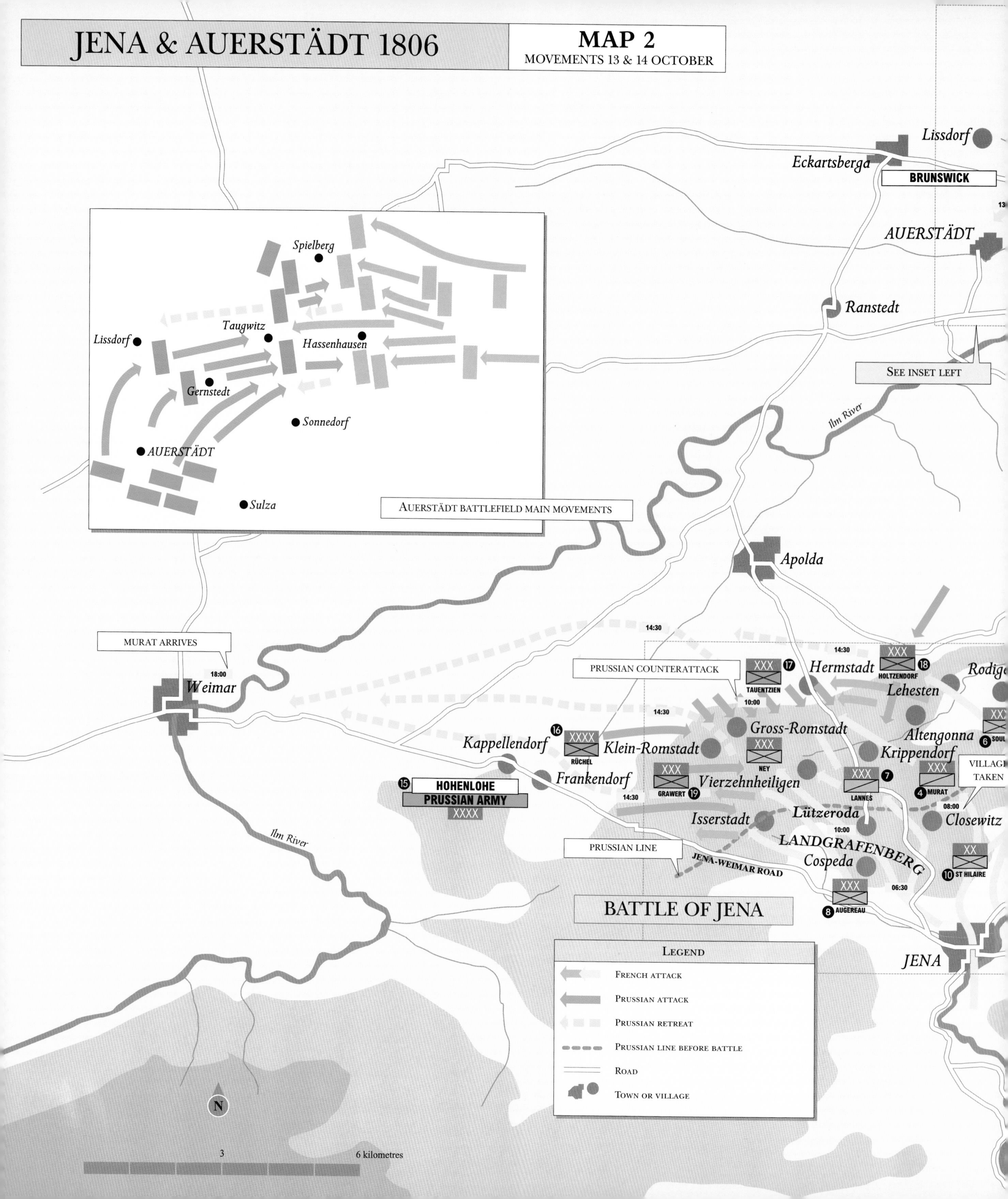

JENA & AUERSTÄDT 1806

MAP 2
MOVEMENTS 13 & 14 OCTOBER

Lissdorf

Eckartsberga

BRUNSWICK

AUERSTÄDT

Ranstedt

SEE INSET LEFT

Ilm River

AUERSTÄDT BATTLEFIELD MAIN MOVEMENTS (inset)

Spielberg

Taugwitz

Hassenhausen

Lissdorf

Gernstedt

Sonnedorf

AUERSTÄDT

Sulza

Apolda

14:30

MURAT ARRIVES

PRUSSIAN COUNTERATTACK

XXX 17 Hermstadt

14:30

XXX 18 HOLTZENDORF

Rodig...

18:00

Weimar

10:00 TAUENTZIEN

Lehesten

14:30

Gross-Romstadt

Altengonna

XXX SOUL

Kappellendorf 16

XXXX RÜCHEL

Klein-Romstadt

XXX NEY

Krippendorf

6

15 **HOHENLOHE**

Frankendorf

14:30

XXX GRAWERT 19

Vierzehnheiligen

XXX 7

VILLAGE TAKEN

PRUSSIAN ARMY

XXXX

LANNES

4 MURAT

08:00

Isserstadt

Lützeroda

Closewitz

PRUSSIAN LINE

JENA-WEIMAR ROAD

LANDGRAFENBERG

10:00

Cospeda

XX 10 ST HILAIRE

06:30

BATTLE OF JENA

XXX 8 AUGEREAU

JENA

Ilm River

LEGEND

←	FRENCH ATTACK
←	PRUSSIAN ATTACK
⇠	PRUSSIAN RETREAT
----	PRUSSIAN LINE BEFORE BATTLE
—	ROAD
▮	TOWN OR VILLAGE

N

3   6 kilometres

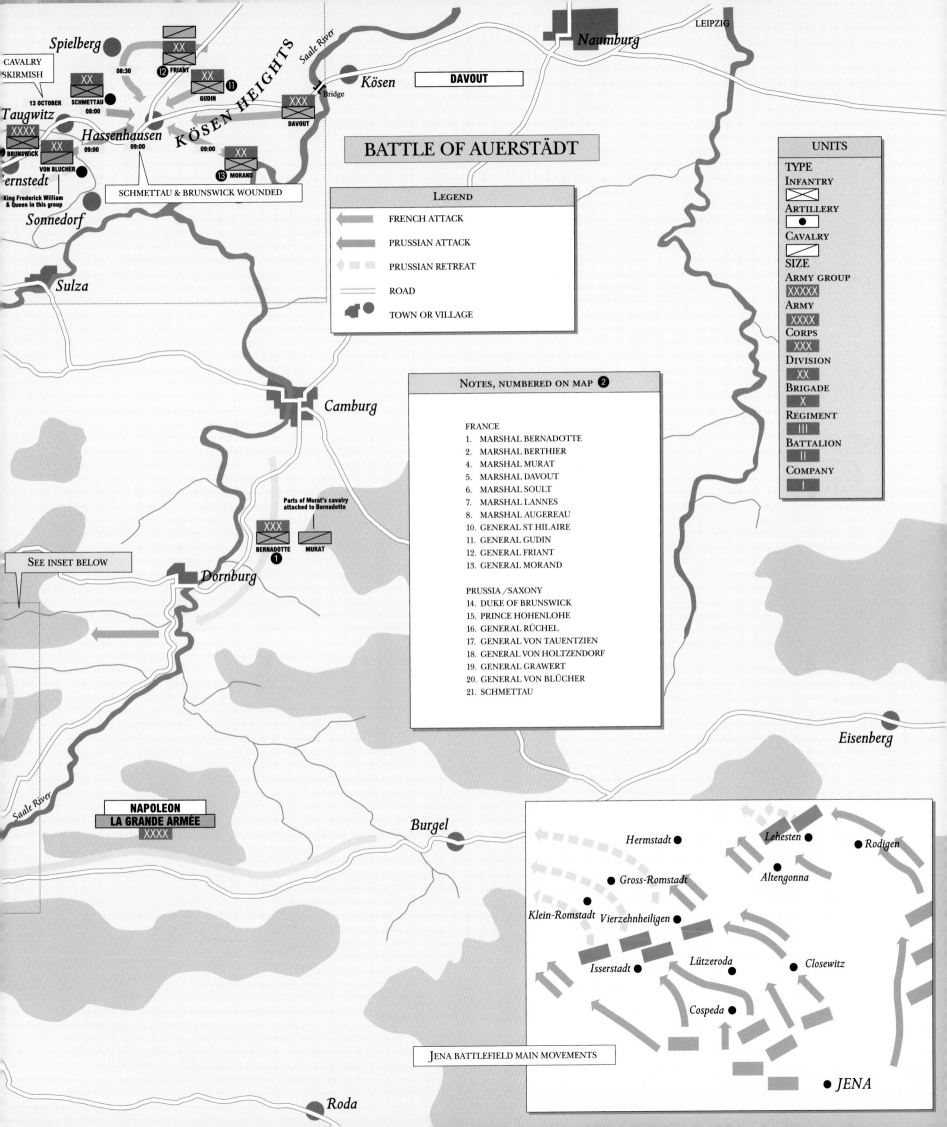

Spielberg

CAVALRY SKIRMISH

13 OCTOBER

Taugwitz

Hassenhausen

KÖSEN HEIGHTS

Saale River

Kösen

LEIPZIG

Naumburg

Bridge

DAVOUT

08:30

12 FRIANT

08:00 SCHMETTAU

GUDIN

11

XXX DAVOUT

BATTLE OF AUERSTÄDT

ernstedt

XXXX BRUNSWICK

09:00 VON BLUCHER

09:00

09:00

MORAND

13

Sonnedorf

King Frederick William & Queen in this group

SCHMETTAU & BRUNSWICK WOUNDED

Sulza

LEGEND

FRENCH ATTACK

PRUSSIAN ATTACK

PRUSSIAN RETREAT

ROAD

TOWN OR VILLAGE

UNITS

TYPE

INFANTRY

ARTILLERY

CAVALRY

SIZE

ARMY GROUP
XXXX

ARMY
XXXX

CORPS
XXX

DIVISION
XX

BRIGADE
X

REGIMENT
III

BATTALION
II

COMPANY
I

Camburg

NOTES, NUMBERED ON MAP 2

FRANCE
1. MARSHAL BERNADOTTE
2. MARSHAL BERTHIER
4. MARSHAL MURAT
5. MARSHAL DAVOUT
6. MARSHAL SOULT
7. MARSHAL LANNES
8. MARSHAL AUGEREAU
10. GENERAL ST HILAIRE
11. GENERAL GUDIN
12. GENERAL FRIANT
13. GENERAL MORAND

PRUSSIA /SAXONY
14. DUKE OF BRUNSWICK
15. PRINCE HOHENLOHE
16. GENERAL RÜCHEL
17. GENERAL VON TAUENTZIEN
18. GENERAL VON HOLTZENDORF
19. GENERAL GRAWERT
20. GENERAL VON BLÜCHER
21. SCHMETTAU

SEE INSET BELOW

Parts of Murat's cavalry attached to Bernadotte

XXX BERNADOTTE 1

MURAT

Dornburg

Eisenberg

Saale River

NAPOLEON
LA GRANDE ARMÉE
XXXX

Burgel

Hermstadt

Lehesten

Rodigen

Gross-Romstadt

Altengonna

Klein-Romstadt

Vierzehnheiligen

Lützeroda

Closewitz

Isserstadt

Cospeda

JENA BATTLEFIELD MAIN MOVEMENTS

JENA

Roda

SALAMANCA 1812

By Christopher L. Scott

With the key border fortresses of Ciudad Rodrigo and Badajoz secure by 1812, General Lord Arthur Wellesley, Viscount Wellington, planned a series of strategic moves enabling him to invade Spain and pit his Anglo-Portuguese army against Marshal Auguste Marmont's Army of Portugal. Marmont arrived in the Peninsula with the reputation of being a first-class field general, adept in aggressive movement and decisive in battle, and by mid-summer there had been a campaign of manoeuvre as each commander sought to gain an advantage to attack the other, until finally, on 22 July, Wellington saw his chance near the city of Salamanca.

MARMONT DEPLOYS FOY AND FEREY TO FACE ALLIES ACROSS THE VALLEY

The Allied army had deployed on the western ridge of the Pelagarcia Valley which ran south from the River Tormes. Wellington kept a large part of his army unseen, but had three of his seven divisions on this high ground with an outpost across the valley at the

ABOVE *In this engraving by J. T. Willmore, Allied cavalry attack the squares of French infantry, which break before them. The dramatic charge of Le Marchant's heavy brigade enabled Wellington to defeat Marmont.*

chapel of Nuestra Señora de la Peña. Marmont ordered General Maximillian Sebastien Foy's division on his extreme right to go north and attack this outpost, and General Jean Guillaume Thomières' division on his extreme left to march westwards and turn Wellington's flank. Instead of concentrating his army he began overextending it.

BOTH SIDES TRY TO SEIZE THE TWO ARAPILES HILLS

Both commanders had seen the importance of two prominent, steep and rugged hills further south. Marmont dispatched General Bonnet's division to seize the Arapil Grande, while Wellington had Major General Lowry Cole's division take the Arapil Chico. The Allies tried to secure the Grande, but the French won the race, tumbled the attackers back, and hauled guns onto its commanding position.

WELLINGTON REALIGNS HIS ARMY FACING SOUTH BEHIND THE RIDGE

Using the Grande as a pivot, the French prepared to advance along a low, east-west ridge south of the village of Los Arapiles to turn the Allied right flank and threaten their supply lines. However, Wellington, not having a significant advantage to offer battle, started to retire, marching his baggage for Ciudad Rodrigo. He shifted his hidden divisions westwards to stop his right being turned and faced them southward. He also moved Major General Sir Edward Pakenham's division and Brigadier General Benjamin d'Urban's cavalry, further west to Aldeatejada, to a defensive line on the Zurguen Rivers, behind which the whole army could retire if pressed. The day seemed just another phase in the campaign of manoeuvre, and Wellington ordered his traditional rearguard, Major General Sir Charles von Alten's light division and Brigadier General Eberhardt Bock's brigade of heavy cavalry, to take over on the ridge. However, behind it, he not only changed his line of battle to face south but redeployed his army for attack.

From the Arapil Grande, Marmont could see a lot, but not everything, and he had learnt that if he could not see most of Wellington's army, it was usually stealing a march. He saw the Allies' westward shift and dust on the Ciudad Rodrigo road, so, believing Wellington was withdrawing, he thought that he could pin the rearguard and turn their southern flank, enveloping and destroying them before reinforcements could return to their aid. He saw his chance and ordered his army to march.

MARMONT ORDERS A LEFT HOOK AND THOMIÈRES TO THREATEN THE CIUDAD RODRIGO ROAD

Generals Sarrut's and Ferey's divisions were sent north to help Foy's pin the Allied rearguard on their ridge. Bonnet's division was the anchor on the Grande and General Maucune's pushed westward along the southern ridge to turn the Allies' flank. It then faced north opposite Los Arapiles only to discover they were opposite Lieutenant General James Leith's division, while those of Generals Thomières, Antoine François (Count) Brennier and Bertrand (Count) Clausel moved westward, south of the Arapil Grande to extend the left hook and threaten the Ciudad Rodrigo road.

THOMIÈRES OUTSTRIPS BRENNIER

Thomières' division marched past Maucune's and was soon hurrying along the southern ridge, going further west. Brennier was to support them but had not yet moved. Wellington was having a late lunch when told the French were extending their left even more. After studying the movement he snapped his telescope shut with the words, 'This will do, at last!' and galloped the 5km (3 miles) to Aldeatejada and Pakenham and d'Urban.

The rapid French advance westward strung the French Army out over 6km (4 miles) and had opened a kilometre-wide gap between Thomières and Maucune, with Brennier too far back to cover it. This was the advantage Wellington had been seeking. He would attack across the valley, split the French, and launch a flank attack from Aldeatejada. It was time for battle. Having launched his right

MAIN CHARACTERS FEATURED

ALLIED ARMY OF SPAIN
General Lord Arthur
   Wellesley, Viscount
   Wellington
Major General Lowry Cole
Major General Sir Edward
   Pakenham
Brigadier General Benjamin
   d'Urban
Major General Sir Charles von
   Alten
Brigadier General Eberhardt
   Bock
Lieutenant General James
   Leith
Lieutenant General Sir Henry
   Clinton
Major General Sir John Hope
Lieutenant General Sir
   Stapleton Cotton
Major General John Gaspard
   Le Marchant
Brigadier General George
   Anson
Brigadier General Victor Alten

Brigadier General Sir Denis
   Pack
Major General Sir Colin
   Campbell
General Don Carlos d'España

FRENCH ARMY OF PORTUGAL
Marshal Auguste Marmont,
   Duke of Ragusa
General Maximillian
   Sebastien Foy
General Jean Guillaume
   Thomières
General Bonnet
General Sarrut
General Ferey
General Antoine François
   (Count) Brennier
General Bertrand (Count)
   Clausel

| *General Lord Arthur Wellesley, Viscount Wellington* | *Marshal Auguste Frédéric de Marmont* |

hook, Wellington ordered Cole's and Leith's divisions to attack in the centre covered by Portuguese brigades on their flanks, with Lieutenant General Sir Henry Clinton's and Major General Sir John Hope's divisions as a second line. Lieutenant General Sir Stapleton Cotton's cavalry supported both attacks: Major General John Gaspard Le Marchant's heavy and Brigadier General George Anson's light brigades swung right to cover the central attack, while Brigadier General Victor Alten's light cavalry joined d'Urban on the extreme right.

Marmont saw the danger and was riding along the southern ridge to issue orders to counter it when a shell blast dashed him from his horse. Command devolved upon Bonnet, but he too was soon severely wounded. Clausel was next in line, and aides quickly rode to his division to find him, but the French army was deprived of its command and control when the Allies struck.

PAKENHAM STRIKES THE HEAD OF THOMIÈRES' DIVISION

Pakenham's division struck at a time when Thomières' division, advancing rapidly in column of battalions (one behind the other), had lost its cohesion and had outpaced its cavalry support. Appearing out of dead ground, d'Urban's cavalry flank-charged the leading French battalion, which did not have time for a coordinated volley. It was broken and scattered. Behind the jubilant horsemen, Thomières saw Pakenham's men bearing down upon him. He quickly deployed several battalions and guns and blasted the leading British brigade. The Allied attack faltered, but then pressed on with fixed bayonets. Some French cavalry tried to intervene, but they were driven off by Alten's light brigade, which Wellington had sent over for just this purpose. The French took heavy casualties, Thomières himself was killed and his division broke under the

ABOVE Battle of Salamanca, 22 July 1812, *etched by J. Clarke, coloured by M. Dubourg (aquatint) by William Heath. Wellington orders the central attack. Behind the general is the Arapil Chico, with artillery deployed upon it, while to the right of the picture we see the British heavy cavalry beginning the charge that would sweep the Allies to victory.*

pressure, having a regimental eagle and six guns taken. The survivors fell back seeking shelter within Maucune's formation. They arrived at the same time as the Allies attacked.

Leith's division was to attack Maucune's and Cole's was aimed at Clausel's.

WELLINGTON'S CENTRAL ATTACK GOES IN

Leith's division crossed the valley and climbed the slopes opposite; the light companies driving off their French counterparts and their support artillery. Having Allied cavalry on his flank, and seeing Leith had more cavalry in support, Maucune retired from the ridgeline and formed squares. Leith's line crested the ridge. The French fired, but being in square their fire was severely reduced, and their guns were too far back and partially masked. Leith's men volleyed and charged. 'No struggle for ascendancy took place; the French squares were penetrated, broken and discomfited' reported Major Leith Hay in *A Narrative of the Peninsular War*. At this juncture Wellington ordered Le Marchant to 'charge at all hazards'. The heavies and Anson's lights went in, and utterly destroyed Maucune's division.

The unformed Allied cavalry then charged again; this time into the hastily brought-up leading battalions of Brennier's division. They, too, were in square and ready to fire. Firing at close range they brought down many of the dragoons but the impetus of the charge carried it forward into the French who momentarily resisted, then broke under the force of the big horses and the jabs and slashes of the heavy sabres. Le Marchant fell with a musket ball in his spine, but the Allies had destroyed three whole French divisions in just 40 minutes!

CLAUSEL COUNTERATTACKS

However, everything did not go Wellington's way. Cole's formation had been disrupted passing through Los Arapiles village, and they had been under constant artillery fire. They were under-strength due to leaving one brigade to hold the Chico and they attacked in a single line of battalions. They were also deprived of

their flank guard as Brigadier General Sir Denis Pack sent his Portuguese to storm the Grande. They failed. To add to Cole's problems, Clausel had assumed command of the French army. He recalled Sarrut's and Ferey's divisions from the right; Sarrut's to stem the progress of Pakenham and Leith, who now held the western end of the southern ridge, and Ferey's to act as a reserve in woods southeast of the Grande.

COLE IS DRIVEN BACK

Unseen from across the valley there is a lateral fold in the southern ridge west of the Grande. There Clausel formed his division to meet Cole's frontally, while ordering several of Bonnet's battalions from behind the Grande to attack Cole's open left flank. When Cole's men reached the lip of the fold Clausel's men fired and four battalions charged. The division was also taken in the flank and outnumbered by Bonnet's men. Cole was wounded; the Allies gave ground. Clausel attacked again and Cole's went reeling back.

CLINTON REPLACES COLE

Unfortunately, Clausel's division's counterattack also left them exposed. Clinton's fresh division replaced Cole's broken one, taking Clausel's in front and Bonnet's in flank. There was a short sharp musketry exchange, but the French were overlapped at both ends. Meanwhile, as Pakenham, Leith and d'Urban attacked Sarrut's division along the southern ridge, part of their force launched a diagonal attack into the rear of Clausel's struggling formation, which disintegrated. Then, outflanked by cavalry and overwhelmed by infantry, Sarrut's division also collapsed. The Allies had won the right.

FEREY STEMS THE ONSLAUGHT BUT GETS OUTFLANKED

Wellington switched his attention to his left. With the Light Division fighting Foy's, he ordered Major General Sir Colin Campbell's division to come off their ridge and take the Grande. The remaining French quit the position, leaving their guns. Two of the Army of

---

HEAVY AND LIGHT HORSEMEN

The 'heavies' were shock-action, melee troops riding into battle, boot to boot for maximum impact, with their long, straight swords pointed directly at their enemy.

The 'lights' were mounted on smaller, lighter horses (below 14.2 hands). Theoretically they were not part of the battle line, but performed reconnaissance and security roles, only joining in pursuits to disperse and slice down runaways with their curved sabres.

In practice both heavy and light horsemen saw themselves as 'battlefield cavalry' for whom charge at the gallop was the principal tactic.

ABOVE *Wellington rides into Salamanca at the head of a regiment of Hussars.*

Portugal's seven divisions remained intact, but Foy's was being hard pressed and only Ferey's, on high ground southeast of the Grande across the French line of retreat, could prevent a rout.

Wellington ordered Clinton's division to go straight at Ferey's. Making excellent use of broken country, rising ground and open slopes, Ferey poured musket and canister into Clinton's leading regiments and a devastating firefight ensued. Clinton's first line was shattered. Units from Cole's and Leith's formations made up an ad hoc second line, and Hope's division came up as support. Cohesion was breaking down as tiredness grew and the divisional generals improvised as best they could. Ferey's men doggedly clung to their ground. Another bloody firefight caused Clinton's second line to retire and, almost crippled, this brave French division prepared to meet the next wave. As the two exhausted forces began volleying each other the remnants of Pakenham's arrived and drove into their flank. Ferey was killed

SQUARES, INFANTRY AND CAVALRY

Infantry formed tight squares as protection against cavalry, because the formation has no flank or rear and horses will shy away from the massed bayonets. However, squares are densely packed, easy targets for cannon. Massed infantry can march up close to the square, stop and fire, because three sides of the square are looking in different directions and cannot fire back. Napoleonic generals tried to use their cavalry to force enemy infantry into squares which they then battered with their cannon and then broke with their infantry bayonets, finally letting the cavalry chase and destroy the remnants.

and the line broke. Now only Foy's could offer any resistance, and the light division ensured they were absorbed in trying to get off without being overwhelmed.

The wreck of the Army of Portugal fled southeastward towards the deep, wide River Tormes which curved south, behind the French position. There were only two crossings: the fords of Huerta and the bridge at Alba de Tormes. Believing a Spanish garrison of 2000 held the bridge, Wellington ordered Hope's division to advance upon Huerta. Apparently only Foy used the fords. General Don Carlos d'España had withdrawn his Spaniards from Alba without orders two days before, so the French escaped over the bridge. However, they were a defeated force. They had lost over 14,000 men, two divisional generals, 20 guns, two eagles and six standards, and Wellington had confirmed himself a master of the offensive battle.

VISITING THE BATTLEFIELD TODAY

The battlefield is not as wooded as it was in 1812 and the rear of the Arapil Grande has been lost to quarrying! Most roads have been surfaced and a new road and a railway line cut across the southern valley with a disused station at the foot of the Chico. Wellington could recognize his battlefield.

Leave Salamanca on the N630. After 5km (3 miles) you will pass Las Torres on your left; further on is a crossroads where you turn left for Los Arapiles. The Arapil Chico lies ahead, the Arapil Grande is to its right. Go into the village, supposedly unaltered since the fight raged around it, and stop at the town hall where there is a plaque, a map of the battle, and several cannon and muskets balls found in the area. To your left is the high ground from where Wellington watched the gap in the French line developing. It is climbable – and take a telescope, if only to survey the opposite ridge and dramatically snap it shut!

Keep on the road to reach the ruined station where you can park. Both Arapiles are within walking distance. Negotiate the fence; a track leads up the Chico for a magnificent panorama of the undulating field. To the north is the rearguard's ridge, running back to the Tormes, and to the northeast is the knoll of Nuestra Señora de la Peña. The heights directly eastwards are where Foy's division fought its retreat with the Light Division, while due south is the Grande. Around the railway station Clinton's division defeated Clausel's counterattack, while beyond it Leith's division attacked Maucune's men.

If you're fit, climb the Grande. It can be tough going, but it is easier round the back. The views are stunning and you will be able to appreciate the size and scale of the whole engagement. You will also see just how restricted was Marmont's view of Wellington's deployment. It is a long hike to follow the railway, but across the valley, where the ground climbs, you will see a ridge to your left. More wooded in 1812, it was on this eastern rise that Ferey's division made their heroic stand before crumbling and streaming back to Alba de Tormes.

VISITORS' FACT FILE

Visiting Salamanca is rewarding whether you self-drive and explore, or go with a battlefield tour company.

- The current major operator is Holts Tours Ltd., HiTours House, Crossoak Lane, Salfords, Redhill, Surrey, RH1 4EX.
- Specializing in arranging small, personally-designed visits is Cooper's: Waterloo Tours, Cooper's Court, Morton, Ongar, Essex, CM5 0NE. 01 277 890 214, and
- Chris Scott, 174, Ermin Street, Stratton St. Margaret, Swindon, Wiltshire, SN3 4NE. Also available as a guide.
- There are others, so choose whichever suits your needs.

Hire car companies are plentiful in Spain if you wish to fly-drive. You can book from home, fly into Madrid or Bilbao and be on the

RIGHT *The old bridge at Salamanca, over which Wellington's baggage filed during the morning's move west and the victorious general rode in triumph later in the day. Although now largely disused and falling into disrepair, it can still be seen today.*

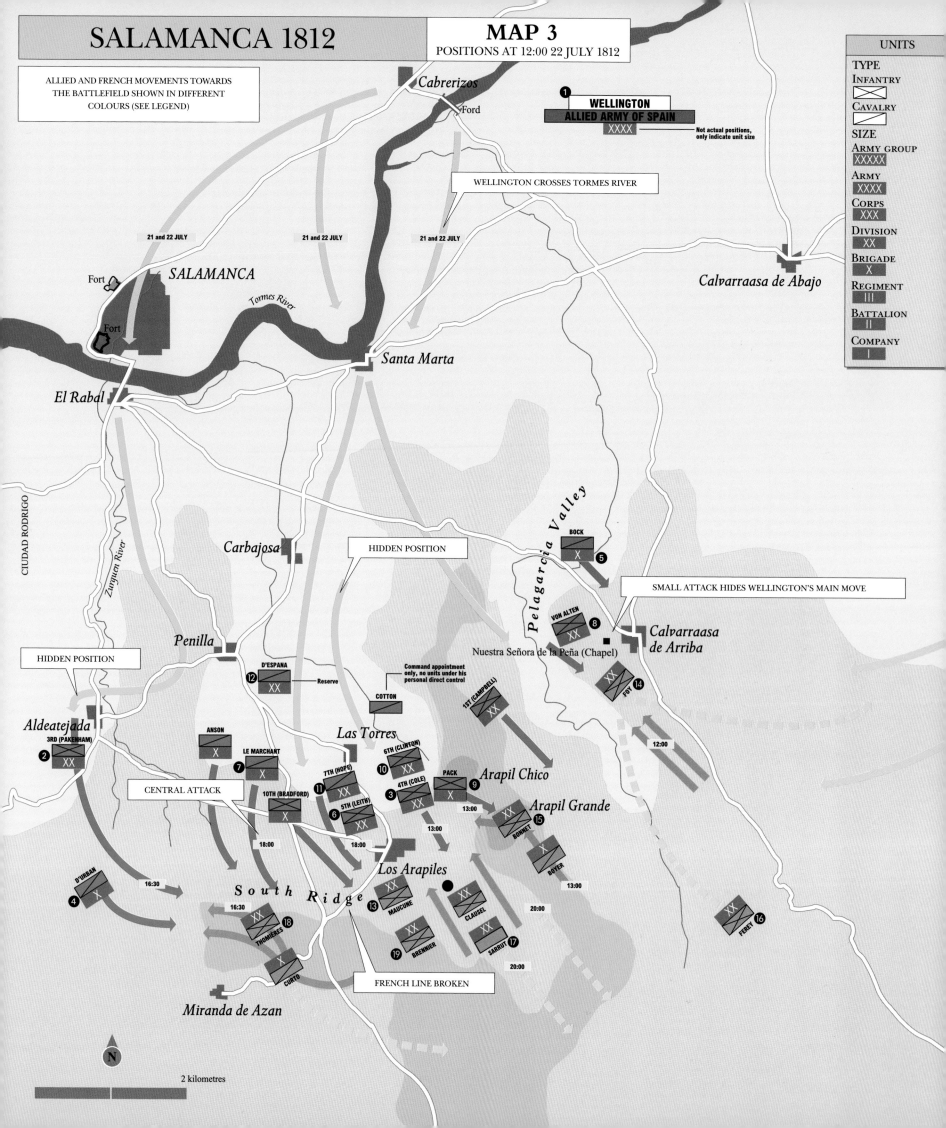

SALAMANCA 1812

MAP 3
POSITIONS AT 12:00 22 JULY 1812

ALLIED AND FRENCH MOVEMENTS TOWARDS
THE BATTLEFIELD SHOWN IN DIFFERENT
COLOURS (SEE LEGEND)

UNITS

TYPE

INFANTRY

CAVALRY

SIZE

ARMY GROUP
XXXX

ARMY
XXXX

CORPS
XXX

DIVISION
XX

BRIGADE
X

REGIMENT
III

BATTALION
II

COMPANY
I

Cabrerizos

Ford

❶ WELLINGTON
ALLIED ARMY OF SPAIN
XXXX

Not actual positions,
only indicate unit size

WELLINGTON CROSSES TORMES RIVER

21 and 22 JULY

21 and 22 JULY

21 and 22 JULY

Fort

SALAMANCA

Tormes River

Calvarraasa de Abajo

Fort

Santa Marta

El Rabal

CIUDAD RODRIGO

Zurguen River

Carbajosa

HIDDEN POSITION

Pelagarcia Valley

BOCK
X ❺

SMALL ATTACK HIDES WELLINGTON'S MAIN MOVE

VON ALTEN
XX ❽

Calvarraasa de Arriba

HIDDEN POSITION

Penilla

D'ESPANA
❶❷ XX — Reserve

Command appointment
only, no units under his
personal direct control

COTTON

Nuestra Señora de la Peña (Chapel)

FOY
XX ❶❹

12:00

Aldeatejada

3RD (PAKENHAM)
❷ XX

ANSON
X

LE MARCHANT
❼ X

7TH (HOPE)
❶❶ XX

Las Torres

6TH (CLINTON)
❶⓪ XX

4TH (COLE)
❸ XX

PACK
X ❾

Arapil Chico

1ST (CAMPBELL)
XX

CENTRAL ATTACK

10TH (BRADFORD)
X

5TH (LEITH)
❻ XX

13:00

Arapil Grande

BONNET
XX ❶❺

13:00

D'URBAN
❹ X

16:30

16:30

South Ridge

Los Arapiles

MAUCUNE
❶❸ XX

CLAUSEL
XX

BOYER
XX

13:00

18:00

18:00

THOMIÈRES
❶❽ XX

BRENNIER
❶❾ XX

SARRUT
XX ❶❼

20:00

FERRY
XX ❶❻

CURTO
X

FRENCH LINE BROKEN

20:00

Miranda de Azan

N

2 kilometres

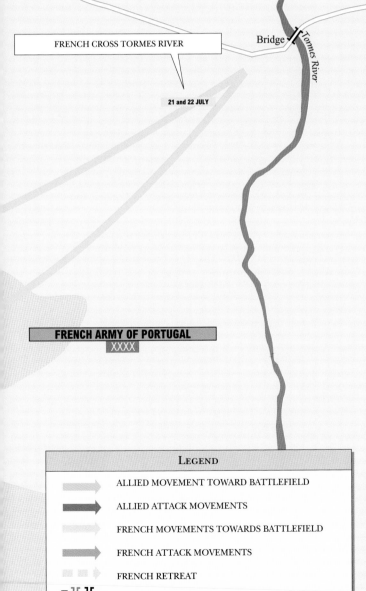

NOTES, NUMBERED ON MAP ❸

THE ALLIED ARMY OF SPAIN
1. GENERAL LORD ARTHUR WELLESLEY, VISCOUNT WELLINGTON
2. GENERAL EDWARD PAKENHAM (3RD DIVISION)
3. GENERAL LOWRY COLE (4TH DIVISION)
4. BRIGADIER GENERAL BENJAMIN D'URBAN
5. BRIGADIER GENERAL BOCK
6. LIEUTENANT GENERAL LEITH (5TH DIVISION)
7. GENERAL JOHN GASPARD LE MARCHANT (HEAVY BRIGADE)
8. MAJOR GENERAL VON ALTEN (LIGHT DIVISION)
9. BRIGADIER GENERAL PACK
10. LIEUTENANT GENERAL CLINTON (6TH DIVISION)
11. HOPE (7TH DIVISION)
12. GENERAL D'ESPANA (SPANISH)

THE FRENCH ARMY OF PORTUGAL
13. GENERAL MAUCUNE
14. GENERAL FOY
15. GENERAL BONNET
16. GENERAL FEREY
17. GENERAL SARRUT
18. GENERAL THOMIÈRES
19. COUNT BRENNIER
20. COUNT CLAUSEL

FRENCH CROSS TORMES RIVER

Bridge

Tormes River

21 and 22 JULY

FRENCH ARMY OF PORTUGAL
XXXX

LEGEND

→ ALLIED MOVEMENT TOWARD BATTLEFIELD

→ ALLIED ATTACK MOVEMENTS

→ FRENCH MOVEMENTS TOWARDS BATTLEFIELD

→ FRENCH ATTACK MOVEMENTS

⇢ FRENCH RETREAT

■)[ )[BUILDING, FORD AND BRIDGE

ROAD OR TRACK

TOWN OR VILLAGE

road in 30 minutes with most international companies. UK-based travellers can car-ferry from Plymouth to Santander. From either Bilbao (E805-E05-E80) or Santander (623), the roads go via Burgos and Valladolid (620-A62/E80), and from Madrid through L'Escorial and Avila (505-501) – all places well worth visiting. The university town of Salamanca lies on a major route to Portugal and a visit can be linked to see the siege sites of Ciudad Rodrigo and Almeida, the battlefields of the Coa and Fuentes d'Onoro and the ruins of Fort Conception.

Salamanca boasts an array of hotels ranging from the inexpensive, even on the Plaza Mayor, to the Salamanca Parador, which is modern and recently refurbished. Out of the city, Santa Martha has a camping site behind the Hotel Regio. The Spanish Tourist Board www.tourspain.co.uk will help with almost everything. The regional tourist information office is in Valladolid www.jcyl.es/turismo; and contacted on sotur@sotur.cyct.jcyl.es. Road maps are available from garages and hotels and European atlases are stocked by AA shops or Halfords. Detailed maps of the area can be ordered from Stanford's in Covent Garden, London.

SALAMANCA TIMELINE

(Approximate as very few time references exist)
22 July 1812

Daybreak   Allied troops occupy ground overlooking the Pelagarcia Valley.

12:00   Marmont deploys Foy and Ferey to face Allies across the valley.

13:00   Skirmishing begins and both sides try to seize the two Arapiles hills; Wellington realigns his army facing south behind the ridge.

14:00   Marmont orders a left hook and Thomières to threaten the Ciudad Rodrigo road. Thomières outstrips Brennier, his support.

15:00   Wellington is informed of the gap in the French line of march.

16:30   Pakenham strikes the head of Thomières' division.

17:30   Wellington's central attack, consisting of Leith, Cole and Cotton, goes in;
Le Marchant breaks Maucune's and Brennier's divisions.

18:00   Clausel counterattacks.

18:10   Sarrut stems Allied attack and Ferey forms reserve; Cole is driven back, and Clinton replaces him.

19:00   Clausel's and Sarrut's divisions collapse and an Allied general advance is ordered.

20:00   Ferey stems the onslaught but gets outflanked and finally breaks.

22:00   Pursuit called off.

WATERLOO 1815

By Michael Rayner

The Battle of Waterloo was an epoch-closing event, ending the Revolutionary and Napoleonic wars, which had begun in 1792 and continued, virtually without pause, for 23 years. Following Napoleon's escape from exile on Elba in February 1815, the coalition against him was re-formed and expanded, with the sovereigns of Europe determined to remove Napoleon for good. It rapidly became clear to Napoleon that he would have to fight to retain his position, therefore he planned to go onto the offensive as quickly as possible. He determined to strike at the enemy forces nearest to Paris – gathered in the newly formed Kingdom of the Netherlands – which led to what became known as the Campaign of the Hundred Days.

There were two allied armies facing Napoleon, the Prussians under the command of Field Marshal Gebhard von Blücher and the other under the British field marshal, Arthur Wellesley, Duke of Wellington. Blücher had a largely homogenous force of 128,000 men and 312 guns under his command from the border town of Charleroi to the east, while Wellington's army comprised 107,000 soldiers of several

nationalities, with 216 guns. His forces were spread through much of modern western Belgium, protecting not only the capital, Brussels, but also the court of the deposed French monarch, Louis XVIII, at Ghent, and his own supply and escape route to the Channel. To defeat these two enemies, Napoleon had in l'Armée du Nord (Army of the North) some 128,000 men with 366 guns. Although heavily outnumbered, Napoleon held the initiative and planned to defeat each of the Allied armies in detail, before they could combine.

NAPOLEON'S DECEPTIVE MOVE

To this end Napoleon manoeuvred his forces toward the border, hiding his true intentions from Wellington and Blücher, until the French attack began on 15 June 1815. The former remained convinced, until the early hours of 16 June and possibly well beyond this time, that Napoleon intended to swing a massive 'left hook' against him, to cut his army off from the coast, with the attack from Charleroi being a mere diversion. This successful deception enabled Napoleon, despite some delays within his own army, to brush aside the initial Prussian defenders and send a large part of his army northward along the main Charleroi to Brussels road, under the command of Marshal Michel Ney, by the evening of 15 June. It was hoped that this force would capture a key road junction at Quatre Bras before nightfall, but a combination of a

ABOVE Battle of Waterloo (oil on canvas) by Sir William Allan, showing the battle at about 19:30 as Napoleon's Imperial Guard advances. Napoleon is in the right foreground, Wellington in the left middle-distance.

small Netherlands (or Dutch-Belgian) force under the command of Prince Bernard of Saxe-Weimar just to the south at Frasnes and the uncharacteristic caution of Marshal Ney, led to the French stopping short of the junction after a skirmish. At that point it looked as if Napoleon's plan was still succeeding, as the two Allied armies were close to being driven apart by the French army's advance. On 16 June the situation became even more perilous for the Allies, as Napoleon in person defeated Blücher's army at the Battle of Ligny, while Ney fought out the day against a steadily reinforced Wellington at Quatre Bras. The key turning points of the campaign came during 17 June.

Firstly, in the early hours, the Prussian Chief of Staff, General Augustus von Gneisenau, formalized the direction of the Prussian retreat after Ligny, already begun by the bulk of the army, toward the town of Wavre. Secondly, during the morning, Napoleon spent much time inspecting the battlefield of Ligny, delaying the pursuit of the Prussians. Crucially he also missed the opportunity to crush Wellington while the latter was still at Quatre Bras. Instead, Wellington was able to make an orderly retreat northward, aided by thunderstorms which prevented cross-country movement once Napoleon had finally stirred himself.

After these events, Wellington's and Blücher's armies found themselves retreating northward, parallel and within less than a day's march of each other. With this in mind, Wellington halted his army on the ridge of Mont St Jean, just to the south of the village of Waterloo during the evening of 17 June. He knew it would be too great a gamble to risk battle against the bulk of Napoleon's army (Napoleon had detached 33,000 men under Marshal Grouchy to pursue the Prussians) without a promise of support from Blücher. Anxious hours followed during the night of 17–18 June, until this assurance arrived at 02:00 on 18 June. Wellington hoped for the first Prussians to arrive on what was to become the battlefield of Waterloo at about 11:00 on 18 June, but due to various factors, not least the poor condition of the local tracks after the heavy rain, the first Prussian forces would only commence fighting at 16:30.

Thus the stage was set for a hard-fought battle on 18 June, which would only be decided late in the evening after Napoleon had made several nearly successful attempts to break Wellington's line on the ridge of Mont St Jean. Wellington commanded about 68,000 men on the battlefield, of whom just over a third were British, about a third German and the remainder Dutch-Belgians. Napoleon had about 73,000 men on the field, while about 28,000 of Blücher's army fought at Waterloo, with a further 20,000 reaching the field before the fighting ceased. Much of the remainder of Blücher's men fought a delaying action at Wavre against Grouchy's forces during the 18th and part of the 19th June, before the latter retreated back into France.

THE ACTION

The battle of Waterloo has a clear pattern to it, with the French trying to win the battle by breaking Wellington's army. This became increasingly important as the Prussians drew ever closer until they arrived on the battlefield. From that point the shape of the battle changed with Prussian attacks against and behind the French right flank, while Napoleon continued to try and smash his way through Wellington's position. The battlefield had an important influence on the outcome of the battle, especially as Wellington had been able to choose his position.

The key to the battlefield was a low west–east ridge, fronted by a number of large farmhouses that were occupied by Wellington's

MAIN CHARACTERS FEATURED

FRENCH
Emperor Napoleon
   (Bonaparte)
Marshal Michel Ney
Marshal Emmanuel de
   Grouchy
General Jean Baptiste Drouet,
   comte D'Erlon

FACING NAPOLEON
Anglo-Dutch Army
Field Marshal Arthur
   Wellesley, Duke of
   Wellington

Major General
   Sir Colin Halkett
Major General
   Sir Peregrine Maitland
General Prince Bernard of
   Saxe-Weimar
General Baron David Chassé
Colonel John Colborne
Prussian Army
Field Marshal Gebhard
   Leberecht von Blücher
General Augustus von
   Gneisenau, Chief of Staff

Field Marshal Gebhard Leberecht von Blücher

Marshal Michel Ney

ABOVE An Incident at the Battle of Waterloo *(oil on canvas) by Thomas Jones Barker, shows British infantry in square being assailed by various types of French cavalry, seemingly in front of the farm of La Haie Sainte, whereas such battalions were behind the farm on higher ground.*

forces. To the south, about 1200m (1300 yards) away, ran a parallel, slightly higher, broader and longer ridge on which the French army deployed. The northern ridge's flanks were protected by steeper ground and by farmhouses which became strongpoints. The nature of the ridge, covered by standing corn before the arrival of the armies, was to prove crucial. Not only did it provide cover for Wellington's troops on its northern reverse slope, but as the day wore on its cloying clay soil, badly affected by the previous day's downpours, became more and more churned up by the boots and hooves of Napoleon's army. The battle opened at about 11:30, more than two hours later than Napoleon had intended. He had delayed to give the ground more time to dry out, in the hope that his artillery would be more effective, and since at that point he did not anticipate any interference from Blücher, it meant he did not have to rush. The battle opened with a diversionary attack launched by one of Napoleon's three main infantry corps against the farmhouse of Hougoumont, guarding Wellington's right. The farmhouse and its grounds, defended initially by light companies of the British Foot Guards and Hanoverian and Nassau light troops, did not fall during the whole day, despite being subjected to numerous attacks. With

the diversion failing to draw in significant numbers of Wellington's reserves, Napoleon sent in what he hoped would be the decisive assault. This attack, by D'Erlon's infantry corps, supported by some cavalry and the fire of the French massed artillery, went in against Wellington's left-centre. It very nearly succeeded, but at the critical point two brigades of British heavy cavalry sent the massed columns back down the slope. Many cavalry pursued too far, became isolated, cut off and destroyed, but Wellington still held the ridge.

The next French attempt came at about 16:00, when Ney ordered forward cavalry against Wellington's right-centre. It seems likely that Ney had seen Wellington's infantry in that sector retreat, and hoped to turn this into a rout. Although there had been a limited withdrawal, due to the desire to gain better cover from the incessant artillery fire, the retreat was controlled and limited, meaning that Wellington's infantry was able to form squares in good time and fight off charge after charge. While these charges continued, the first Prussian troops arrived and began to form up for an attack against the village of Plancenoit, hastily garrisoned by Napoleon's remaining corps of infantry, with support from the Young Guard. It was now clear that Wellington had to be beaten quickly, before more Prussians could arrive. Ney threw what he could muster against the central farm of La Haie Sainte, capturing it – due in large part to the fact that the garrison of light troops of the King's German Legion ran out of rifle ammunition. This gave the French an opportunity to rush guns to the farm to fire at the centre of Wellington's line. However, instead of launching an attack at that time, Napoleon was distracted by a worsening situation at Plancenoit. This required the intervention of two battalions of the Old Guard and the deployment of most of the remainder of the Imperial Guard to face the Prussian threat.

ADVANCE OF NAPOLEON'S IMPERIAL GUARD

It was only at about 19:30 that Napoleon was ready to launch a final attack against Wellington's line on the ridge, in what was to be the climactic point of the battle. The breathing space given to Wellington by Napoleon's distraction at Plancenoit had been used to good effect, as he had brought across relatively unscathed units to bolster his centre, in the form of Lieutenant-General Chassé's Dutch-Belgian division and light cavalry brigades, who had been holding the village of Braine-L'Alleud on the right flank. Napoleon advanced with nine battalions of the Imperial Guard just to the south of La Haie Sainte, where command was passed to Marshal Ney. Even though only nine battalions were with Ney, these units were rarely used in battle, but kept as a last reserve. Rather than advance straight up the main road for the centre of Wellington's line, the Guard turned off to the left of the road, so that their attack climbed the same slopes as had been badly churned up by the earlier massed cavalry charges. The attack was delivered by just five battalions of the Middle Guard, probably in their hollow square formation as protection against possible cavalry attacks, although they were supported by the remnants of other line units, especially on their right, as well as by a battery of Guard artillery and other available guns. The other four battalions (three of the Old and one of the Middle Guard) remained in close support.

The Imperial Guard attacked in echelon from the right – that is, the first battalion to make contact was on the French right, with each subsequent battalion reaching Wellington's line slightly later in turn. Shortly after leaving the road, Marshal Ney had his fifth horse of the day shot from underneath him, so he carried on leading the troops on foot, sword in hand. The Allied troops sensed a lull in the firing and at least some of them knew that their final test was about to come. Wellington himself had received a warning that the Imperial Guard was on its way, thanks to a deserting French cavalry officer, enabling him to make some last-minute adjustments to his formations. The first contact was made by the 1st Battalion 3rd Grenadiers, followed closely by the 4th Grenadiers. They had initial success against part of the Brunswick division, before a confused fight ensued with the four British battalions of Colin Halkett's brigade. It seems likely that two British battalions were pushed back in confusion, but as this occurred, Chassé brought up an artillery battery and Colonel H. Detmers' infantry brigade which, together with Halkett's other two battalions, sent the two battalions of French Guards back down the slope in confusion.

The two battalions of the French 3rd Chasseurs of the Middle Guard headed straight for the British Foot Guards of Maitland's brigade, with Wellington stationed behind them. Here, one British Guardsman remembered 'the bearskin caps rising higher and higher, as they ascended the ridge of ground which separated us and advanced nearer and nearer to our lines': the crisis point was clearly at hand. The calming authoritative voice of Wellington rang out: 'Now, Maitland! Now is your time!' Followed shortly after by: 'Up Guards! Make ready! Fire!' Maitland's two battalions of the 1st Foot Guards gave a withering fire to the head of the French formations, which tried to deploy into line, but were instead forced to retreat.

The final French battalion, that of the 4th Chasseurs, made its way up the ridge. They must have had some cause for hope as Maitland's brigade was in some confusion, since, having repulsed the 3rd Chasseurs, they appear to have misunderstood an order and were attempting to rally as the new French assault materialized. At that point Colonel Colborne, commanding the 52nd Light Infantry battalion, took his men out of the line in an audacious move. He wheeled them to their right, so that they ended up parallel to the left flank of the French formation. Being a large battalion and relatively fresh, their fire was devastating, forcing this

final battalion to crumble and retreat. As word spread that the Guard was retreating the entire French army turned and ran, with the exception of the final reserve of the Old Guard.

Wellington saw this as his chance to come off the ridge and finish the battle. Urging Colborne forward he ordered a general advance which, combined with renewed Prussian advances, cleared the battlefield of formed French units. The Prussians took up the pursuit of Napoleon's army, nearly capturing the Emperor. Instead, Napoleon reached Paris, where he was forced to abdicate for the second time.

TOURING THE SITE TODAY

The battlefield of Waterloo is a most rewarding site to visit, being largely open farmland. The best approach is from the south, after visiting the battlefields of Ligny and Quatre Bras, and having followed the route of Napoleon's advance through Genappe (don't follow the modern bypass, but go through the town). The battlefield is some way south of the small town of Waterloo, where Wellington had his headquarters at an inn, now the Wellington Museum. Approaching the battlefield from the south one first reaches Le Caillou, Napoleon's headquarters the night before the battle, but since rebuilt. It now contains a small museum. Further north is La Belle Alliance, where Wellington met Blücher at the end of the battle. There are several monuments close to the building. Once at La Belle Alliance, the view from the French-held ridge can be appreciated, as well as a smaller intermediate ridge slightly to the north, which was used for the grand battery. At that point you may wish to turn off right, to visit Plancenoit, with its rebuilt church and several memorials, or this could be saved for the end of a visit. Further north from La Belle Alliance stands the farm of La Haie Sainte, still largely intact. The farm itself is not open to the public. Once

ABOVE *The Lion Mound stands at the point where the Prince of Orange was wounded by a spent musket ball in the left shoulder.*

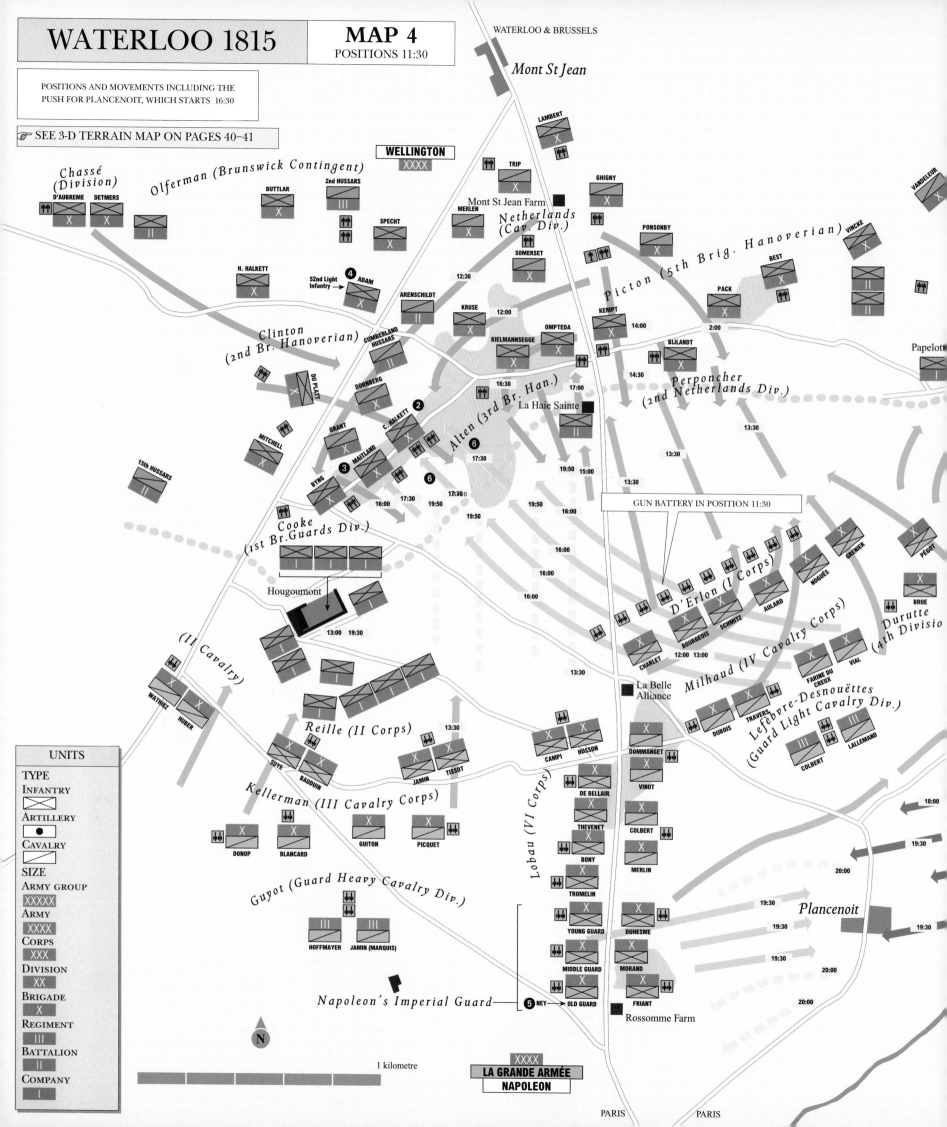

WATERLOO 1815

MAP 4
POSITIONS 11:30

POSITIONS AND MOVEMENTS INCLUDING THE
PUSH FOR PLANCENOIT, WHICH STARTS 16:30

☞ SEE 3-D TERRAIN MAP ON PAGES 40–41

WATERLOO & BRUSSELS

Mont St Jean

LAMBERT

WELLINGTON

Chassé
(Division)

Olferman (Brunswick Contingent)

D'AUBREME   DETMERS

BUTTLAR

2nd HUSSARS

SPECHT

TRIP

GHIGNY

Mont St Jean Farm

MERLEN

Netherlands
(Cav. Div.)

PONSONBY

VINCKE

VANDELEUR

Picton (5th Brig. Hanoverian)

SOMERSET

BEST

H. HALKETT

52nd Light
Infantry →   ❹ ADAM

ARENSCHILDT

KRUSE

12:30

12:00

PACK

2:00

Papelott

Clinton
(2nd Br. Hanoverian)

CUMBERLAND
HUSSARS

KIELMANNSEGGE

OMPTEDA

KEMPT

14:00

DU PLATT

DORNBERG

BIJLANDT

14:30

Perponcher
(2nd Netherlands Div.)

MITCHELL

GRANT

C. HALKETT

❷

La Haie Sainte

16:30   17:00

13:30

Alten (3rd Br. Han.)

❻

13:30

MAITLAND

❸

BYNG

❻

17:30

17:30

19:50   15:00

16:00   17:30   19:50

17:30

13:30

15th HUSSARS

19:50

16:00

GUN BATTERY IN POSITION 11:30

Cooke
(1st Br.Guards Div.)

19:50

16:00

PEGOT

16:00

GRENIER

Hougoumont

16:00

D'Erlon (I Corps)

NOGUES

BRUE

(II Cavalry)

13:00   19:30

SCHMITZ

AULARD

Durutte
(4th Division)

BOURGEOIS

WATHIEZ

HUBER

Milhaud (IV Cavalry Corps)

CHARLET

12:00   13:00

FARINE DU
CREUX

VIAL

Reille (II Corps)

13:30

DUBOIS

TRAVERS

Lefebvre-Desnouëttes
(Guard Light Cavalry Div.)

SOYE

BAUDUIN

JAMIN

TISSOT

CAMPI

HUSSON

DOMMANGET

La Belle
Alliance

COLBERT

LALLEMAND

Kellerman (III Cavalry Corps)

DE BELLAIR

VINOT

DONOP   BLANCARD

GUITON   PICQUET

THEVENET

COLBERT

18:00

BONY

MERLIN

19:30

Lobau (VI Corps)

TROMELIN

19:30

Guyot (Guard Heavy Cavalry Div.)

YOUNG GUARD

DUHESME

Plancenoit

19:30

19:30

HOFFMAYER   JAMIN (MARQUIS)

MIDDLE GUARD

MORAND

20:00

19:30

Napoleon's Imperial Guard —— ❺ NEY → OLD GUARD

FRIANT

Rossomme Farm

20:00

UNITS

TYPE

INFANTRY
☒

ARTILLERY
●

CAVALRY
╱

SIZE

ARMY GROUP
XXXX

ARMY
XXXX

CORPS
XXX

DIVISION
XX

BRIGADE
X

REGIMENT
III

BATTALION
II

COMPANY
I

N

1 kilometre

LA GRANDE ARMÉE
NAPOLEON
XXXX

PARIS   PARIS

NOTES, NUMBERED ON MAP ❹

ALLIED
1. FIELD MARSHALL GEBHARD LEBERECHT VON BLÜCHER
2. MAJOR GENERAL SIR COLIN HALKETT
3. MAJOR GENERAL SIR PEREGRINE MAITLAND
4. COLONEL COLBORNE

FRENCH
5. MARSHAL MICHEL NEY
6. ADVANCE OF THE IMPERIAL GUARD

BLÜCHER ❶
PRUSSIAN ARMY
XXXX

THE PUSH FOR PLANCENOIT
STARTS 16:30

SYDOW   WATZDORFF

Saxe-Weimar

Smohain

La Haie

Bülow
(IV Corps)

Perponcher
(2nd Netherlands Division)

Frichermont

LOSTHIN   HILLER

17:00

17:00

MARBOT

Jacquinot
(1st Cavalry Division)

BRUN

14:00

GOBRECHT

Bülow
(IV Corps)

LOSTHIN   SYDOW

WATZDORFF

HILLER

18:00

LEGEND

→	WELLINGTON INITIAL MOVEMENTS
→	BLÜCHER PRUSSIAN MOVEMENTS
→	NAPOLEON INITIAL MOVEMENTS
→	NAPOLEON FINAL MOVEMENTS
Plancenoit	TOWN OR VILLAGE
Mont St Jean ■	FARM OR BUILDING
19:30	TIME OF MOVEMENT
⊞	ARTILLERY BATTERY
⊡	ROCKET
░	HIGHER GROUND
••••	LINE OF BATTLE

beyond La Haie Sainte you are soon onto Wellington's ridge. To the right (east) is the slope up which D'Erlon's infantry attacked and to the left (west), the site of the attack by French cavalry and the Imperial Guard. Tourist attractions connected with the battle include the massive Lion Mound, built as a memorial to the Prince of Orange, who was wounded at that spot. The panoramic views from the top of the mound are tremendous, although one should remember that in creating the mound huge quantities of soil were removed from the ridge, changing the profile of this key feature forever. The farm of Hougoumont has many of the original buildings.

VISITORS' FACT FILE

- Bartletts Battlefield Journeys: www.battlefields.co.uk
- The War Research Society: www.battlefieldtours.co.uk
- Tours with Experts Ltd: www.tours-with-experts.com
- Midas Tours: www.midastours.co.uk
- Middlebrook-Hodgson Battlefield Tours. Lancaster Farm, Tumby Woodside, Boston, PE22 7SP. Tel: +44 (0) 1526 342249
- Holt's Tours: www.battletours.co.uk
- Somme Normandy Battlefield Tours. www.somme-normandy-tours.com
- Travel and Learn (Royal British Legion organiser). www.travelandlearn.com

WATERLOO TIMELINE

15 June

03:30 French troops cross into Kingdom of the Netherlands, close to Charleroi.

16 June Battle of Quatre Bras between French and Anglo-Dutch armies.
Battle of Ligny between French and Prussians.

17 June

10:00 Anglo-Dutch withdrawal from Quatre Bras.

18 June

11:30 French attacks against Hougoumont farm begin and continue throughout the day.

18 June

13:00 French massed artillery bombardment.

13:15 First Prussian troops sighted by French.

13:30 D'Erlon's infantry attacks Wellington's left-centre.

16:00 Massed French cavalry attacks against Wellington's right-centre.

c.16:30 First Prussian attacks near Plancenoit.

18:00 French capture farm of La Haie Sainte.

19:30 Attack by French Middle Guard against Wellington's right-centre.

c.21:15 Wellington and Blücher meet at La Belle Alliance.

WATERLOO 18 JUNE 1815

THE ADVANCE OF THE IMPERIAL GUARD

As the day waned, Napoleon faced a difficult decision. The approach of the Prussian army made it imperative that the French break the British line and force a decision. The British, together with their allies, had held Mont St Jean for the whole day, having withstood repeated French assaults and a lethal bombardment from the French artillery. Napoleon decided on one last stroke: he ordered the Imperial Guard into battle. The Imperial Guard were the Emperor's personal troops, fiercely loyal and devoted and relatively privileged compared with the rest of La Grande Armée. By tradition, the Imperial Guard were kept in reserve, and sent into battle only when circumstances demanded it. But with the approach of dusk and the battle far from won, Napoleon knew he had to gamble. The illustration on these pages shows the situation at about 19:30, when the first battalions of the Imperial Guard reached the crest of the ridge.

(1) Hougoumont: By 19:30, the chateau of Hougoumont was still in Allied hands, having endured a desperate see-saw battle throughout the day. Its defenders, a mixture of Coldstream and Scots Guards and Nassau troops, were reinforced by the King's German Legion and by Hanoverians and Brunswickers.

(2) La Haie Sainte: The small farm, a key strongpoint anchoring Wellington's centre, fell to the French around 18:00. Its small garrison of the King's German Legion was unable to repel the French, who attacked in vastly superior numbers.

(3) Mont St Jean: Although only 30m (100ft) high, the long ridge of Mont St Jean offered a strong defensive position.

(4) Sunken road: Running along the crest of the Mont St Jean ridge, the sunken road offered concealment to the British and Allied troops.

(5) Reverse slope: Invisible to the French, though well within range of their artillery, the reverse slope of the Mont St Jean ridge permitted Wellington and his commanders to conceal bodies of troops and their movements.

(6) Start line: Located 500m (550 yards) south of La Haie Sainte. Napoleon himself led the Imperial Guard to the farm's orchard, where he handed command to Marshal Ney.

(7) Leading battalions: Five battalions of the Middle Guard, a mix of Chasseurs and Grenadiers, led the advance. The Guard advanced and attacked in squares. Each battalion was under the command of a general.

(8) The Old Guard: Three battalions of the Old Guard marched in the second line. Even when the advance faltered, these formations retreated in good order.

(9) Artillery: Horse artillery advanced with the Guard, with the guns positioned between the squares. The Guard artillery inflicted heavy losses on the British and their allies.

(10) Reserve: A ninth Guard battalion, of Grenadiers, was posted between Hougoumont and La Haie Sainte. Two more battalions of the Old Guard, as well as the entire Young Guard, were deployed to the east, at Plancenoit, to face the threat from the advancing Prussians.

(11) Guards Brigade: The British Guards Brigade, commanded by Maitland, lay concealed behind the crest of the ridge. At a signal from Wellington, the Guards emerged from hiding and fired at close range into the packed French squares, inflicting heavy casualties.

(12) Colin Halkett's Brigade: Made up of the 30th, 73rd, 33rd and 69th regiments of Foot, and deployed in a line four deep, the brigade suffered from the accurate fire of the Guard artillery. However, with supporting fire from a Belgian battery, they turned back two battalions of the Middle Guard.

(13) Detmer's Brigade of Dutch-Belgian troops from Chassé's Netherlands Division were brought into the line to repulse two battalions of the French Middle Guard, aiding Colin Halkett's Brigade.

(14) 52nd Regiment of Foot: The massed volley of

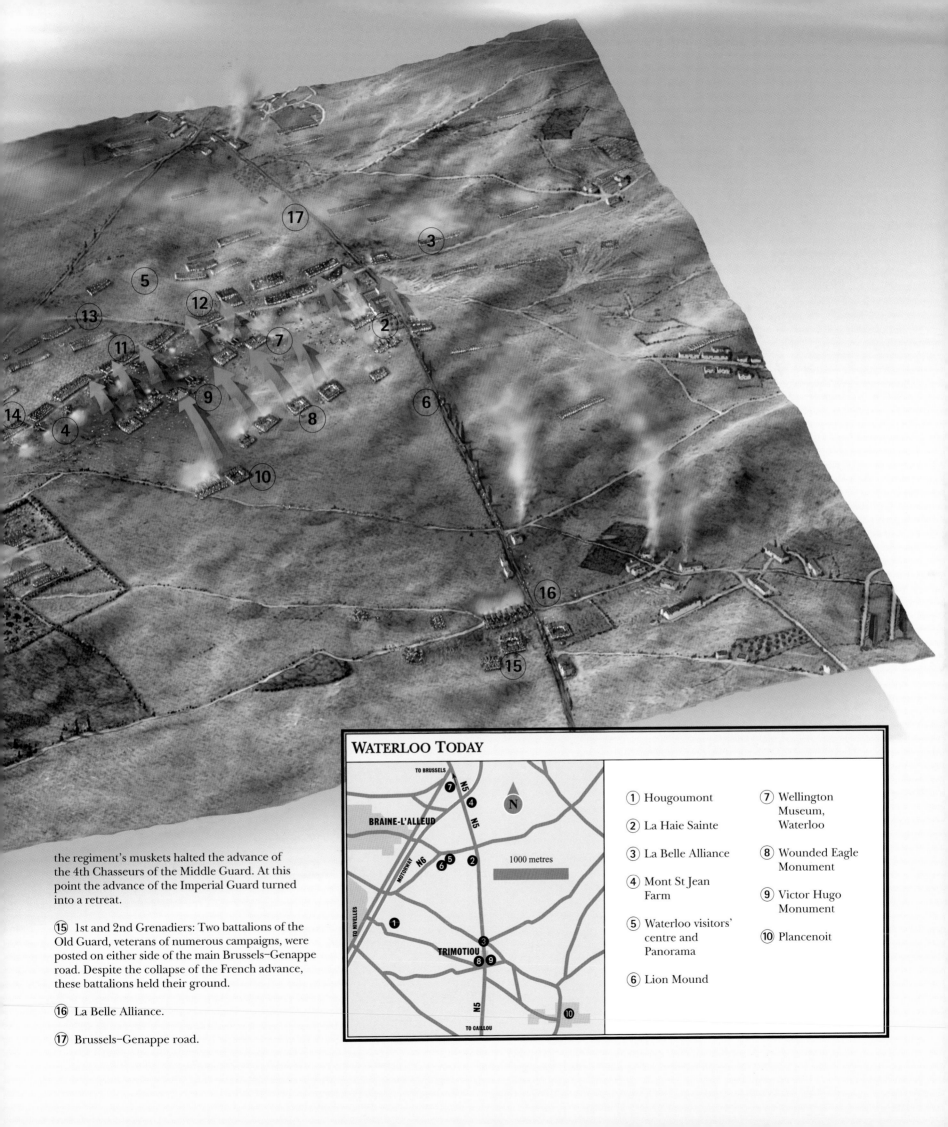

the regiment's muskets halted the advance of
the 4th Chasseurs of the Middle Guard. At this
point the advance of the Imperial Guard turned
into a retreat.

⑮ 1st and 2nd Grenadiers: Two battalions of the
Old Guard, veterans of numerous campaigns, were
posted on either side of the main Brussels–Genappe
road. Despite the collapse of the French advance,
these battalions held their ground.

⑯ La Belle Alliance.

⑰ Brussels–Genappe road.

WATERLOO TODAY

TO BRUSSELS

N5

BRAINE-L'ALLEUD

N5

MOTORWAY N6

TO NIVELLES

1000 metres

TRIMOTIOU

N5

TO CAILLOU

① Hougoumont

② La Haie Sainte

③ La Belle Alliance

④ Mont St Jean
Farm

⑤ Waterloo visitors'
centre and
Panorama

⑥ Lion Mound

⑦ Wellington
Museum,
Waterloo

⑧ Wounded Eagle
Monument

⑨ Victor Hugo
Monument

⑩ Plancenoit

American Civil War

1861 - 1865

By Joshua Moon

The costs to the nation of the American Civil War were immense. It was the baptism in blood for a fledgling republic. Over one million Americans lost their lives, and hundreds of thousands of others lost their homes and livelihoods during the conflict. The battles of Bull Run, Shiloh, Gettysburg and Antietam claimed more American dead and wounded than the Korean and Vietnam wars combined. No four battlefields better typify the horror and ferocity of the American Civil War than the four represented in this book.

Neither North nor South predicted a long struggle in 1861, and most felt it would be decided by a single, decisive battle. The first Battle of Bull Run, or Manassas Junction, in July 1861, foreshadowed the long and costly war that was to come. A Southern victory at Bull Run gave a brief ray of hope to the great myth that every Southerner, due in large part to 'God-given' talents to ride and shoot, could 'whip ten Yankees'. This, unfortunately, was to prove more tunnel than light, and the ensuing four years of war would devastate the South.

The truth was much more complex. Outmatched by the Union's ever-expanding population and burgeoning economic might, the Confederacy's only chance was a quick war. The Confederacy also believed that any economic pressure it could apply on European cotton and tobacco markets would result in diplomatic recognition. However, the false hope of British and French recognition disappeared with Union victories at Antietam and Gettysburg and with Europe's ability to find cotton elsewhere. It also crumbled under the steadfast leadership of President Abraham Lincoln.

The war was also decided on the battlefield. The war in the eastern theatre, dominated by the Army of Northern Virginia under Robert E. Lee, was waged for control of capital cities and to obtain European recognition. The war in the western theatre, ultimately won by Ulysses S. Grant and William Tecumseh Sherman, was fought for control of the Mississippi River and the far more important strategic transportation networks that brought food, replacements and munitions from the Confederacy's heartlands to Virginia and the Carolinas. In the end, the Union's victory in the west was the death knell for the Confederacy.

The hundreds of hills and fields, whose names before the war were known only to the farmers who ploughed them, are now national battlefield shrines. A large pile of rocks in a southern Pennsylvania wheatfield became the 'Devil's Den' at Gettysburg and a clump of trees in a depression at a corner of a peach orchard on the bank of the Tennessee River was transformed into the infamous 'Hornet's Nest' at Shiloh. All of these places have become fixtures in American military heritage and are recognized throughout the world as defining tactical events.

Even the names of some of the great battlefields reflect the struggle between the states. While the Union commanders referred to the battlefields by nearby rivers or creeks, Confederate generals often named the battlefields by the closest city or town. Therefore, the battle of Antietam was named by the Union commanders for the small creek that meanders through the field. It is known to southerners as the battle of Sharpsburg. Regardless of the names of the places, America's Civil War battlefields left an indelible scar on the American landscape. The American Civil War was the defining moment for the American nation and its effects can be felt even today.

THIS PAGE The Battle of Gettysburg *by Sebastian Mayer. Gettysburg, 1–3 July 1863, coupled with the surrender of Vicksburg the next day, signified the end of the South's ability to conduct offensive operations and sounded the death knell of the Confederacy.*

FIRST BULL RUN (MANASSAS) 1861

By Anthony Hall

After the surrender of the Federal garrison at Fort Sumter, Charleston, South Carolina, on 14 April 1861, the focus of the war between the Northern and Southern states moved to Virginia (the Old Dominion). On 7 May Virginia was admitted to the Confederacy and on 20 May its legislature invited the Confederate government to relocate its capital from Montgomery, Alabama, to Richmond, Virginia, 180km (110 miles) south of Washington, DC. This made the defence of Richmond a priority for the Confederacy in the east, and ensured that the war's first battle would be fought somewhere on the farmlands of northern Virginia, as Union forces sought to

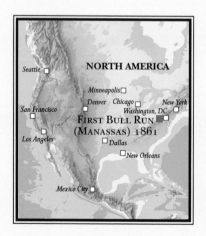

advance from Washington to capture the Confederacy's new capital city. In June, two Confederate armies were established in Virginia to guard the routes to Richmond. To the west, in the Shenandoah Valley, General Joseph E. Johnston commanded a force of 11,000 infantry in four brigades, together with a regiment of cavalry under Colonel James Ewell Brown (Jeb) Stuart. To the east of Johnston, about 160km (100 miles) across the Blue Ridge Mountains, stood the main Confederate army of 18,000 men under the command of General Pierre G.T. Beauregard. Beauregard had his army positioned 40km (25 miles) southwest of Washington, about 6km

ABOVE LEFT *Federal infantry guard the Orange & Alexandria Railroad near Manassas in the summer of 1862. As the only railroad that ran south from Washington into Virginia, it was strategically vital to both sides.*

ABOVE CENTRE *The banks of Bull Run proved an obstacle to the Federal advance in July 1861, but when Manassas was fought over again in August 1862, Federal engineers were prepared and built new crossings.*

ABOVE RIGHT *The location of General Beauregard's headquarters near Manassas. The Confederate general moved his HQ during the battle from around Blackburn's Ford to the Portici house east of Henry Hill.*

(4 miles) northwest of the rail junction at Manassas. The army, organized into seven brigades, was deployed behind a meandering and steep-banked stream called Bull Run that ran northwest to southeast.

Bull Run was largely impassable, and Beauregard positioned his brigades along a 13-km (8-mile) front behind its few vulnerable crossing points. To the northwest, on his far left, stood the Stone Bridge that carried the Warrenton Turnpike (now State Route 29, Lee Highway). Downstream over the next 6km (4 miles) lay Lewis Ford, Ball's Ford and Island Ford. The stream then took a large convex bend where Mitchell's Ford, Blackburn's Ford and

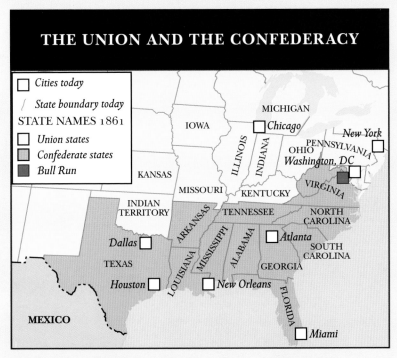

THE UNION AND THE CONFEDERACY

Cities today

State boundary today

STATE NAMES 1861

Union states

Confederate states

Bull Run

MICHIGAN
IOWA
Chicago
New York
PENNSYLVANIA
OHIO INDIANA
Washington, DC
ILLINOIS
KANSAS
VIRGINIA
MISSOURI
KENTUCKY
INDIAN TERRITORY
TENNESSEE
NORTH CAROLINA
ARKANSAS
Dallas
MISSISSIPPI
ALABAMA
Atlanta
SOUTH CAROLINA
TEXAS
LOUISIANA
GEORGIA
Houston
New Orleans
FLORIDA
MEXICO
Miami

ABOVE *Allowing for periodic reversals, Union armies entered the Confederacy in stages moving the line of major fighting through the following areas:* **The Border** *(the most vulnerable parts of the Confederacy and adjacent slaveholding areas): Missouri and Kentucky (both claimed by the Confederacy), Indian Territory (Oklahoma), western Virginia, Maryland, and the District of Columbia with adjacent parts of northern Virginia;* **The Lower South** *(the four Confederate states that seceded in 1861): Virginia, North Carolina, Tennessee, and Arkansas; and* **The Deep South** *(the original seven Confederate states): South Carolina, Georgia, Florida, Alabama, Mississippi, Louisiana, and Texas.*

The Union's subjugation of the Confederate rebellion began with the Border in 1861-62, continued into the Lower South in 1862–63, and entered much of the Deep South by 1863–64.

Notable exceptions are that the heart of Virginia remained in Confederate hands until the close of the war; early Federal offensives secured some important gains in the Deep South, particularly along the coasts; and Confederate counteroffensives periodically, if briefly, pushed back into the Lower South and the Border as late as 1864.

McLean's Ford all lay within a stretch of 5km (3 miles). These three fords, due north of Manassas, provided the best line of advance for the Federals. The crossing at Union Mills Ford lay on the Confederate far right to the southeast.

UNION RESPONSE TO CONFEDERATE DEPLOYMENT SOUTHWEST OF WASHINGTON

The Union response in late June was to order a small army under General George Patterson into the Shenandoah to engage Johnston, while from Washington the main Union force of 33,000, in five divisions under General Irvin McDowell, would advance on Richmond. On 16 July McDowell marched out of Washington towards Manassas Junction, watched by Southern spies. Before dawn on Thursday 18 July, Beauregard had telegraphed Johnston asking him to bring his army to Bull Run. By midday on the 18th, screened by Stuart's cavalry, Johnston left Patterson standing and marched east. On the morning of the 19th, his leading brigade under General Thomas J. Jackson had reached the Manassas Gap Railroad at Piedmont and was boarding a train for Manassas Junction 55km (34 miles) away.

By this time the Federals had begun to attack along Bull Run. On 18 July McDowell had reached the town of Centreville, 6km (4 miles) miles east down the Warrenton Turnpike. He immediately ordered General Daniel Tyler's division south to reconnoitre Blackburn's Ford. What was meant to be a feint turned into a sharp engagement that cost Tyler 83 men. Realizing the strength of the Confederate position here, McDowell's next plan was to flank Beauregard's right over Union Mills Ford, but a lack of good roads made this impractical. He then decided to flank the Confederate left. Two divisions would advance over the Sudley Springs Ford about 3km (2 miles) upstream from the Stone Bridge. Once across the Sudley Road (now State Route 234) heading south would then take the Federals in behind the Confederates and straight on to Manassas Junction. The plan relied on surprise, but it would, however, take another two days before his men would be ready to move.

Meanwhile, Johnston's army was arriving by train at Manassas Junction. By the end of 20 July the brigades of Jackson, Colonel Francis Bartow and General Bernard E. Bee had arrived and the train was on its way back to Piedmont to pick up General Edmund Kirby Smith's brigade. By the end of Saturday 20 July 35,000 Confederates were facing 37,000 Union troops across Bull Run. Beauregard, taking command of the combined Confederate army, planned to launch his own attack from around Blackburn's Ford. Here he concentrated nine brigades and all the cavalry, leaving his left flank protected by only one and a half brigades around the Stone Bridge.

CONFEDERATE

General Pierre G.T.
  Beauregard

Colonel Nathan G. Evans

Colonel Jubal Early

General Joseph E. Johnston

General Thomas J. (Stonewall)
  Jackson

Colonel Francis Bartow

General Bernard E. Bee

General Edmund Kirby Smith

Colonel Arnold Elzey

Colonel Wade Hampton

Colonel James Ewell Brown
  (Jeb) Stuart

UNION

General Irvin McDowell

General Daniel Tyler

Colonel William T. Sherman

General David Hunter

General Samuel Peter
  Heintzelman

General Oliver O. Howard

General George Patterson

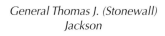

General Thomas J. (Stonewall) Jackson

General Irvin McDowell

McDOWELL'S ATTACK BEGINS

At 02:00 on Sunday 21 July McDowell's army began its advance. Tyler's division marched down the turnpike to make a diversionary attack at the Stone Bridge, while the divisions of generals David Hunter and Samuel P. Heintzelman, accompanied by McDowell himself, took the roads north and west to Sudley Springs Ford. At 06:00 Tyler reached the Stone Bridge and shortly afterwards Hunter and Heintzelman began crossing Bull Run, meeting no opposition.

To counter this attack the Confederates had only half a brigade under Colonel Nathan G. Evans. Fortunately for the South, not only was Evans one of the most aggressive of commanders, he also had the benefit of the finest defensive positions on the field. On either

side of the turnpike west of Bull Run rose two hills. To the north was Matthews Hill, and to the south Henry Hill (which was called Spring Hill in 1861). They both rose over 46m (150ft) and were topped with plateaux broad enough to deploy several brigades. The hills dominated the turnpike, Sudley Road and the Stone Bridge.

EVANS MOVES UP MATTHEWS HILL

At the southern foot of Matthews Hill, for about two hours, Evans held off Tyler's brigades across the Stone Bridge. By about 9:00 Evans had realized that this action was just a feint and, on being told of movement on his left, took most of his men up to the top of Matthews Hill. Evans arrived just in time to attack the lead regiments of Hunter's division as they came out of the woods to the north. Just after 10:00 Beauregard ordered the brigades of Bee and Bartow from McLean's Ford to support Evans. These brigades, plus artillery, established themselves on Evans' right and counterattacked.

This charge was effective at first, but stalled in the face of fresh Union troops of Heintzelman's division, who arrived at the foot of Matthews Hill at about 11:00. First Evans, then Bartow, then Bee were forced back up the hill; but despite heavy losses they managed to regroup and hold off two counterattacks by Heintzelman. Matthews Hill remained in Confederate hands, but the arrival of Colonel William T. Sherman's Union brigade on their right forced the battered Confederates to retreat off Matthews Hill to positions just north of the turnpike. There they stood behind a small tributary stream called Young's Branch that wound round to the east of Henry Hill. Victory now seemed in McDowell's grasp. He ordered the concentration of six brigades north of Young's Branch in preparation for a final assault.

Under increasing pressure, Evans, Bee and Bartow were forced to pull back across the turnpike to the northern slopes of Henry Hill. These rose gently over some 730m (800 yards). A track from the turnpike led to Robinson House, the cabin of freed slave James Robinson. To the right of the cabin and to the southwest across farmland stood Henry House, the home of a widow, Mrs Judith Carter Henry. Behind Henry House the hill began to slope down to surrounding woodland. Sudley Road ran to the west.

The Rebel retreat over Henry Hill slowed from about 11:00 with the arrival of fresh reinforcements. Colonel Wade Hampton's Legion from South Carolina made a short stand around Robinson House, and, by the time it was forced back, General Jackson's four Virginia regiments plus nine pieces of artillery were moving into line on the southern slope behind Henry House. 'Stonewall' Jackson's steadfast defence at this crucial moment was to become part of Confederate legend and provide the story behind his nickname. On Jackson's right, the remnants of Bee's brigade were falling back. Seeing Jackson standing firm, Bee rallied an Alabama regiment with words reported later to be: 'Look! There stands Jackson like a stone wall. Rally behind the Virginians.' Bee's precise words are unknown, but his call to action worked. The Alabamians followed their general back into the line, though it was at that moment that Bee received a mortal wound. The battle now centred on control of Henry Hill. Both Beauregard and Johnston were on the scene by midday and between them redeployed the army. Three brigades were kept at Blackburn's Ford, but the rest were brought up into line with Jackson. It was at this point that Colonel Bartow, moving his brigade onto the left of Jackson's, was also killed.

McDOWELL ADVANCES ON THE CONFEDERATE LEFT

At about 13:00 McDowell began to advance his troops towards the Confederate left. The move turned into a disaster. The infantry, Zouaves of the 11th New York, were routed by a charge of Jeb Stuart's cavalry coming in on their open right flank, from the west of the Sudley Road over Bald Hill. Shortly afterwards the 33rd Virginia, holding the Confederate far left, advanced close enough to the supporting Union artillery to shoot down its gunners and horses. The 33rd Virginia managed to get within range because the regiment was dressed in blue that day, the uniform colour of the US Army. There was no standard colour of dress for the

ABOVE *The rebuilt Henry House, home of the widow Mrs Judith Carter Henry. Behind the house, the hill began to slope down to surrounding woodland. On this slope Stonewall Jackson earned his nickname.*

armies at Bull Run, the war being in its infancy, and on several occasions during the battle there were mistakes of identity that led to fatalities on both sides.

With McDowell's first attack repulsed, the Confederates moved forward to secure the hill. For the next three hours McDowell attempted to take ground, but his attacks were repulsed. The Federals began to lose the initiative just as fresh reinforcements began to swing the battle in the Confederates' favour. The turning point came at about 16:00 with the arrival on the Rebel left of two fresh brigades: those of Colonel Jubal Early and General Kirby Smith. Smith's was the last of Johnston's brigades to arrive, marching straight from Manassas Junction into battle. Smith himself took a wound, and it was Colonel Arnold Elzey who led the brigade in the final charge that broke the Union right. As one side of his line collapsed, McDowell lost control of his army. A retreat turned into a rout as the Federals ran in a panic back up the Sudley Road and down the Warrenton Turnpike to Centreville. Most did not stop until they reached Washington.

It had been a bitter, confused battle, and the casualty figures on both sides were high. Of the men engaged, McDowell lost some 2900 men, while the Confederates lost 2000. In July 1861 the US Army erected a memorial obelisk to the Union dead. It lies to the east of Henry House and was the first of several monuments placed on Henry Hill to commemorate the battle.

VISITING THE BATTLEFIELD TODAY

The whole site is preserved today within the Manassas National Battlefield Park, which is maintained by the US National Park Service. The park also includes the area over which the Second Battle of Bull Run was fought in August 1862. It is open every day except Thanksgiving and Christmas Day.

Two hiking trails take visitors around the main landmarks of the First Battle of Bull Run. Both start from the visitor centre on the southern edge of Henry Hill, east of Route 234 and south of the Route 29 junction. The first of these is a 1.6km (mile-long) loop trail that winds around Henry Hill. The trail moves north to the rebuilt Henry House – which was demolished during the battle – and the grave of Mrs Carter Henry – the battle's only civilian casualty. The trail moves past the Confederate artillery positions facing Matthews Hill and down to the site of Robinson House. Only foundation marks are visible today because a reconstruction of the cabin was burnt down by arson in 1994. The trail then loops south to the approximate positions of Jackson's brigade and the Confederate line at mid-afternoon. Dominating this area to the east of the visitor centre is an equestrian statue of Jackson in bronze erected in 1940. Nearby are stone monuments to Colonel Bartow and General Bee.

The second trail is 8km (5 miles) in length. It loops east from the visitor centre and includes the Stone Bridge and Matthews Hill

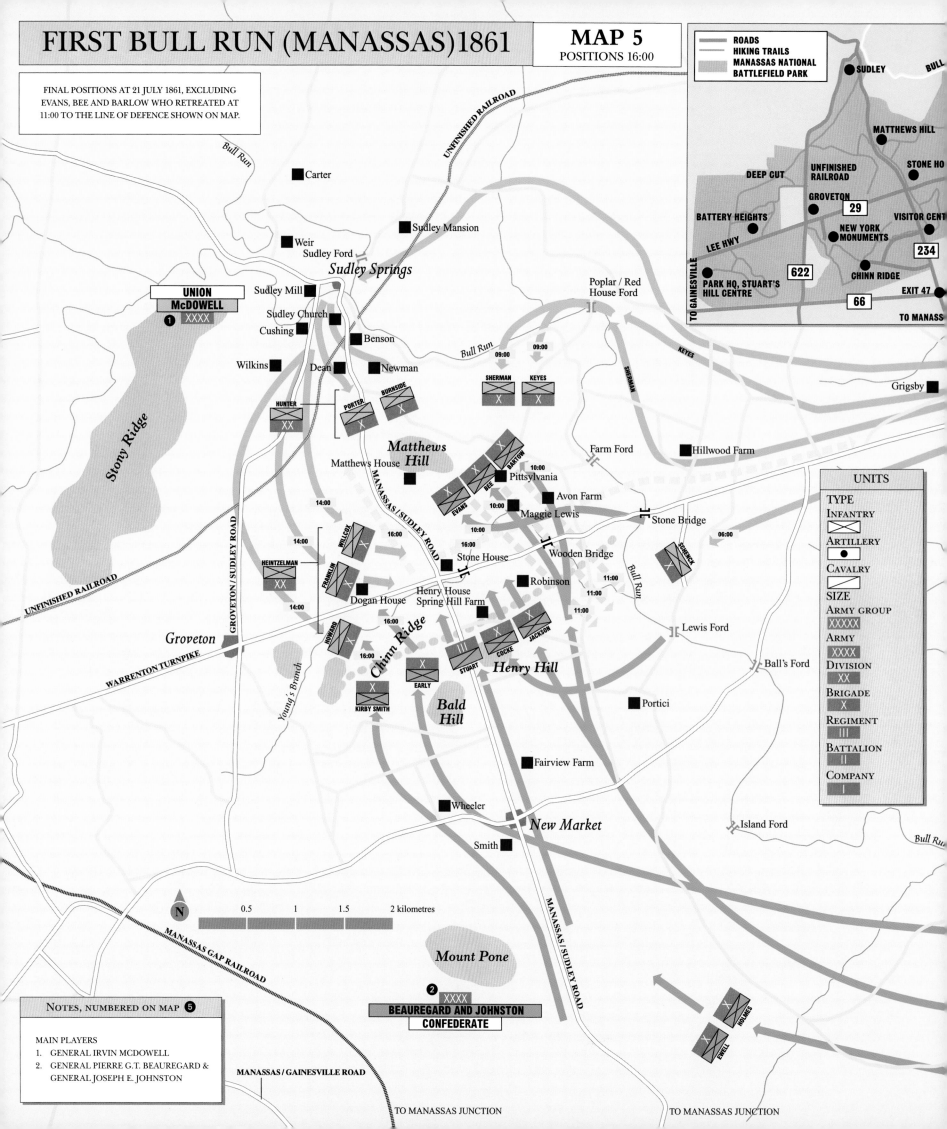

FIRST BULL RUN (MANASSAS) 1861

MAP 5
POSITIONS 16:00

FINAL POSITIONS AT 21 JULY 1861, EXCLUDING EVANS, BEE AND BARLOW WHO RETREATED AT 11:00 TO THE LINE OF DEFENCE SHOWN ON MAP.

Legend (top right)
- ROADS
- HIKING TRAILS
- MANASSAS NATIONAL BATTLEFIELD PARK

Inset map labels: SUDLEY, BULL, MATTHEWS HILL, STONE HO, DEEP CUT, UNFINISHED RAILROAD, GROVETON, 29, VISITOR CENT, BATTERY HEIGHTS, NEW YORK MONUMENTS, LEE HWY, 234, TO GAINESVILLE, 622, PARK HQ, STUART'S HILL CENTRE, CHINN RIDGE, 66, EXIT 47, TO MANASS

Map place labels
Bull Run
Carter
Sudley Mansion
Weir
Sudley Ford
Sudley Springs
UNION McDOWELL 1 XXXX
Sudley Mill
Sudley Church
Cushing
Benson
Wilkins
Dean
Newman
Bull Run 09:00 09:00
Poplar / Red House Ford
Grigsby
HUNTER XX
PORTER X
BURNSIDE X
SHERMAN X
KEYES X
SHERMAN
KEYES
Matthews Hill
Matthews House
Pittsylvania
BARTOW X
BEE X
EVANS X
10:00
10:00
10:00
Farm Ford
Hillwood Farm
Avon Farm
Maggie Lewis
Stone Bridge
14:00
14:00
WILLCOX X
HEINTZELMAN XX
FRANKLIN X
16:00
16:00
16:00
Stone House
Wooden Bridge
SCHENCK X
06:00
Robinson
11:00
11:00
14:00
Dogan House
Henry House
Spring Hill Farm
Bull Run
Stony Ridge
Groveton
GROVETON / SUDLEY ROAD
UNFINISHED RAILROAD
WARRENTON TURNPIKE
HOWARD X
16:00
Chinn Ridge
STUART III
COCKE X
JACKSON X
Henry Hill
11:00
Lewis Ford
Ball's Ford
KIRBY SMITH X
EARLY X
Bald Hill
Portici
Young's Branch
Fairview Farm
Wheeler
New Market
Island Ford
Bull Run
Smith
MANASSAS / SUDLEY ROAD
MANASSAS GAP RAILROAD
N
0.5 1 1.5 2 kilometres
Mount Pone
BEAUREGARD AND JOHNSTON 2 XXXX
CONFEDERATE
HOLMES X
EWELL X
MANASSAS / GAINESVILLE ROAD
TO MANASSAS JUNCTION
TO MANASSAS JUNCTION

UNITS
TYPE
- INFANTRY
- ARTILLERY
- CAVALRY

SIZE
- ARMY GROUP — XXXX
- ARMY — XXXX
- DIVISION — XX
- BRIGADE — X
- REGIMENT — III
- BATTALION — II
- COMPANY — I

NOTES, NUMBERED ON MAP 5
MAIN PLAYERS
1. GENERAL IRVIN McDOWELL
2. GENERAL PIERRE G.T. BEAUREGARD & GENERAL JOSEPH E. JOHNSTON

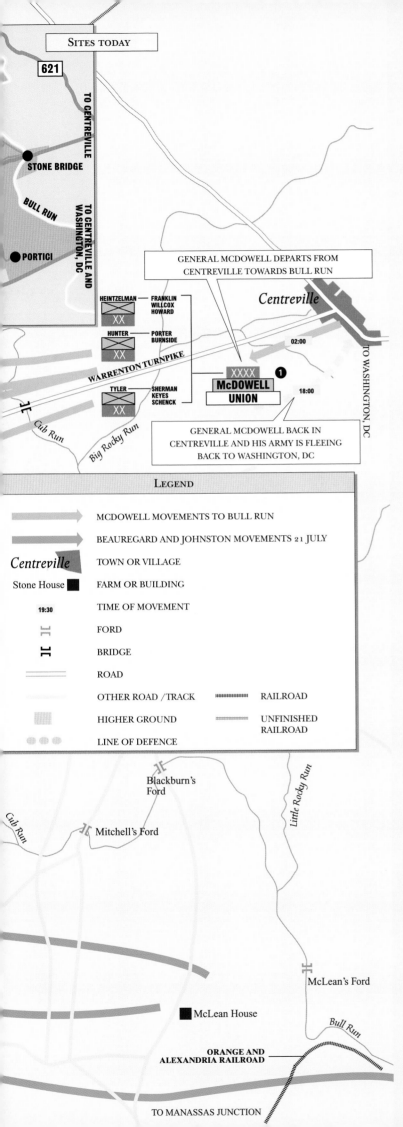

where the positions of Union gun batteries can be seen. The National Park Service has recently removed a car park and a picnic site from Matthews Hill and is endeavouring to return as much of the battlefield to its 1860s condition as is practical. This includes the removal of foreign and exotic plant species over an area of some 600ha (1500 acres). Efforts to preserve the battlefield, however, are constrained by the fact that it is cut through today by two major commuter routes into Washington, DC. The development of the city's suburbs poses a continual threat.

FIRST BATTLE OF BULL RUN TIMELINE

Sunday, 21 July 1861

02:00 McDowell marches out of Centreville towards Bull Run. Hunter and Heintzelman turn north towards Sudley Springs Ford. Tyler takes his men along the Warrenton Turnpike towards the Stone Bridge.

06:00 Tyler reaches the eastern end of Stone Bridge.

08:00 Tyler's attack limited to a skirmish. Evans suspects a feint.

09:00 Evans realizes he is being flanked from the north and takes up a new position on the northern slope of Matthews Hill. Starts attack on Hunter's division.

10:00 Confederate reinforcements begin to reach Evans. General Bee and Colonel Bartow move on to Matthews Hill. General Jackson begins to march from Mitchell's Ford towards Henry Hill.

11:00 Evans, Bee and Bartow are forced off Matthews Hill and retreat across the turnpike and up Henry Hill. The retreating Confederates rally around Jackson's strong line of defence on the hill's southern slope.

12:00 Beauregard and Johnston order brigades from the west banks of the Bull Run to strengthen Jackson.

14:00 Confederates repulse Federal assaults. McDowell extends his right in a flanking manoeuvre. He attempts to enfilade the Confederate left with artillery, but fails to support the move with enough infantry. The Federals are held after a charge by Colonel Stuart's Confederate cavalry.

15:00 McDowell continues to attempt to flank the Confederate left and orders his last reserve brigade, commanded by General Oliver O. Howard, into the attack from west of the Sudley Road.

16:00 Howard's brigade flanked by two fresh Confederate brigades: Colonel Early and General Kirby Smith charging in on its extreme left. Federal line buckles.

17:00 The Federal retreat becomes a rout.

18:00 McDowell back in Centreville; army flees back to Washington. Confederates too exhausted to pursue.

SHILOH 1862

By Jason R. Musteen

In the first true battle of the American Civil War in July 1861, southern forces routed the Union army at Manassas, Virginia, initiating four years of stroke and counterstroke between the two capitals of Richmond and Washington, DC. With the exception of the Antietam campaign, General Robert E. Lee amassed a string of remarkable Confederate victories that continued into 1863. However, while Confederate President Jefferson Davis focused his attention on the successes in the eastern theatre of the war, he was steadily losing it in the west. Abraham Lincoln continued to search in vain for a general capable of defeating Lee in the east, but he could at least look with satisfaction to the west, where a northern general had begun to bring him victory.

Ulysses Grant had left the army following the Mexican War and had failed in business before donning the uniform again at the outbreak of war in 1861. At the head of 23,000 men, Grant won for the Union its first great victory at Forts Henry and Donelson, Tennessee in February 1862. The Confederate surrender removed

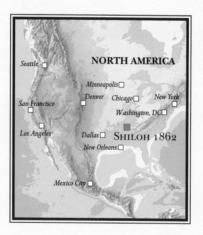

NORTH AMERICA

Seattle
Minneapolis
Denver Chicago New York
San Francisco Washington, DC
Los Angeles Dallas SHILOH 1862
New Orleans
Mexico City

12,000 southerners from the already stretched western theatre, brought northern Tennessee under Union control, and opened the way for Grant to unite his army with Major General Don Carlos Buell's Army of the Ohio, which had occupied Nashville. On 1 March, Major General Henry Halleck, commanding Union forces in the west, ordered Grant to move south to Pittsburg Landing on the Tennessee River in preparation for an attack on the rail junction of Corinth, Mississippi. Once Corinth was secure and the Confederate army in the west defeated, Union control of Tennessee would be complete and Grant could continue down the Mississippi River to Vicksburg and beyond.

The Confederate western army was under the command of General Albert Sidney Johnston, hailed by many in the north and south as the greatest general on either side. With a resumé that included posts like Commanding General of the Army of the Republic of Texas, Texan Secretary of War, and Commanding General of US forces in the Mormon War, he had more experience leading large numbers of troops than anyone else in uniform. 'I hoped and expected that I had others who would prove generals', President Davis once stated, 'but I knew I had one, and that was Sidney Johnston'. Davis placed Johnston second on the seniority list behind Adjutant General Samuel Cooper and assigned him the difficult task of defending the Confederacy from the

ABOVE *These heavy 24-pounder siege guns from the 2nd Illinois Artillery formed part of the Union's 'Last Line' at Pittsburg Landing, Tennessee, on 6 April 1862, that repelled the final Confederate attacks at the Battle of Shiloh.*

Appalachian Mountains to the Mississippi River with a small army centred in Kentucky and Tennessee. Dispersed as his army was, Johnston had been unable to reach Fort Donelson in time to prevent its fall, but as Grant marched south, Johnston determined to move quickly and take the fight to Grant before he could unite with Buell or reach Corinth.

By 10 March, Grant's army had moved down the Tennessee River, occupied Pittsburg Landing, and had begun to organize for the invasion of Mississippi. The consolidation of his forces was necessarily a long process, yet Grant forbade his men from digging trenches at Pittsburg Landing, lest they lose their offensive mindset. While the Union Army continued to arrive, Johnston arrived in Corinth, mustering 44,000 men of the Army of Mississippi by the end of March. On 3 April, the southerners marched into Tennessee.

THE BATTLE

As Johnston approached Pittsburg Landing and then bivouacked only a couple of miles away on the 5th, Grant's 39,000 men maintained their weak position, pinned between the Tennessee River and Owl Creek, waiting for Buell's 50,000 men to arrive. The fields and woods around the landing site had become a major military town, teeming with men and cluttered with supplies in various stages of organization. Convinced that the Confederate Army was still dispersed and miles away, Grant did not reconnoitre the routes to his south. Major General William Tecumseh Sherman, one of Grant's key subordinates, even refused to believe reports of major enemy formations to his front. Subsequently, in the pre-dawn hours of 6 April, Johnston unleashed one of the most successful surprise attacks of the war when his forward divisions poured out of the woods and into the Union camps. Some northern troops were cooking breakfast; many were still asleep when the bullets started to fly.

The opposing armies first clashed near a small church called Shiloh, ironically meaning 'place of peace'. Johnston had planned to attack first on the Union left in order to push Grant north and away from Pittsburg Landing. By seizing the landing site, Johnston could prevent Buell's army, which was still on the far side of the river, from joining the fight while he destroyed Grant's army. However, as the first three Confederate corps marched into action, they hit William Sherman's division on the Union right. Although caught completely by surprise and wounded in the opening moments, Sherman managed to rally his men and hold the Confederate attack for several hours – long enough to fall back in good order into a second defensive position with Major General John McClernand's division by mid-morning. To Sherman's left, in the Union centre, Alabamians of Major General Braxton Bragg's corps caught Brigadier General Benjamin Prentiss's division eating breakfast and drove it back in disorder for over a mile. Major General Leonidas Polk's corps joined Bragg in the attack on the Union centre, practically destroying it

before slowing in the face of Union reinforcement. Although his opening attacks had not progressed exactly according to plan, Johnston had the initiative and was driving Grant back. His early success, however, had led to increasing chaos as his corps became intermingled in the woods. Johnston's quick advance on the Union right and centre also left his own right flank dangerously exposed, so he ordered his remaining forces to attack Colonel David Stuart's brigade on the Union left. Although the southerners repeatedly attacked from 11:00 to 13:00, they were unable to sever Grant's link to the river on his left. The Confederate attack in the centre also stalled around noon when Brigadiers General Stephen A. Hurlbut and William H.L. Wallace's Union divisions occupied positions in a sunken road in front of the Confederate advance. The hail of lead was so thick in the woods around the road that small trees were cut in half by the fire and whole Confederate units were destroyed in minutes in what became known as the Hornet's Nest.

In mid-afternoon, after reorganizing his corps, Johnston reinvigorated his attacks against Sherman on the Union right with more success. Meanwhile, the sunken road still held strong as Bragg continued to hurl his men in assault after assault on the strong Union position.

Recognizing that his corps commander was slaughtering his own men in these futile attacks, Brigadier General Daniel Ruggles, one of Bragg's division commanders, gathered 62 cannon and formed the largest concentration of guns assembled in the war to that

UNIT SIZES

NAME	USUAL SIZES	
	Union Army	**Confederate Army**
Corps	3 Divisions	3 Divisions
Division	3 Brigades	4–5 Brigades
Brigade	4–5 Regiments	4–6 Regiments
Regiment	10 Companies	10 Companies
	1100 officers and men	1100 officers and men
Company	100 men	100 men

Both sides would allow a regiment to dwindle in size due to casualties and then use new recruits to start new regiments rather than reinforce depleted regiments. That way politicians could hand out more commissions. In many cases, especially late in the war, a regiment consisted of only 200 men.

left Grant no retreat. The Confederate command devolved on P.G.T. Beauregard, hero of Fort Sumter and Manassas, who, as second in command, had been managing the fight from the rear and was not completely aware of the situation. After assuming command and assessing Grant's final line around Pittsburg Landing, Beauregard ordered a halt for the night in order to reorganize and begin anew in the morning. Time was one commodity he could not afford to waste, though. During the night, 7500 men from two divisions of Buell's Army of the Ohio crossed the river and joined Grant's line on the left. Also joining the fight was another Union division of 5800 men under Major General Lew Wallace, later author of *Ben Hur* and nemesis of Billy the Kid as governor of New Mexico. Wallace had missed the entire fight to that point and so added fresh men to the Union right. Moreover, two Union gunboats capable of firing into the Confederate lines arrived on the river to the east of Grant and began firing from south of Pittsburg Landing.

Despite the formidable force he faced on the morning of the 7th, Beauregard began the attack again, but quickly realized that total victory was no longer possible. As his force grew weaker and smaller, Buell's men continued to cross the river and had almost 18,000 soldiers in the fight by the end of the battle. No longer in danger of being pushed into the river, Grant assumed the offensive. Although the Confederates mounted an admirable defense, they were forced back throughout the day before retiring from the field in good order by 16:00 that afternoon. Grant's Union army was too spent to mount an aggressive pursuit and allowed Beauregard to fall back on Corinth, ending the battle.

point. Ruggles' massive battery almost immediately forced the Union troops out of the sunken road, where 2000 of them were captured, including Prentiss. Wallace fell mortally wounded.

Ruggles's action had regained the southern initiative for the final push on Grant's line; Union troops were streaming back towards Pittsburg Landing and the entire Confederate front advanced. However, at that critical moment, the southern army was without clear direction. Around 14:30, as Ruggles gathered his cannon, Johnston had decided to personally lead an attack into a peach orchard on the Union left-centre. A penetration there would serve the dual purpose of making the sunken road untenable and breaking the Union anchor on the river. Johnston's bold attack and personal bravery motivated his men at just the right moment and helped lead to a general advance. After allowing the attack to pass him by, Johnston discovered that his uniform was shot through in four places and the sole of his boot shot off. The general continued to issue orders with great spirit, but although he appeared unscathed, he had taken a bullet in the lower right leg. The ball severed an artery and Johnston bled into his boot for half an hour before anyone realized the gravity of the wound. The bleeding could have been easily managed, but Johnston had dispatched his personal physician earlier in the day to care for wounded Union troops. Therefore, with a tourniquet in his own pocket, the Confederate commander slowly bled to death shortly before Ruggles's success in the Hornet's Nest. As a full general and army commander, Sidney Johnston remains the highest-ranking American ever killed in battle.

At the time of Johnston's death, a concerted attack on the Union's far left flank would likely have broken the entire line and

When the smoke cleared, Shiloh had eclipsed anything yet seen in the war in tenacity and in cost. With 23,000 casualties during the two days' fighting, it was by far the bloodiest action ever fought on American soil to that point. The path to Vicksburg lay open and hopes for a short war were destroyed; after the carnage visited on 'the place of peace', both sides knew that the war would not be an affair of mere weeks or months, and that many more would die before peace could be restored.

TOURING THE BATTLEFIELD TODAY

Shiloh is a great battlefield to tour today and all the action can be covered easily in one day whether on foot or in a vehicle. The National Park Service maintains the battlefield, which includes a bookstore, museum, and theatre. Numerous colour-coded plaques and markers indicate the position of units throughout the battle, monuments are plentiful, and it is easy eough to embark on a self-guided tour. For a more focused or ambitious tour, the park also offers 10 different hiking trails ranging from 3km (2 miles) to a 32-km (20-mile) hike that follows Johnston's advance from Corinth. A good way to prepare for an actual tour of the battlefield is to take the virtual tour available at www.cwbattlefields.com/virtualtours/shiloh. The website briefly explains the battle, identifies the monuments, and provides a virtual tour. The US Army War College has also published a guide to the Battle of Shiloh through the University Press of Kansas that is arranged as a self-guided tour, with detailed descriptions and driving directions. The guide includes maps and photos and explains the action at each stop with original reports and quotations, helping the tourist to appreciate the importance of each piece of the battle. When planning a visit, remember that Shiloh is a small town and lodging is scarce, so it is best to stay in nearby Savannah or Corinth, Mississippi.

VISITORS' FACT FILE

Museums, tours, and accommodations:
- Hardin County Tourism Board, 507 Main St., Savannah, Tennessee 38372. (800) 552-3866.
- Shiloh National Military Park, 1005 Pittsburg Landing Road, Shiloh, Tennessee 38376. (731) 689-5450. www.nps.gov/shil.
- McNairy County Historical Museum, 114 North Third Street, Selmer, Tennessee 38375. (731) 646-0018.
- Tennessee River Museum, 507 Main Street, Savannah, Tennessee 38372. (731) 925-2364. www.tourhardincounty.org.
- Northeast Mississippi Museum, Fourth and Washington Streets, Corinth, Mississippi 38834. (601)287-3120. www2.tsixroads.com/~nemma/.
- Shiloh Tours, Guided tours are available at www.ShilohGuides.com.

MAIN CHARACTERS FEATURED

SOUTH (CONFEDERATES)
General Albert Sidney
  Johnston
Major General Braxton Bragg
Major General Leonidas Polk
Brigadier General Daniel
  Ruggles
General Pierre G.T.
  Beauregard

NORTH (UNION)
Major General Ulysses Grant
Major General Don Carlos
  Buell (Army of the Ohio)

Major General Henry Halleck
Major General William
  Tecumseh Sherman
Major General John
  McClernand
Brigadier General Benjamin
  Prentiss
Brigadier General Stephen A.
  Hurlbut
Brigadier General
  William H.L. Wallace
Major General Lew Wallace
Colonel David Stuart

General Albert Sidney Johnston

Major General Ulysses Grant

ABOVE *The headquarters of the Shiloh National Military Park.*

SHILOH 1862

MAP 6
POSITIONS 6 APRIL

POSITIONS AT 09:30 6 APRIL, JOHNSTON'S ADVANCE TO 17:00 ON 6 APRIL, AND THE FINAL COUNTERATTACK ON THE 7TH OF APRIL, BY GRANT AND BUELL

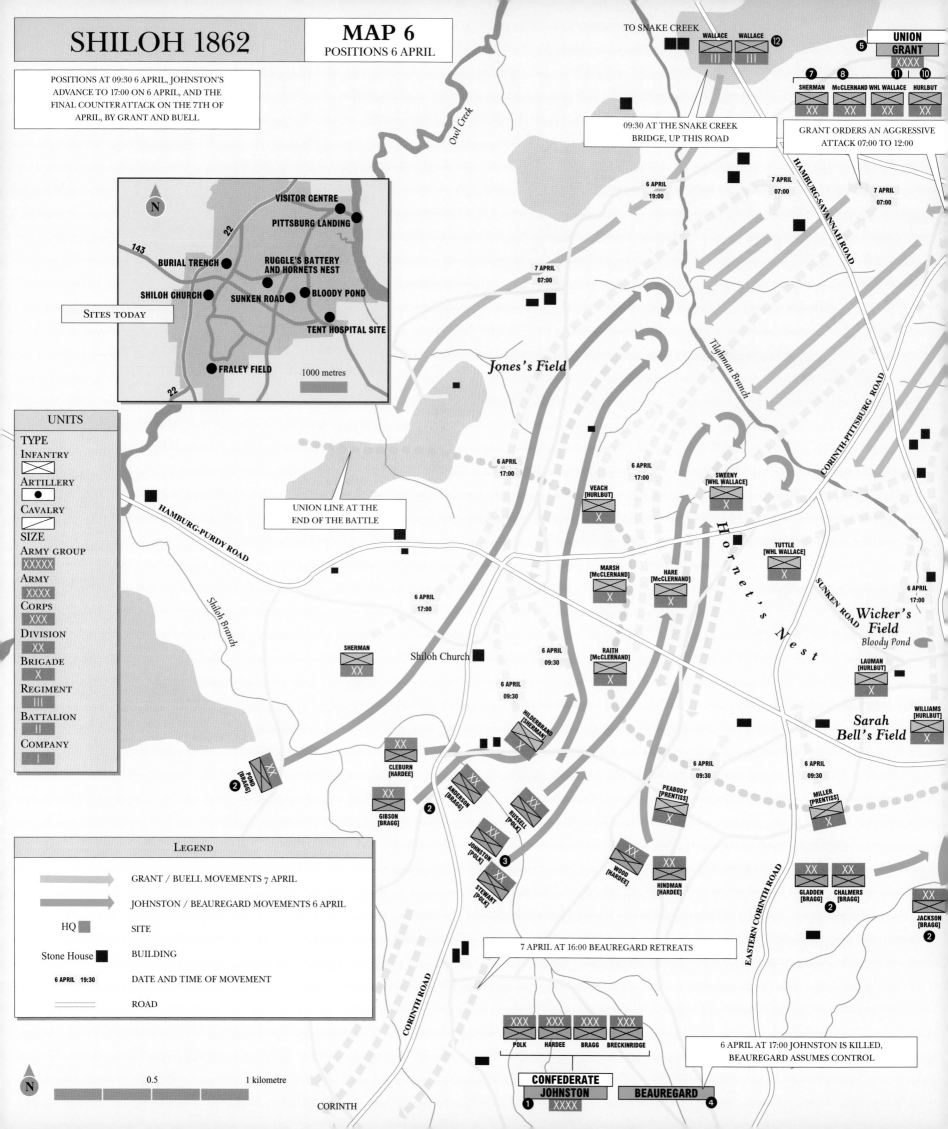

TO SNAKE CREEK

WALLACE ⅲ   WALLACE ⅹ ⑫

⑤ UNION
GRANT XXXX

⑦ SHERMAN XX   ⑧ McCLERNAND XX   ⑪ WHL WALLACE XX   ⑩ HURLBUT XX

09:30 AT THE SNAKE CREEK BRIDGE, UP THIS ROAD

GRANT ORDERS AN AGGRESSIVE ATTACK 07:00 TO 12:00

Owl Creek

6 APRIL 19:00

7 APRIL 07:00

7 APRIL 07:00

HAMBURG-SAVANNAH ROAD

Tilghman Branch

7 APRIL 07:00

Jones's Field

6 APRIL 17:00

6 APRIL 17:00

SWEENY [WHL WALLACE] X

CORINTH-PITTSBURG ROAD

SITES TODAY

- VISITOR CENTRE
- PITTSBURG LANDING
- RUGGLE'S BATTERY AND HORNETS NEST
- BURIAL TRENCH
- SHILOH CHURCH
- SUNKEN ROAD
- BLOODY POND
- TENT HOSPITAL SITE
- FRALEY FIELD

1000 metres

143   22

22

UNION LINE AT THE END OF THE BATTLE

VEACH [HURLBUT] X

TUTTLE [WHL WALLACE] X

Hornet's Nest

Sunken Road

Wicker's Field
Bloody Pond

6 APRIL 17:00

UNITS

TYPE
- INFANTRY ⊠
- ARTILLERY ■
- CAVALRY ⊘

SIZE
- ARMY GROUP XXXX
- ARMY XXXX
- CORPS XXX
- DIVISION XX
- BRIGADE X
- REGIMENT Ⅲ
- BATTALION Ⅱ
- COMPANY Ⅰ

HAMBURG-PURDY ROAD

Shiloh Branch

6 APRIL 17:00

SHERMAN XX

Shiloh Church

MARSH [McCLERNAND] X

HARE [McCLERNAND] X

6 APRIL 09:30

RAITH [McCLERNAND] X

LAUMAN [HURLBUT] X

WILLIAMS [HURLBUT] X

6 APRIL 09:30

HILDERBRAND [SHERMAN] X

Sarah Bell's Field

CLEBURN [HARDEE] XX

② POND [BRAGG] XX

ANDERSON [BRAGG] XX

GIBSON [BRAGG] XX ②

RUSSELL [POLK] XX

6 APRIL 09:30

PEABODY [PRENTISS] X

6 APRIL 09:30

MILLER [PRENTISS] X

JOHNSTON [POLK] XX ③

WOOD [HARDEE] XX

HINDMAN [HARDEE] XX

GLADDEN [BRAGG] XX   CHALMERS [BRAGG] XX ②

JACKSON [BRAGG] XX ②

STEWART [POLK] XX

LEGEND

⟹	GRANT / BUELL MOVEMENTS 7 APRIL
⟹	JOHNSTON / BEAUREGARD MOVEMENTS 6 APRIL
HQ ■	SITE ●
Stone House ■	BUILDING ■
6 APRIL 19:30	DATE AND TIME OF MOVEMENT
——	ROAD

EASTERN CORINTH ROAD

7 APRIL AT 16:00 BEAUREGARD RETREATS

CORINTH ROAD

N

0.5   1 kilometre

POLK XXX   HARDEE XXX   BRAGG XXX   BRECKINRIDGE XXX

6 APRIL AT 17:00 JOHNSTON IS KILLED, BEAUREGARD ASSUMES CONTROL

CONFEDERATE
JOHNSTON ①   **BEAUREGARD** ④
XXXX

CORINTH

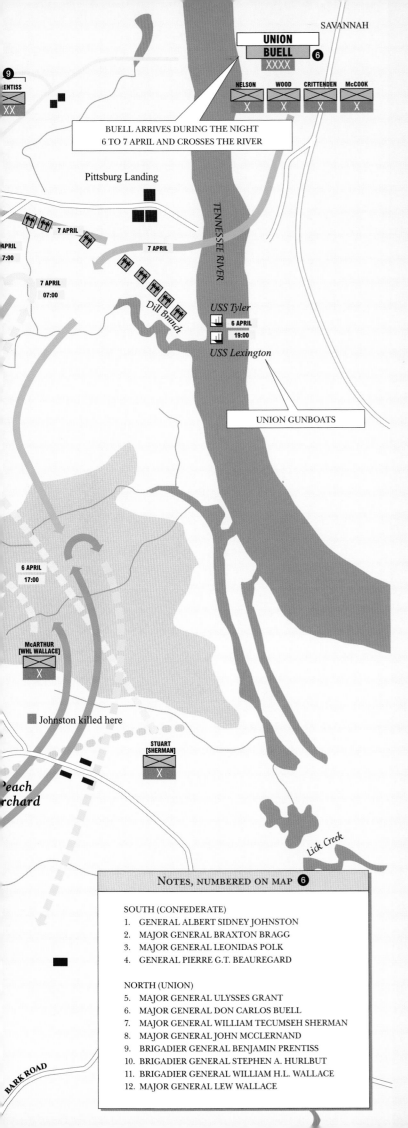

SHILOH TIMELINE

5 April   Grant based at Pittsburg Landing.

5 April   Johnston's army bivouacked within 8km (5 miles) of Grant.

6 April

5:15   Johnston launches surprise attack.

4:55–6:30   A Union patrol discovers Johnston's forward units, opens fire and withdraws.

6:30–9:00   Bragg and Polk's Confederate corps attack the Union centre, forcing Prentiss to flee.

8:00–9:30   Hurlbut and W.H.L. Wallace occupy a sunken road in the centre of the Union frontline.

7:00–10:00   Sherman arrests the advancing Confederates before falling back to join McClernand.

9:00–10:30   To keep his frontline uniform, Johnston orders an attack on the Union left.

10:00–11:30   The Confederate army continues the attack against the Union right, pushing Sherman and McClernand further back.

11:00–13:00   Stuart's division repulses the Confederate attack on the Union left.

12:00–14:30   Sherman and McClernand mount a counterattack, but after initial success, are forced to withdraw.

12:00–15:30   While the Union right counterattacks, the Confederate attack fails repeatedly to dislodge Hurlbut and Wallace in the Hornet's Nest at the sunken road.

13:00–16:00   Johnston personally leads an attack near the Peach Orchard on the Union left centre. The attack succeeds, but Johnston dies at 14:30.

14: 30–17:30   Ruggles gathers 62 cannon and breaks the Union defence in the sunken road. Wallace is killed and Hurlbut captured.

15:00–17:30   Sherman and McClernand withdraw and establish a stronger defence on the Union right.

15:00–18:00   Beauregard takes command of the Confederate army and halts the advance in front of Pittsburg Landing for the night.

19:00   Lew Wallace's division begins to arrive on the battlefield after spending the entire day trying to find the right road to reach the fight.

18:30   Buell's Army of the Ohio begins to arrive at Pittsburg Landing. Union gunboats *Lexington* and *Tyler* begin firing into Confederate positions.

7 April

7:00–14:00   A general Union advance pushes Beauregard back across the ground taken the previous day.

14:00–16:00   The Union advance slowed to a halt, allowing Beauregard to withdraw to Corinth.

ANTIETAM 1862

By Joshua Moon

The South's failure to gain a major operational victory on Union soil hindered their attempt to gain formal diplomatic status from Europe. Following the bitter defeat at Shiloh in April 1862, and mindful of this nagging short-coming, the rebel president, Jefferson Davis and his ministers devised a strategy to separate the Border States of Kentucky and Maryland from the Union. In order to politically weaken the Union and garner European support, a two-pronged military strategy was planned: General Robert E. Lee would invade Maryland and possibly Pennsylvania, and General Braxton Bragg would attack into Kentucky in the west.

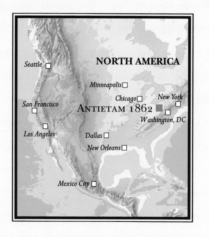

ABOVE LEFT *'Burnside Bridge' over the Antietam Creek. The action on the Union left flank hinged on the successful crossing of this obstacle. General Burnside's inability to coordinate his attack bought valuable time for Confederate General A.P. Hill to arrive from Harpers Ferry with reinforcements.*
ABOVE CENTRE *A sunken road is littered with dead men and equipment. While offering protection as natural trenches to defending infantry, it could become deadly with enfilading fire.*
ABOVE RIGHT *Confederate artillery crew lie dead near their caisson on the east side of Hagerstown Pike looking towards the Dunker Church. They fell close to where the visitor centre is today.*

LEE MOVES NORTH

Lee's invasion plan was to have the added benefit of relieving the stress upon war-torn northern Virginia, which had been forced to shoulder the burden of feeding both Union and Confederate armies for over a year. As Lee moved north-ward, on 8 September, he sent a proclamation to the people of Maryland: 'The people of the South have long wished to aid you in throwing off a foreign yoke, and to enable you to again enjoy the inalienable rights of freemen ... in obedience with this wish the army has come to you.' To his dismay, Lee found little sympathy in the state. Mary-landers did not rally to his cause. Worse yet, they also did not volunteer supplies for his army. Unwilling to punish the people he sought to free from Union occupation, Lee decided to push north-ward into Pennsylvania.

In order to confuse the Union army, which had been ably organ-ized by General George McClellan to pursue and defeat the invader, Lee boldly divided his army into four formations. On 9 September he issued Special Order 191, which directed his army's drive towards Pennsylvania. Lee's subordinates were experienced and competent and included generals Thomas 'Stonewall' Jackson, James Longstreet, and Daniel H. Hill. Lee also had General Jeb Stuart's cav-alry. Stuart's cavalry was far superior to those of his Union counterparts and maintained a constant vigil on the Union's Army of

'McClellan is an able general but a very cautious one. His army is in a very demoralized and chaotic condition and will not be prepared for offensive operations – or he will not think so – for three or four weeks. By that time I hope to be on the Susquehanna River.'

Robert E. Lee, 8 September 1862

'To the President: I have the whole rebel force in front of me … I have a difficult task to perform but with God's blessing will accomplish it. I think Lee has made a gross mistake and he will be severely punished for it. The army is in motion as rapidly as possible.'

George B. McClellan, 13 September 1862

the Potomac as it lumbered west in pursuit of Lee. With his talented group of subordinates, Lee ordered Jackson to seize the Federal arsenal and key transportation hub at Harpers Ferry, and moved General Longstreet north towards Hagerstown. Against a more aggressive foe, Lee might not have risked dividing his force. However, he was fighting 'cautious' George McClellan, and therefore assumed that his columns could reunite before the Union army could strike.

While Lee's army pushed northward, the winds of chance blew in the direction of the Yankees: four days after Lee issued his instructions, McClellan's troops found a copy of Special Order 191 at an abandoned Confederate campsite. In the hands of a

bold and aggressive leader, the captured order would have spelled doom for Lee's divided force, but McClellan was neither – and waited 24 hours to issue his directives. McClellan's troops lost valuable time and instead of aggressively moving in between Longstreet and Jackson, the Union columns advanced methodically. The crucial delay gave Lee the time he needed to bring his troops together.

Lee chose the town of Sharpsburg to defend. Located on the eastern bank of the Potomac River, Sharpsburg was a quiet, modest place. Cornfields covered the undulating terrain. A small creek, the Antietam, meandered through the farmland east of the town until it flowed into the Potomac River. Lee's artillery occupied the high ground that overlooked the Antietam. To the west lay the town of Sharpsburg, and the only 'escape route' for Lee's army was one narrow bridge across the Potomac. With the river at his back, Sharpsburg was a risky position to defend, but Lee felt that the terrain and the quick Union pursuit had dictated his choices.

In accordance with Lee's original instructions, Jackson captured the important transportation hub of Harpers Ferry and its Union garrison of 12,000 men on 15 September. (It marked the largest surrender of United States troops until the fall of Corrigedor in 1942.) As soon as the town was captured, Jackson left a division under General Ambrose P. Hill to process the prisoners and then hastily marched the 27km (17 miles) towards Sharpsburg. Jackson did not arrive until the morning of the 16th. By that time, McClellan's forces had pushed Longstreet's troops back to Sharpsburg and were in position to strike. However, once again, McClellan waited, giving Lee the afternoon of the 16th to organize his defense. Lee moved Jackson into position on the left and Longstreet's troops defended the right.

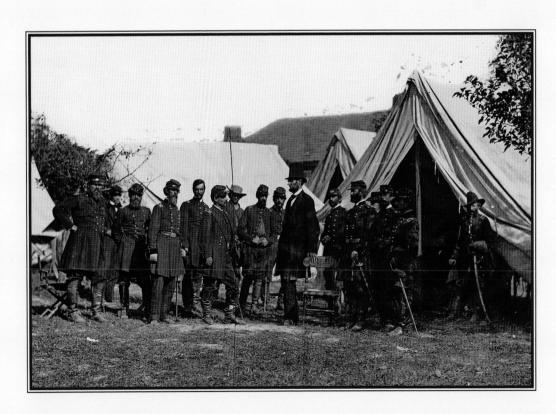

RIGHT *President Lincoln and McClellan's staff. Lincoln used the victory to issue the Emancipation Proclamation. However, he relieved McClellan (sixth from left in the picture) for his failure to pursue Lee's shattered army aggressively. The photo was taken by Alexander Gardner, who took 70 photographs of the battlefield starting just two days after the battle. This was the first time an American battlefield had ever been photographed before the dead had been buried. Gardner returned in early October when President Lincoln visited General George McClellan and the Army of the Potomac and took another series of images. Gardner worked for a photography gallery in Washington.*

CONDUCT OF THE BATTLE

At dawn on the 17th, McClellan intended to attack both Confederate flanks and then commit his reserves to smash Lee's centre. It required a double envelopment by forces separated by the Antietam Creek against forces in defensive positions and with the advantage of interior lines (being able to reposition forces from flank to flank because the distance within the defensive perimeter is less than on the outside – although it didn't help Custer). Not surprisingly, the plan miscarried.

The primary attack against Lee's left flank became a series of blows delivered by individual divisions as they reached the battlefield, while General Ambrose Burnside's attack against the right was late in materializing. There was no cohesion, no unified command, no definite objective, and at the climax of the battle, McClellan was unwilling to commit his reserves in the centre. Antietam was in fact a soldier's battle, waged by separate units with very little direction from above.

The early morning Union attack began on the Confederate left. The attack traversed a cornfield, where Jackson's men met them. After the battle, General Joseph (Fighting Joe) Hooker commented, 'every stalk of corn was cut as closely as could have been with a knife ... the slain lay in rows precisely as they stood in their ranks a few moments before.' Hooker added 'It was never my for-

tune to witness a more bloody, dismal battlefield.' As Hooker's attack pressed across the cornfield, it was hit in the flank by a violent counterattack by General John Bell Hood's Texas troops. 'Hood's troops always fight well', one southern general had commented earlier and, at Antietam, he said 'they fought like devils'. Hood's attack sent the Federals reeling, but by 09:00, the Federals formed another attack. However, Confederate reinforcements arrived from Harpers Ferry to shore up the rebel line and these Federal attacks failed. Back and forth the two armies fought all morning on the Confederate left. Each time a Federal attack was defeated, it was pursued by a rebel counterattack that encountered stiff resistance and overwhelming Federal artillery. At about noon, the two bloodied and exhausted armies formed defensive lines in roughly the same positions they had occupied in the morning; the fight for the Confederate left was over.

The fight shifted to the centre of the two opposing lines. Here the fighting was no less violent, but was equally uncoordinated as Federal troops surged forward to a sunken road which was lined by a fence and defended by Confederate troops. The road served as a natural trench, and as the Federal troops reached a crest just before the trench, they were met by a withering fire. A Confederate commander recalled: 'For five minutes, the Union troops bravely stood a telling fire at 80 yards [73m], which my brigade delivered ... then

ABOVE *Confederate dead along the west side of Hagerstown Pike, killed by enfilading fire when Union troops outflanked their positions.*

fell back.' In one of the few flanking movements of the battle General Israel Richardson's division of II Corps arrived and outflanked the rebel trench. Pouring enfilading fire down the sunken road, it quickly became 'Bloody Lane' for the rebel defenders. However, Richardson's attack stalled when he was killed, and the fighting in the centre stalled just as it had on the Confederate left.

CLIMACTIC ACTION

As the day drew on, the fighting at last flared up on the Confederate right, where McClellan had been prodding General Burnside, for over two hours, to storm the bridge to his front and charge the slopes beyond. Defending the bridge, were Georgians under General Robert Toombs. Two Federal assaults over the bridge were repulsed as Toomb's troops punished them from an

enfilading artillery position on the opposite bank and from the cover of boulders and trees that overlooked the bridge. Finally, at 13:00, two regiments, from New York and Pennsylvania, dashed across the bridge and gained a foothold on the Confederate side. While another unit outflanked the rebels by fording the creek further south, it took Burnside over two hours to advance up the slopes from the bridgehead. By 15:00 the Union attack had gained momentum and advanced towards Sharpsburg. Led by the New York Zouaves with their distinctive red trousers, one observer noted, 'with arms and banners glittering in the sun, following the double line of skirmishers dashing forward at a trot, loading and firing as they moved ... it was one of the most brilliant exhibitions of the day.'

To halt the Union tide, Lee shifted all available artillery to support the defense of the southern flank. By 16:00 the Union troops were approaching Sharpsburg, and only a half-mile lay between them and Lee's line of retreat. Disaster seemed at hand for Lee's exhausted troops.

As fate would allow, the timely arrival of General A.P. Hill's division saved Lee's army. Having covered the 27km (17 miles) from Harpers Ferry in less than seven hours, Hill's veteran troops crossed the Potomac and marched headlong into the firestorm. As Hill's exhausted troops slammed into Burnside's left flank, confusion and fear ran through the Union ranks. As men turned to run, Hill's men pushed forward. The Union line, sagging from Hill's attack and the blistering rebel artillery fire, retreated back to the sheltering banks of the Antietam.

While McClellan still retained the numerical advantage, he did not press the attack. An hour and a half after Hill halted Burnside's attack, the battle of Antietam set with the Maryland sun. Bloodied and beaten, the two commanders were unwilling to pursue action the next day. It had been a meat grinder.

Tactically the battle was a draw. Operationally and strategically, it was a Union victory because it halted Lee's invasion. However, because Lee's army, with its back to the Potomac River, escaped, President Lincoln relieved McClellan of command. Furthermore, the battle ended any serious consideration of European recognition for the Confederacy, and made it possible for Lincoln to issue the Emancipation Proclamation on 22 September. With the formal abolition of slavery in the United States 'or any state or district in rebellion' the war took on a new purpose. In the north, the cause of American union became synonymous with human liberty. In the south, it forced the people into a desperate struggle for survival.

Antietam might have ended the war; instead the battle only prolonged it. The official reports, survivor's testimony, and the 12,410 Union and 10,700 Confederate dead left behind in field hospitals and shallow graves, all bear witness that Antietam was the bloodiest day of the Civil War, and probably any day in American history.

MAIN CHARACTERS FEATURED

SOUTH (CONFEDERATES)	NORTH (UNION/FEDERAL)
General Robert E. Lee	General George McClellan (Army of the Potomac)
General Braxton Bragg	
General Thomas 'Stonewall' Jackson	General Ambrose Burnside
General James Longstreet	General Joseph (Fighting Joe) Hooker
General Daniel Harvey Hill.	General Israel Richardson
General JEB Stuart (cavalry)	
General Ambrose Powell Hill	
General John Bell Hood	
General Robert Toombs	

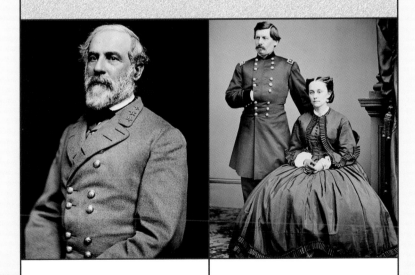

General Robert E. Lee

General George McClellan and his wife Ellen Mary Marcy

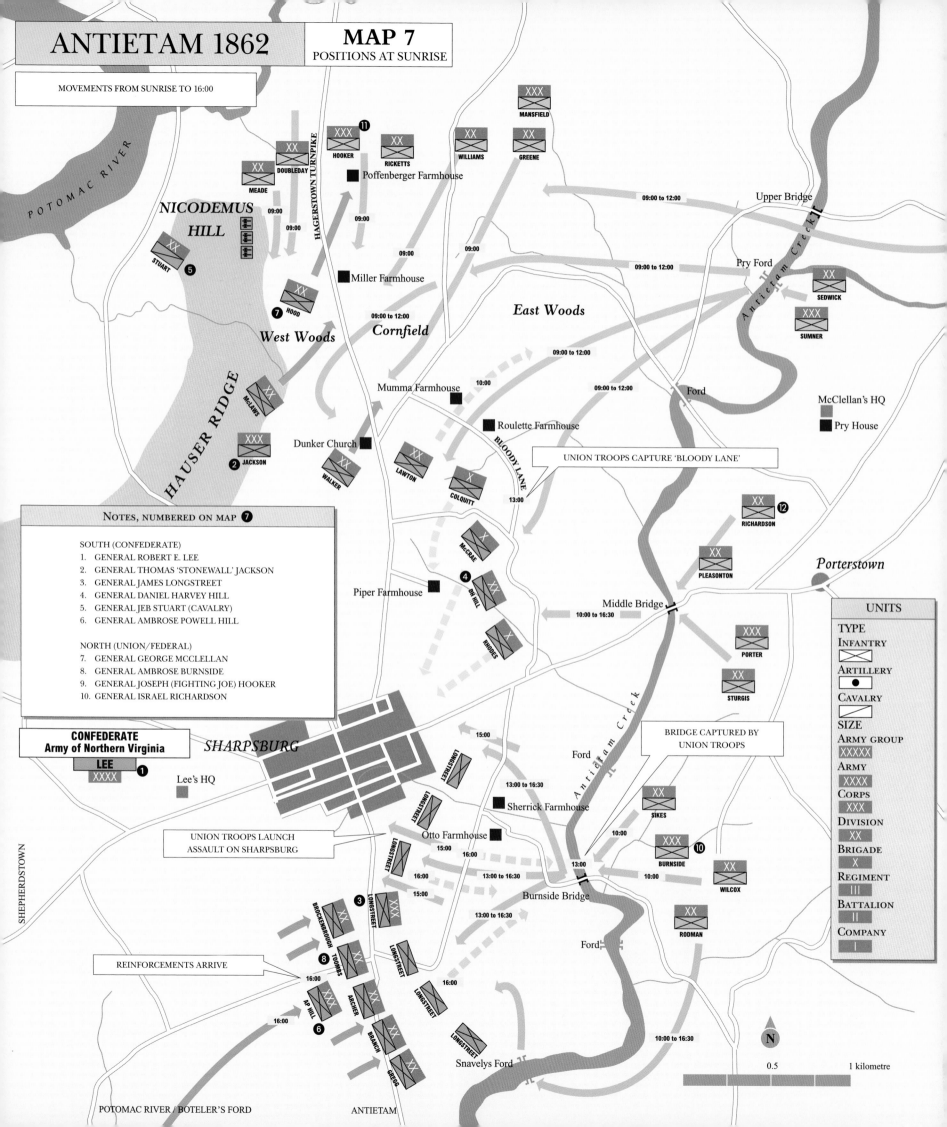

ANTIETAM 1862

MAP 7
POSITIONS AT SUNRISE

MOVEMENTS FROM SUNRISE TO 16:00

POTOMAC RIVER

NICODEMUS HILL

MANSFIELD

DOUBLEDAY

MEADE

HOOKER ⑪

RICKETTS

WILLIAMS

GREENE

Poffenberger Farmhouse

Upper Bridge

STUART ⑤

09:00

09:00

09:00

09:00

09:00

09:00

09:00 to 12:00

Pry Ford

09:00 to 12:00

SEDWICK

SUMNER

HOOD ⑦

Miller Farmhouse

HAGERSTOWN TURNPIKE

West Woods

Cornfield

East Woods

09:00 to 12:00

09:00 to 12:00

09:00 to 12:00

Ford

McLAWS

HAUSER RIDGE

JACKSON ②

Mumma Farmhouse

10:00

Roulette Farmhouse

McClellan's HQ

Pry House

Dunker Church

WALKER

LAWTON

COLQUITT

BLOODY LANE

UNION TROOPS CAPTURE 'BLOODY LANE'

13:00

RICHARDSON ⑫

McCRAE

Porterstown

Piper Farmhouse

④

DH HILL

PLEASONTON

Middle Bridge

10:00 to 16:30

RHODES

PORTER

NOTES, NUMBERED ON MAP ⑦

SOUTH (CONFEDERATE)
1. GENERAL ROBERT E. LEE
2. GENERAL THOMAS 'STONEWALL' JACKSON
3. GENERAL JAMES LONGSTREET
4. GENERAL DANIEL HARVEY HILL
5. GENERAL JEB STUART (CAVALRY)
6. GENERAL AMBROSE POWELL HILL

NORTH (UNION/FEDERAL)
7. GENERAL GEORGE McCLELLAN
8. GENERAL AMBROSE BURNSIDE
9. GENERAL JOSEPH (FIGHTING JOE) HOOKER
10. GENERAL ISRAEL RICHARDSON

STURGIS

UNITS

TYPE

INFANTRY

ARTILLERY

CAVALRY

SIZE

ARMY GROUP
XXXXX

ARMY
XXXX

CORPS
XXX

DIVISION
XX

BRIGADE
X

REGIMENT
III

BATTALION
II

COMPANY
I

CONFEDERATE
Army of Northern Virginia

LEE ①
XXXX

Lee's HQ

SHARPSBURG

15:00

Antietam Creek

Ford

BRIDGE CAPTURED BY
UNION TROOPS

SIKES

LONGSTREET

LONGSTREET

13:00 to 16:30

Sherrick Farmhouse

BURNSIDE ⑩

10:00

UNION TROOPS LAUNCH
ASSAULT ON SHARPSBURG

Otto Farmhouse

15:00

16:00

13:00 to 16:30

13:00

10:00

WILCOX

SHEPHERDSTOWN

LONGSTREET

16:00

13:00 to 16:30

LONGSTREET

Burnside Bridge

RODMAN

REINFORCEMENTS ARRIVE

BROCKENBROUGH

③ LONGSTREET

TOOMBS

⑧

16:00

16:00

15:00

LONGSTREET

16:00

Ford

AP HILL
⑥

ARCHER

16:00

BRANCH

GREGG

Snavelys Ford

N

0.5   1 kilometre

POTOMAC RIVER / BOTELER'S FORD

ANTIETAM

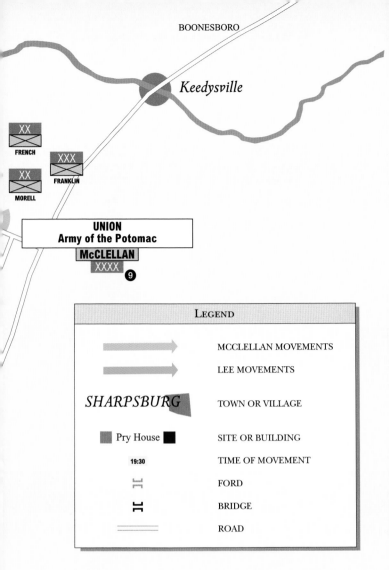

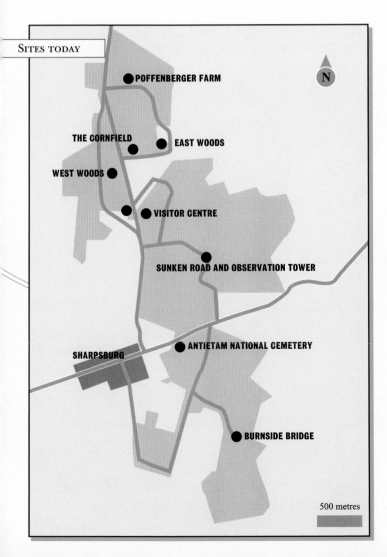

VISITING THE BATTLEFIELD TODAY

The first thing that strikes most visitors is the size of the battlefield. Compared to other famous Civil War battlefields, Antietam is very small, and for that reason is a great place to visit. Unlike Gettysburg, which stretches along nearly 10km (6 miles), the Antietam battlefield, from flank to flank, is less than 5km (3 miles). The best way to see it is by starting from the Confederate left flank, where the attacks began in the morning, and finishing on the Confederate right flank. There are great vantage points all along the battlefield, but highlights include the large observation tower that overlooks Bloody Lane in the centre of the field, the Pry House, which served as McClellan's headquarters, and the National Cemetery, which is where Lee's headquarters was situated. Touring the battlefield by car is also possible as car paths run to all the major stops.

All first-time visitors should begin their tour in the Antietam visitor centre, which overlooks the battlefield from the centre of the Confederate line. Like all American Civil War battlefields, admission to the battlefield and visitor centre is free. It features a small museum and bookstore, but there is no interpretive map presentation or movie. There are no recommended groups which give tours of the field.

Unlike Gettysburg, which receives thousands of guests each year, the town of Sharpsburg has remained very small and does not feature many options for lodging or meals. For that reason, the best place to stay and eat while visiting Antietam is Shepherdstown, Maryland. From Shepherdstown, visitors can also drive to Harpers Ferry, Maryland (the scene of John Brown's famous raid in 1859, and Jackson's siege during 1862.)

ANTIETAM TIMELINE

1862

3–13 September	Lee invades Maryland.
12–15 September	Siege of Harpers Ferry, MD.
14 September	Battle of Turner's Gap/Battle of Crampton's Gap.
15 September	Lee's 'Lost Order' discovered by McClellan.
17 September	Battle of Antietam.
06:00–07:30	Attack of Union 1st Corps (Cornfield).
07:30–09:00	Attack of the Union 12th Corps.
09:00–13:00	Attack of the Union 2nd Corps (Confederate centre – Bloody Lane).
10:00–16:30	Attack of the Federal 9th Corps (Burnside Bridge).
16:30–18:30	Confederate (General A.P. Hill) counterattack.
19–20 September	Lee withdrawals across Potomac – Maryland invasion ends.
26 October	McClellan crosses the Potomac.
7 November	McClellan relieved of command.

1863

1 January	Effective date of the Emancipation Proclamation.

GETTYSBURG 1863

By Joshua Moon

Despite crushing the Union Army at the battle of Chancellorsville in May 1863, General Robert E. Lee faced an operational and strategic dilemma. In order to replenish the war-ravaged countryside of northern Virginia, and to gain European recognition for the Confederacy, he once again had to invade the northern states. However, he would be invading the Union heartland and doing so with inexperienced commanders. The victory at Chancellorsville had come at great cost, since his most trusted subordinate, General Thomas (Stonewall) Jackson, was accidentally killed by his own soldiers. Jackson's death greatly affected Lee's performance at Gettysburg. His absence forced Lee to restructure his army from two to three corps, and it also forced Lee to promote two men, generals Richard Ewell and Ambrose P. Hill, to command the two new corps. While Lee maintained the services of his 'Old Warhorse', General James Longstreet, the advancement of Ewell and Hill forced Lee to rely on men who had never commanded a corps in battle. Their lack of aggressiveness and inability to incorporate Lee's intent into their attacks played a significant role in the South's failure at Gettysburg.

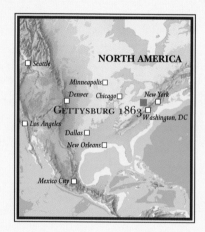

ABOVE *General George Meade and his staff. Meade was fortunate to be able to rely on an experienced staff, despite replacing General Hooker only days before the battle.*

Chancellorsville also forced change in the Union's Army of the Potomac. President Abraham Lincoln relieved General Joseph (Fighting Joe) Hooker and replaced him with General George Meade. With a reputation for caution, Meade immediately felt the pressure of his task. Because Lee was operating on northern soil, Meade was expected to act quickly to find and defeat the rebels with a degree of urgency not previously felt by the Union commanders. Meade's major advantages were the support of a seasoned group of corps commanders and an experienced cavalry commander, General John Buford, who located Lee's army and provided Meade with an accurate assessment of Lee's position and strength. In contrast to Lee's corps commanders, generals John Reynolds, Daniel Sickles and Winfield Hancock were experienced and would play pivotal roles in the Union victory at Gettysburg.

LEE MOVES NORTH

In late May, Lee moved his army across the Mason-Dixon line and into Pennsylvania. Using the Shenandoah Valley, the Blue Ridge and South Mountains to screen his army's movement, Lee penetrated deep into the Union interior. Under pressure from Lincoln to repel the invader, Meade moved his army north from Washington, DC, ultimately to meet Lee at the town of Gettysburg.

MAIN CHARACTERS FEATURED

SOUTH	NORTH
General Robert E. Lee	General George Meade
General Richard Ewell	General John Buford (cavalry)
General Ambrose Powell Hill	General John Reynolds
General James Longstreet	General Daniel Sickles
General George Pickett	General Winfield Hancock
Colonel William C. Oates	General Gouverneur K. Warren (chief engineer)
	Colonel Strong Vincent
	Colonel Joshua Chamberlain

General George Pickett

Colonel Joshua Chamberlain

The two armies resumed the battle the next day. Lee resolved to defeat the Yankee force by first attacking their flanks. However, his commanders were unable to coordinate the attacks, and the main attack started several hours late. Despite the late start, they launched wave after wave against positions in the southern and northern flanks of the Union line. In the south, Longstreet was given the task of rolling up the Yankee line. In order to manoeuvre his troops into position, he conducted a foot march that delayed his attack several hours.

On the rolling hills and peaceful meadows, names such as the Devil's Den and the Peach Orchard became synonymous with death in the American military lexicon. However, as darkness fell the Union line held and hopes of a Confederate victory on the second day slipped away with the setting sun.

As dawn broke on 3 July, most of Lee's subordinates favoured either another series of flank attacks or a withdrawal to more favourable ground. Lee disagreed with them and ordered his last fresh division to attack the one place which he felt was weakest, the Union centre. The Union position on Cemetery Ridge was an unassailable line of muskets and artillery firmly entrenched behind stone walls, overlooking nearly 1½km (1 mile) of gently sloping killing ground. Nevertheless, Lee ordered General George Pickett to lead his Virginians in one last push to break the Union line. In what would become known as Pickett's Charge, the attack was a disaster for the South as the Union troops poured artillery and musket fire from their prepared defensive positions into the exposed rebel troops as they advanced gallantly to their deaths.

Gettysburg was the bloodiest battle in American history. In all, the three-day fight cost Lee's army over 21,000 casualties, or nearly 30 per cent of its force. The Union army suffered over 23,000 casualties or 24 per cent of its force. This Union victory,

In the only battle of the Civil War where the Confederate army advanced from the north and the Union army from the south, they met on the hot and humid morning of 1 July 1863. The Confederates gained control of the town after an all-day fight, but were unable to prevent the Union army from occupying high ground south of the town. From here the Union army was able to view the disposition of the entire Confederate army. On the first night, the Union army entrenched itself along a fish-hook-shaped defensive line that ran from Culp's Hill in the north, south along Cemetery Ridge and ended at two hills in the south, called Little and Big Round Top.

RIGHT *Meade's headquarters on Cemetery Ridge. Situated on the reverse slope of the centre of the Union line, the building was nearly destroyed by the Confederate artillery preparation before Pickett's Charge.*

combined with the fall of Vicksburg on the Mississippi River the next day, dashed the Confederacy's hope for European recognition. It also shattered the confidence of Lee's army. Never again would Lee be on the offensive.

CLIMACTIC ACTION

Pickett's Charge is the best known action of the battle, but it proved to be a waste of manpower which the South could ill afford. It was precipitated by the decisive action of battle, the Union defence of the southern flank during day two. Made famous by the film *Gettysburg*, and the book *Killer Angels* by Michael Shaara, the Union defence of Little Round Top against multiple flanking attacks throughout the second day preserved the Union line and led to Meade's victory.

At the close of the first day's fighting, the Union defensive line extended south from Cemetery Ridge to two hills named Little Round Top and Big Round Top. As the rebels began their uncoordinated attacks in the afternoon, Meade's chief engineer, General Gouverneur K. Warren, became aware of the rebels' plan to turn the Union southern flank and hastily ordered a brigade to occupy the key terrain that anchored it.

At around 16:00 hours the following day, on 2 July, Colonel Strong Vincent manoeuvered his brigade, consisting of regiments from Pennsylvania, Michigan and Maine, into position. He placed the 20th Maine, commanded by Colonel Joshua Chamberlain, on the extreme southern end of the Union line, where it occupied nearly three times the recommended frontage for an

infantry regiment of the day. Furthermore, his men were tired, having marched continuously since early that morning. Rushing into position, Chamberlain's men felt the brunt of the Confederate assault and throughout the next few hours repelled six attacks by the veterans of the 15th and 47th Alabama Regiments. At times throughout the fight, Chamberlain said there were more enemy soldiers around him than his own. Nevertheless, each time the Union line held. During the continued attacks Chamberlain assessed the rebel attempt to turn his left flank. Therefore, he ordered a portion of his force to break off from their positions, hurry down to the end of their line and to form

ABOVE RIGHT *Hat and sword in hand, General Lewis Armistead leads the final assault of Cemetery Ridge. Ironically, he was killed by troops commanded by his best friend and West Point classmate, Winfield Scott Hancock.*

RIGHT *View from a Confederate artillery position along Seminary Ridge looking east towards Cemetery Ridge. The 'copse of trees' in the centre of the horizon marks the location of the Union position. Lee's order to cross this open ground and assail the fortified Union line ended in disaster for the South.*

ABOVE *A statue of the hero of the second day, General Gouverneur K. Warren, stands on Little Round Top. It looks down on the Devil's Den and Valley of Death. Deforestation of this area by the National Park Service has successfully recreated the actual battlefield conditions of July 1863.*

a new line which formed a 90-degree angle at the end of his old line. Chamberlain's thin defensive line might be overwhelmed, but would not be outflanked.

The situation was rapidly becoming desperate for Chamberlain. There was a lull in the battle after the sixth charge. A third of his men were down, and the survivors were frantically rummaging through the cartridge boxes of their fallen comrades. Chamberlain was convinced there would be another charge and, unwilling to receive it, he ordered a bayonet charge. In doing so, Chamberlain knew that he would have the advantage of charging downhill and that the enemy would not expect it. Chamberlain recalled that 'the command "Fix Bayonets!" ran like fire along the line, from man to man, and rose into a shout.'

Anchored on the 83rd Pennsylvania Regiment to his right, Chamberlain ordered his men on the left flank to start the charge down the hill. As soon as these men cleared their positions, the remainder of the unit would follow in a violent charge aimed at clearing the rebels to their front. Similar to the action of a door swinging open on its hinges, the sequenced Yankee attack drove the Confederates down the hill away from the exposed left flank. Surprised and not completely understanding the tactical situation, the rebel commander, Colonel William C. Oates, feared that Union cavalry had charged into the rear of his unit. In the face of the bayonet charge and with the majority of

his weapons fouled and unable to fire, Oates ordered the Alabamians to retreat down the hill. Chamberlain pressed his attack and eventually took over 200 prisoners.

Chamberlain's defence of Little Round Top was not the only critical action of day two, since rebel attacks continued into nightfall. However, it was the most significant. Had his position been overrun, the Confederates could have turned the entire Union line. It was a gallant display of courage and initiative, which earned the 20th Maine a place in American military history and also won Colonel Chamberlain the nation's highest honour, The Congressional Medal of Honor.

TOURING GETTYSBURG TODAY

The battlefield is hallowed ground for Americans from both north and south. Thousands of civil war re-enactors flock to the battlefield where, dressed as Confederates and Yankees, they participate in battle re-enactments and conduct weapon demonstrations. They are always friendly and glad to share their knowledge of the period.

Due to its size, the battlefield is best toured by car. The visitor centre and Gettysburg Museum are situated on Cemetery Ridge in the centre of the Union line. As with all observation towers and car parks, access to the visitor centre is free. There is a bookstore and an auditorium where an excellent battlefield orientation is presented on a large electronically lit map. There is a minimal cost for the 30-minute overview, which is well worth it. The auditorium has

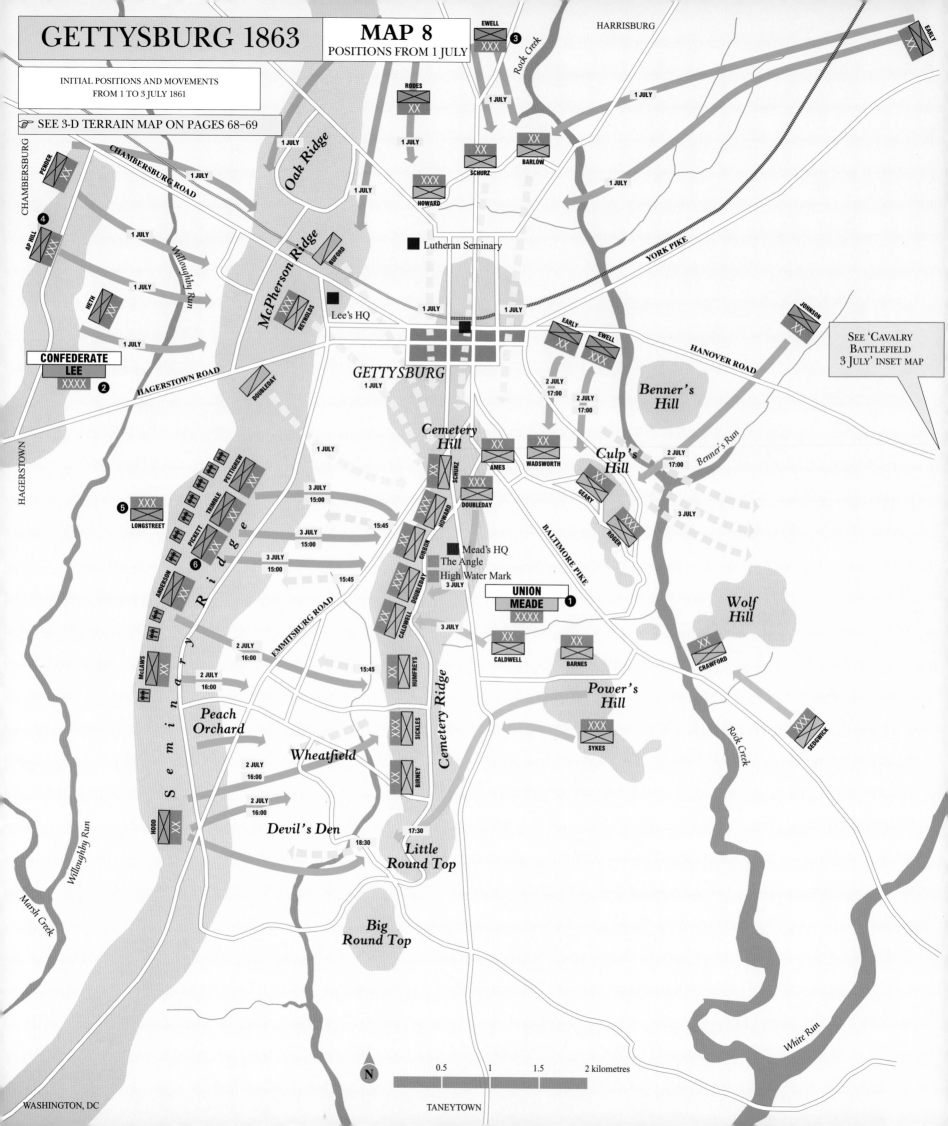

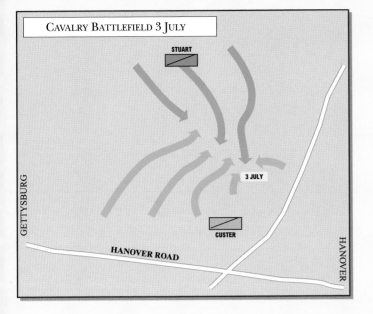

CAVALRY BATTLEFIELD 3 JULY

STUART

GETTYSBURG

3 JULY

CUSTER

HANOVER ROAD

HANOVER

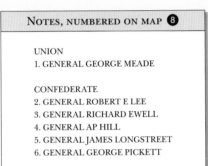

UNITS	
TYPE	
INFANTRY	⊠
ARTILLERY	●
CAVALRY	╱
SIZE	
ARMY GROUP	XXXXX
ARMY	XXXX
CORPS	XXX
DIVISION	XX
BRIGADE	X
REGIMENT	III
BATTALION	II
COMPANY	I

NOTES, NUMBERED ON MAP ❽

UNION
1. GENERAL GEORGE MEADE

CONFEDERATE
2. GENERAL ROBERT E LEE
3. GENERAL RICHARD EWELL
4. GENERAL AP HILL
5. GENERAL JAMES LONGSTREET
6. GENERAL GEORGE PICKETT

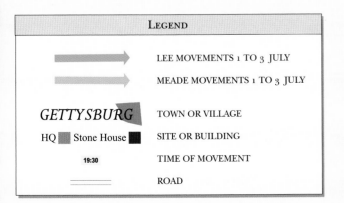

LEGEND

➤ LEE MOVEMENTS 1 TO 3 JULY

➤ MEADE MOVEMENTS 1 TO 3 JULY

GETTYSBURG TOWN OR VILLAGE

HQ ▮ Stone House ▮ SITE OR BUILDING

19:30 TIME OF MOVEMENT

ROAD

360-degree seating, but first-time visitors should sit at either the south or north end of the auditorium to ensure they can visualize the famous fish-hook of the defensive line.

Due to the size of the battlefield, terrain association and orientation is important. Therefore, first-time visitors should also consider participating in a guided tour. There are a number of companies that provide tours. Gettysburg Battlefield Tours (www.gettysburgbattle-fieldtours.com) offers a two-hour bus trip that stops at all the major points of interest. Once familiar with the layout, visitors should again tour the battlefield themselves. While Little Round Top and the site of Pickett's Charge garner large crowds, the most tranquil point on the battlefield is Culp's Hill. Located on the extreme northern end of the Union line, Culp's Hill is the site of a large observation tower that gives the visitor a unique perspective of the battlefield.

In addition to the battlefield, Gettysburg is the site of the Gettysburg National Cemetery, where Abraham Lincoln delivered the Gettysburg Address. It is also situated on the farm of the 34th President of the United States, General Dwight D. Eisenhower, the Supreme Allied Commander in Europe during World War II. Both Eisenhower's farm and the cemetery are close to the visitor centre, and both are great places to visit.

GETTYSBURG TIMELINE

1 July 1863

08:00	Buford's Union cavalry and Heith's division skirmish.
10:00	Reynolds's I Corps arrives (Reynolds is killed; battle ensues).
14:30	Lee arrives on the battlefield.
16:30	Union troops retreat through Gettysburg (Hancock orders troops to fortify a line from Culp's Hill to Cemetery Ridge to the Round Tops).
17:00	Ewell chooses not to attack Culp's Hill.
21:30	Meade orders all eight Union corps (80,000 men) to converge on Gettysburg.

2 July

03:00	Meade arrives at Gettysburg; Lee plans the day's attack.
09:00	Lee issues the orders for Longstreet's attack on the Union left flank.
11:00–16:00	Longstreet moves his corps into attack position.
15:00	Sickles extends his line forward of the Union line (occupies the Peach Orchard).
16:00–18:00	Longstreet attacks the Union left flank. (Chamberlain's defense of Little Round Top)
19:00–22:30	Ewell attacks Culp's Hill.

3 July

04:00–08:00	Fighting resumes on Culp's Hill.
13:00–15:00	Confederate cannonade of Union centre.
15:00	Confederate attack on Union centre (Pickett's Charge).
16:00	Confederate attack fails.

4 July

	Confederate Army begins withdrawal; Grant seizes Vicksburg.

CRISIS ON THE UNION FLANK

Union and Confederate forces faced each other for four days at Gettysburg in a climactic battle that held the fate of the divided nation in the balance. After Gettysburg, the Confederacy was increasingly forced on the defensive, but the struggle at Gettysburg exacted a heavy price on both sides. On Day 2, Confederate commander Robert E. Lee ordered General James Longstreet to attempt a flanking maneouvre around the southern edge of the Union line. The Union troops held the high ground, with their positions terminating at two hills named Big Round Top and Little Round Top. The illustration on these pages shows the position at the extreme southern end of the Union line, which formed a fish-hook around the base of Little Round Top.

① Cemetery Ridge: The Union army under General George G. Meade was deployed along the high ground of Cemetery Ridge, which runs in a roughly southerly direction from the town of Gettysburg. Across the intervening wide shallow valley was Lee's Army of Northern Virginia, deployed along Seminary Ridge.

② Big Round Top: A large conical hill dotted with glacial boulders, and heavily forested, Big Round Top was the most prominent landmark.

③ Little Round Top: The lower slopes of Little Round Top were thinly held by the 20th Maine Regiment, commanded by Colonel Joshua Chamberlain. The men from Maine were deployed behind a low stone wall.

④ Peach Orchard: On 2 July, Union General Daniel Sickles led his 3rd Corps to take up positions in the Peach Orchard. Although not authorized by Meade, Sickles' move created a bulge in the Union line that threatened Longstreet's flanking manoeuvre. The Peach Orchard became the scene of fierce fighting, as Sickles'men were driven back towards Cemetery Ridge.

⑤ The Wheatfield.

⑥ Devil's Den: A narrow wooded valley studded with glacial boulders, the Devil's Den lay between Big and Little Round Top. When their ammunition ran out, Chamberlain's troops fixed bayonets and charged down towards the Devil's Den, throwing the Confederate attack off balance and thereby preserving the Union line.

⑦ 1st Minnesota Regiment: The Confederate drive through the Peach Orchard threatened to punch a hole through the thinly held Union line along Cemetery Ridge. The veterans of the 1st Minnesota Regiment were ordered to drive back the advancing Confederates. They succeeded, but at a heavy cost in lives.

⑧ Seminary Ridge: The main Confederate positions lay along this low ridge.

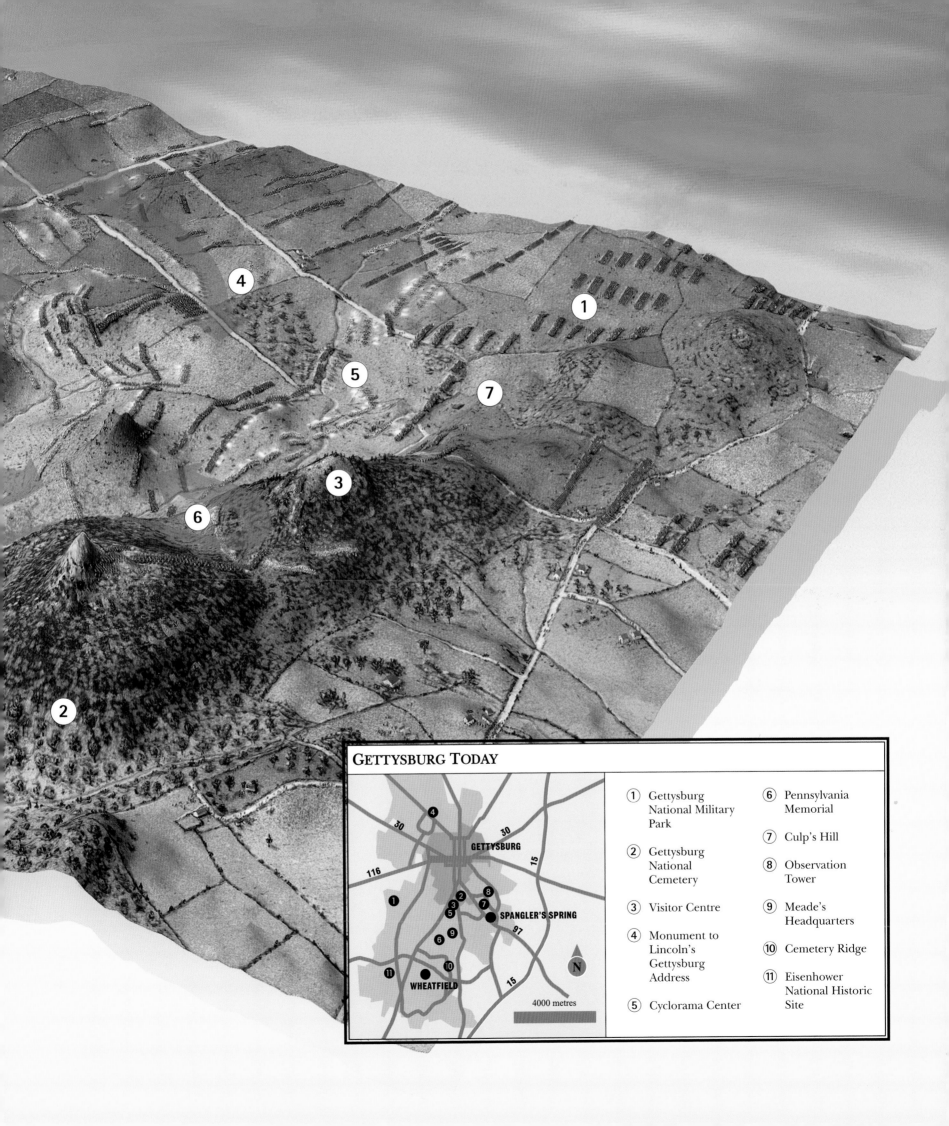

Gettysburg Today

1. Gettysburg National Military Park
2. Gettysburg National Cemetery
3. Visitor Centre
4. Monument to Lincoln's Gettysburg Address
5. Cyclorama Center
6. Pennsylvania Memorial
7. Culp's Hill
8. Observation Tower
9. Meade's Headquarters
10. Cemetery Ridge
11. Eisenhower National Historic Site

GETTYSBURG

SPANGLER'S SPRING

WHEATFIELD

30

30

116

15

97

15

N

4000 metres

Anglo-Zulu War

1879

By David Rattray

The British had been involved in South Africa since their successful occupation of the Cape Colony in 1806. The area under British jurisdiction was to expand eastwards over the following decades as the Xhosa tribesmen were pushed out of their traditional territories in a series of Frontier Wars.

In 1842 Britain annexed the territory known as Natal and in 1877 the landlocked Republic of the Transvaal. The British wanted to establish a confederation of states in southeastern Africa, following the mould that Lord Carnavon had used in Canada in 1867. These political aspirations were no doubt stimulated by the promise of great mineral wealth in the country.

The Boers (people of Dutch and French Huguenot extraction) in the interior were perceived to constitute a threat to this plan. A guarded peace ensued, broken in 1880 when a war broke out between the British and the Boers, which the British lost after a disastrous engagement at the Battle of Majuba.

A greater perceived threat to Lord Carnavon's confederation plans came from the territory known as Zululand, north of the British Colony of Natal, where King Cetshwayo, nephew of the progenitor of the Zulu nation, King Shaka, reigned. King Shaka had shaped the Zulu nation with great, and often brutal, military conquests into a highly motivated and successful force in the region. King Shaka was assassinated in September 1828 and was succeeded by one of his brothers, Dingane. The Boers allied themselves to Mpande, King Dingane's brother, who was killed in 1840. Mpande, much assisted by the Boers, became king. The Boers encroached into Zululand and King Mpande found himself powerless to resist. King Mpande died of old age in 1872 and the monarchy passed to his son, Cetshwayo.

King Cetshwayo resisted the Boer encroachments, appealing to the British for help. The Zulus had hitherto enjoyed a good relationship with the British, and verbal support for the Zulus was forthcoming.

The Boers considered the Zulu territories that they occupied as part of the Transvaal, and when the British annexed the Transvaal in 1877, they resisted Zulu claims to that 'Disputed Territory' despite a judicial commission's finding in favour of these Zulu claims. As a consequence the relationship between the British and the Zulus began to sour.

The British High Commissioner in South Africa, Sir Bartle Frere, in fear of the threat that he believed the great Zulu military machine constituted in the region, began to plot against King Cetshwayo. In this he was much assisted by Lord Chelmsford, commander in chief of the British forces in South Africa. Chelmsford had recently defeated the Xhosa people in the eastern Cape Colony, and believed that, with the forces he had at his disposal in South Africa, military success against the Zulus was assured. The relationship between the British and the Zulus deteriorated, culminating in Frere issuing the Zulu king with an ultimatum in December 1878.

The terms were unreasonable, demanding among other things the disbanding of the Zulu army within 30 days. Predictably the Zulu king did not submit to these terms and Lord Chelmsford, whose plans for the invasion were already well advanced, prepared to invade the Zulu territory on 11 January 1879.

The Zulu king never understood why his country was invaded by his friends, the British.

ISANDLWANA AND RORKE'S DRIFT 1879

By David Rattray

Lord Chelmsford's plan was to invade the Zulu territory with three huge and two small columns. Colonel Pearson was to move north from the port city of Durban along the coastal plain, across the Tugela River into Zululand near its mouth and move thence to the Zulu capital, Ulundi. Colonel Evelyn Wood was to come into the Zulu territory from Utrecht in the north. The strongest of the three major columns, the central column, was to move from Pietermaritzburg via Greytown to Helpmekaar and to ford the Buffalo River frontier at Rorke's Drift. It was accompanied by the commander in chief, Lord Chelmsford, and consisted of 4850 men, 220 wagons and carts and 4500 oxen. One of the small

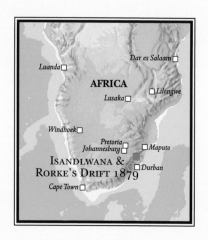

columns was placed up in the north to keep the Swazis out of the fight. The other was originally intended to operate between the coastal column and the central column, but as it happened this force later joined the central column.

The central column descended from the Help-mekaar plateau to Rorke's Drift in early January. Here the British commandeered the mission station, converting it into a depot and a hospital and waited for the ultimatum (see p 71) to expire.

The ultimatum duly expired at midnight on 10 January 1879, and the next morning the invasion of Zululand began. Chelmsford had at his command both battalions of the 24th Regiment of Foot, a highly disciplined force of well-trained and well-equipped men, many of whom had been fighting in the eastern Cape Colony.

On 12 January, Lord Chelmsford had a successful skirmish against some warriors in rough terrain east of Rorke's Drift. This did much to instill complacency in the breast of the British general as he continued his advance into Zululand. By 20 January, Lord Chelmsford had set up a temporary camp at the foot of the crag known by the Zulus as Isandlwana, 16km (10 miles) east of Rorke's Drift.

PREVIOUS PAGE *The Last Stand of the 24th Regiment of Foot (South Welsh Borderers) by Charles Fripp depicts the frantic fighting in the closing moments of the battle, with the ominous sphinx of Isandlwana looming behind.*
ABOVE *Historic photograph of 50 Rorke's Drift survivors of B Company, 2/24th. The dog in the bottom right of the picture warned defenders of approaching Zulus during the fighting.*

THE ZULU RESPONSE TO THE ULTIMATUM

The Zulu king and his councillors were confused by the aggression of the British and tried to prevent the invasion of Zululand by diplomacy. Nevertheless, Cetshwayo refused to disband his army and called all his warriors to Ulundi, about 80km (50 miles) east of Rorke's Drift. The bulk of his mobile force, comprising some 25,000 warriors, was sent in the direction of Rorke's Drift to repulse the British invasion.

Although the Zulu forces could cover large distances in a very short time, the King directed the commander of the detachment on its way to Rorke's Drift, General Ntshingwayo-ka-Mahole Khoza, to move slowly so as not to tire the warriors. Every warrior carried in his pouch a quantity of dried maize biscuit, which he was told to eat sparingly. The Zulu force was not encumbered with great logistical support. The warriors would carry this 'iron ration', and the great 'impi' or body of fighting men would be accompanied by hundreds – even thousands – of teenage boys, who would run along behind the army, carrying their older brothers' sleeping mats and spare porridge. They would also chase along a number of slaughter cattle.

THE ZULU ARMY

The Zulus, contrary to popular belief, had no standing army. They were merely an armed people. Young men were drafted into regiments in a system of 'national service'. Their training was thorough and vigorous, and a warrior would be taught all the combat tactics that had been developed over more than 60 years. They were taught to use their great stabbing spears and to deploy in the famous 'Horns of the Buffalo' formation: the younger, faster warriors take position in the flanks to encircle the enemy, while the experienced, older warriors are in the head of the formation, where the enemy would be destroyed in the 'killing field'.

After their initial period of training, they would be released and could be called up for active service at short notice.

The Zulus could put about 50,000 men into the field. Each regiment was made up of men of the same age. They were drawn from all over Zululand. This served the important political function of uniting the people of Zululand. It also equipped every regiment with an astounding knowledge of their territory, because each regiment would have men from every part of Zululand. Often these regiments had regimental songs and traditions, and had identifying patterns on their shields to distinguish them from other regiments.

If the impi was to move very far afield, the chiefs who lived in those areas would be expected to provide slaughter cattle. If action was contemplated outside the borders of Zululand, cattle would be captured from the enemy.

This impi of superbly motivated and disciplined men could move very quickly if necessary, and the Zulu commanders would use the folds in the field to conceal their movements. Spies kept the Zulu command well informed of every British move.

In the main the warriors were barefoot. The soles of their feet were extremely tough, and their barefoot condition was a huge advantage: they never suffered from the terrible fungal infections that afflicted their British counterparts. Every warrior was equipped with a broad-bladed stabbing spear and two or three long, thin, throwing spears. He also carried a great wooden club, a deadly weapon at close quarters. Many Zulus had firearms, bartered from white traders, and Zulu firepower played a role in every battle on this campaign.

On 17 January General Ntshingwayo left Ulundi. Moving slowly and conserving energy, he could expect to make contact with Lord Chelmsford's force within a few days. Zulu custom dictated that he should avoid fighting if he could on 22 January because the phase of the moon (first day of the first quarter) was considered inauspicious. However, circumstances forced the Zulus to fight on this day.

THE BRITISH PREPARE

By 21 January, Lord Chelmsford had established a temporary bivouac beneath the crag of Isandlwana, 16km (10 miles) east of Rorke's Drift. His intention was to shuttle supplies from his rear and then to advance deeper into Zululand in the direction of the Zulu capital, Ulundi.

His camp was a huge, sprawling affair, which he failed to entrench or laager: the ground was too hard and the wagons too bulky to draw into a defensive arrangement. Chelmsford no doubt expected to remain at this site for a few days only – not enough time to implement any of these measures. He ignored the good advice given him by the Boers and left the camp spread out and vulnerable to attack. History would judge him harshly for this.

Chelmsford duly received information that the Zulu army was on its way. British scouting parties were sent out to the east and reported seeing numbers of Zulus, and when a large reconnaissance party under the command of Major John Dartnell reported finding a great force of Zulus to the southeast on 21 January, Lord Chelmsford incorrectly deduced that Dartnell had made contact with the main Zulu army.

Chelmsford, anxious to reinforce Dartnell with all speed, decided to split the column at Isandlwana. His intention was to move out of the camp before dawn the next day with a force consisting of four

BRITISH
Lord Chelmsford, commander
   in chief of the British forces
   in South Africa
Major John Dartnell
Brevet Lieutenant Colonel
   Henry Pulleine
Colonel Anthony Durnford,
   Royal Engineers
Major Francis Russell, Royal
   Artillery
Captain Reginald
   Younghusband (C Company
   1st/24th)

Lieutenant Teignmouth Melvill
Lieutenant Neville Coghill

ZULU
King Cetshwayo
General Ntshingwayo-ka-
   Mahole Khoza
Chieftain Mkhosana (Chest of
   the Zulu Buffalo)

Lord Chelmsford	*King Cetshwayo*

At 08:05, Pulleine's pickets on the rim of the plateau to the north-east of the camp reported seeing numbers of Zulus. A defensive firing line of infantry was put in place on the forward crest of a low, grassy ridge to face that threat. The men were deployed in skirmishing order, standing 3–5m (10–16ft) apart. The line extended across the northeastern quarter of the camp, about 730m (800 yards) beyond its outer perimeter. Two 7-pounder guns were placed on the centre of this line.

Before leaving Isandlwana, Lord Chelmsford had ordered Colonel Anthony Durnford, Royal Engineers, to move across from Rorke's Drift to Isandlwana with his considerable force of mounted men.

By 10:30, Durnford had arrived at Isandlwana. He became concerned that the Zulus, seen earlier to the northeast, might threaten Lord Chelmsford's movements in the southeast. As a result he decided to move out from Isandlwana in an easterly direction to protect Chelmsford's flank.

On reaching the prominent conical hill that lies 2½km (1½ miles) east of Isandlwana, Durnford ordered his Rocket Battery, under the command of Major Francis Russell, Royal Artillery, to move up onto the plateau to the north, while the rest of his force continued east.

Durnford also sent patrols onto the plateau, and, at about 11:30, one of these stumbled upon the unimaginable: as they crested a stony ridge they saw the main Zulu army, made up of some 25,000 warriors, lying concealed along the course of the Ngwebini stream in the valley below.

The Zulus were not in the southeast – they were in the northeast. The patrol dismounted and fired into the packed mass of warriors.

The battle of Isandlwana had started.

THE HORNS OF THE BUFFALO

Chief Ntshingwayo's men would indeed have to fight on the Day of the Dead Moon in order to retain the element of surprise. This great, disciplined force of warriors moved rapidly out of the head of the ravine. They spread out into The Horns of the Buffalo, and raced for the rim of the plateau.

Back in the British camp, the men were unaware of the patrol's discovery until they saw a force of Zulus descend off the plateau and destroy the Rocket Battery which, at that moment, was still clawing its way up the steep slope. Thousands of warriors followed this force, dropping onto the plain below. They engaged Colonel Durnford and his men, driving them back towards the camp at Isandlwana. Durnford and his men made a famous stand in a dry watercourse known thereafter as Durnford's Donga, 2000m (2200 yards) east of the Isandlwana Mountain, where they successfully pinned thousands of warriors down for some time.

guns, six companies of the 2nd/24th Regiment and the Native Pioneers. Chelmsford decided to accompany this force. He was to have the most unsatisfactory day skirmishing with small parties of Zulus in the southeast.

Chelmsford left Brevet Lieutenant Colonel Henry Pulleine in command of the camp and its garrison which consisted of five companies of the 1st/24th and one company of the 2nd/24th, two guns of the Royal Artillery and some 600 members of the Natal Native Contingent (NNC) – a total force of over 1700 men. Pulleine was told to defend the camp and to expect an order to move to the new campsite, the location of which would be determined that day.

The guns of the Royal Artillery were limbered up and fired accurately into the warriors that had been checked by Durnford and all was apparently well for the British. The soldiers on the firing line and those in the camp would have had their eyes trained on Durnford's Donga.

A soldier then glanced to the north and gasped: the whole extent of the summit of the plateau had turned black with Zulus, as the impi crested the skyline.

A great wing of this force separated from the mass on the plateau. Despite the fact that they were fired upon by two companies of soldiers that had been sent up onto a low ridge to the north of the camp, they continued to move away from the camp and out of sight. These warriors, taking brilliant advantage of terrain, used a valley to hide their movements as they made their way south until they reached the road back to Rorke's Drift. Retreat for the British was no longer an option.

BLACK AUXILIARY FORCES

Natal Native Contingent (NNC), consisting of Zulu-speaking black men from the British Colony of Natal, was formed to deal with this particular emergency, but there were other units, with a long history of fighting in South Africa, consisting of black soldiers led by white officers. Many of them were of Zulu origin who had fled to Natal from Zululand a generation or two earlier and still bore a grudge or for various other reasons had an axe to grind with the Zulu king. The British made use of these old enmities, but failed to train and equip these soldiers properly. The black men in the NNC were poorly trained and poorly equipped: one rifle for 10 men, five cartridges per rifle. The black horsemen of the Natal Native Horse, on the other hand, were highly trained and disciplined and probably constituted the finest black cavalry unit South Africa ever produced.

The Horns of the Buffalo were now in position. Until this moment the British didn't believe that the Zulus could deploy their tactic on this grand scale with the horns some miles apart.

Isandlwana was not a British blunder: it was a great Zulu victory.

Chief Ntshingwayo, sitting on the great rocks at Nyoni on the plateau, gave the order for the Chest of the Zulu Buffalo to descend, and this great body of excited warriors, regiment upon regiment, dropped down into the killing field with awesome precision, and finally the Zulu impi lapped up against the British firing line!

This line was made up of highly disciplined, well-trained men, armed with modern, breech-loading Martini-Henry rifles. The redcoats fired into the warriors, but the Zulus held their position.

Despite terrible casualties, the Zulu force held their position in the depression beyond the British firing line, inspired by the leadership of the Chieftain Mkhosana, who lost his life in this battle.

The Zulus in the Left Horn then began edging their way south of Colonel Durnford's position in the donga. Durnford came under pressure here, and the possibility that he might be outflanked became obvious to the British officers on the southern extremity of the British firing line, 900m (984 yards) behind Durnford. About 170 men on the British firing line were immediately ordered forward to support Durnford but, at that moment, Durnford, unable to hold his position in the donga, retired on the camp. The Zulus of the Left Horn charged, catching the 170 redcoats, who were then out in the open, off guard. They were destroyed where they stood.

Durnford fought his way back to camp, making a stand on the lower slope of the stony hill south of the saddle. Here this brave man died, surrounded by his force of mostly colonial soldiers.

The warriors of the Chest, having been kept in check for some time, were inspired by the success of their comrades of the Left

Horn. They rose up and charged the British firing line. A bugler sounded the Retire, whereupon these British soldiers attempted a tactical withdrawal across the 800m (875 yards) of open grassland to the camp.

The British withdrawal failed, ending ignominiously in the tented camp. The tents had not been struck, adding to the confusion. Some British soldiers managed to fight in reasonable order for a considerable distance down the boulder-strewn, bush-clad wilderness towards the Buffalo River, along the path now known as the Fugitives' Trail. The last stand of the 24th was probably fought on the banks of the Manzimyama River, at least a mile southeast of Isandlwana. No British infantryman on the firing line lived to tell the tale. One company of soldiers, thought to be C Company, 1st/24th, under Captain Reginald Younghusband, made a stand high up on the shoulder of the Isandlwana Hill. Zulu sources tell us that the last British soldier to die on the battlefield was an infantryman who crept into a cave from where he held off his assailants for some time. By coincidence, in the closing moments of the battle, there was a significant partial eclipse of the sun. At this time, Lieutenant Colonel Pulleine entrusted the Queen's Colour of the 1st/24th to the Adjutant, Lieutenant Teignmouth Melvill who, with Lieutenant Neville Coghill, died in an heroic attempt to get this regimental treasure back into the British Colony of Natal. They are buried where they fell on the lip of the gorge on the Natal side of the Buffalo River.

The colour, which they lost in the flooded river, was later miraculously retrieved. It hangs today in Brecon Cathedral in Wales. Melvill and Coghill were among the first recipients of posthumous Victoria Crosses, which their families received 28 years later, in 1907.

At least 1329 men, including 52 British officers, were killed on the British side. The Zulu casualties were probably much higher than originally thought, possibly as high as 3000 killed.

This battle, a pivotal event in South Africa's story, left Lord Carnavon's plan for the confederation of Southeastern Africa in tatters. It encouraged the Boers in the Transvaal to contemplate rebellion and did much to ensure Gladstone's victory over Prime Minister Disraeli in the Midlothian Campaign of 1880.

Lord Chelmsford returned to the destroyed camp at Isandlwana that night with the force that had gone off to the southeast. The famished, exhausted and demoralized men stumbled about in the

LEFT *Isandlwana, visible in the background here, has, ironically, an uncanny resemblance to the sphinx, the central emblem in the badge of the regiment destroyed beneath it. This photograph shows the graves of men who died close to the 'saddle' in the last moments of the battle.*
OPPOSITE *A memorial at Fugitive's Drift honouring British soldiers killed in the Battle of Isandlwana.*

RORKE'S DRIFT

When Lord Chelmsford crossed the Buffalo River at Rorke's Drift on 11 January, he left a garrison to hold Otto Witt's mission station, which he had commandeered and turned into a supply depot. This force was left under the command of Major Henry Spalding, whose brief was to keep the column supplied with commissariat.

On the morning of 22 January, Spalding, frustrated that two companies of the 24th Regiment had not arrived from Helpmekaar, left Lieutenant John Chard, Royal Engineers, in command and rode away on horseback to see what had happened to them. Chard had been busy mending the *ponts* (ferries) at the Buffalo River half a mile from the undefended mission station when two riders appeared on the Zulu bank and blurted out the news of Isandlwana. Chard galloped up to the post to find that Lieutenant Gonville Bromhead, commanding B Company of the 2nd Battalion of the 24th, had already been informed of the disaster at Isandlwana and had been told that a huge force of Zulus was on its way to attack the British garrison.

Chard and Bromhead, ably assisted by Assistant Commissariat Officer James Dalton hastily threw up a defensive arrangement of *mielie* (maize) bags and biscuit-box walls, following a plan devised by Dalton. They used the men of B Company and some hundreds of men of the Natal Native Contingent (NNC). They ingeniously linked the missionary's house (which had been converted into a hospital) with a storeroom and a stone cattle kraal, using 90kg (200 lb) bags of maize meal and 45kg (100 lb) boxes of army biscuits. As the 4000 warriors of the Zulu army approached, the men of the NNC broke and fled, leaving a total of 139 men on the British side, many of whom were sick in the hospital. The hospital was a strange building,

darkness among the dead and disembowelled bodies of their comrades. Alerted by the dim crackle of distant gunfire, they gazed off to the west where, 16km (10 miles) away, the Oskarberg mountain at Rorke's Drift loomed against the glow of a great fire. Their worst fear was being realized: the mission station at Rorke's Drift was on fire; the Zulus were in the British Colony of Natal.

ISANDLWANA TIMELINE

22 January 1879

08:05 Pulleine's pickets report seeing Zulus.

10:30 Durnford moves out in an easterly direction to protect Chelmsford's flank.

11:30 A Durnford patrol sees the main Zulu army lying concealed along the course of the Ngwebini stream. Durnford pins down thousands of warriors. Horns of the Buffalo in position. Chest of the Buffalo descends to the British firing line. Left Horn charges, annihilating Durnford and his men. Chest charges. Bugler sounds the Retire, but the withdrawal fails in confusion.

that night Chelmsford returns to Isandlwana. Gunfire and a glow at Rorke's Drift alerts them that the mission station is on fire.

MAIN CHARACTERS FEATURED

BRITISH
Major Henry Spalding
Lieutenant John Chard, Royal Engineer
Lieutenant Gonville Bromhead (commanding B Company of the 2nd Battallion of the 24th)
James Dalton (Assistant Commissariat Officer)

Lieutenant Gonville Bromhead

consisting of a series of little 'cubbyhole' rooms which, for the most part, communicated only with the exterior. These rooms were filled with sick men. Men from B Company were detailed to defend them. Late in the afternoon of 22 January the Zulu army appeared. Initially the Zulus attempted to rush the British position with a frontal assault, but concentrated Martini-Henry rifle fire checked this attack. The Zulus then attacked a corner of the British position and succeeded in occupying the area to the front of the hospital and the verandah of that building. They set fire to the south end of the hospital, necessitating a withdrawal from the building by the sick men and their defenders.

The building's architecture, however, denied its occupants the ability to retire through the building, because of a lack of interleading doors and passages, so the defenders were left no choice but to bash holes through the unfired mud-brick walls in order to effect an escape. The withdrawal through this building that night constitutes one of the most dramatic events in British military history. Some men were dragged out and stabbed by the Zulus. Others were killed in their beds as the building's defenders, with the sick, attempted to fight their way through the blazing building to its northern face.

When they eventually got there, they found that the rest of the garrison had withdrawn across the open area between themselves and the area immediately in front of the storeroom. In effect they constituted an island, separated from their comrades by 46m (50 yards) of no-man's-land. Immediate evacuation of the burning building was imperative. Two brave men ran from an area in front of the storeroom to assist with the evacuation of the sick, and eventually most of the occupants of the hospital were brought in behind the wall of biscuit boxes that had been hastily erected as a second line of defence. When the hospital building finally burned out, the British found themselves that night fighting an enemy they could not see. The Zulus attacked repeatedly, eventually taking the stone cattle *kraal* (enclosure). The British built themselves a great redoubt of *mielie* (maize) bags which was to have been the position of their last stand, but the Zulu attacks, which continued throughout most of the night, eventually petered out, and in the dawn of 23 January, the exhausted Zulu army withdrew.

ABOVE *At Rorke's Drift 139 British soldiers, 35 of whom were sick, were attacked by 4000 Zulus, who set fire to the thatched roof of the hospital.*

Hundreds of Zulu warriors had been killed and 17 men died on the British side. The 11 Victoria Crosses that were awarded was a record for a single action, and much was made of this gallant stand in the aftermath of one of the most serious reverses ever suffered in the colonies by the British army.

POSTSCRIPT

Six months later the Zulus were finally defeated at the Battle of Ulundi. The British had been defeated again at the battles of Ntome (12 March) and Hlobane (28 March), and a whole column was besieged at Eshowe for 10 weeks. The Prince Imperial of France was killed (1 June) while out on a patrol with the British, the death of the last of the Napoleons adding a twist to the story.

But the British turned the tide at the Battle of Khambula (29 March) and the Battle of Gingindlovu (2 April). The siege of Eshowe was lifted, and eventually the old Zulu order was smashed at Ulundi on 4 July. The King was captured and exiled and this tragic chapter in South Africa's story eventually came to a close.

VISITORS' FACT FILE

Fugitives' Drift Lodge is a guest house from where guests can set out to visit the battlefields of Isandlwana and Rorke's Drift.

- Fugitives' Drift Lodge and Guest House, PO Rorke's Drift, 3016 KZN
  www.fugitives-drift-lodge.com
  Tel +27 34 6421843/2718051
  Fax +27 34 2718053

TOP *Rorke's Drift, showing the mission station at the foot of the Oskarsberg Mountain. In this illustration the building used as a hospital is on fire and the Zulus have surrounded the defensive arrangement, which had been hastily thrown up by the British.*
ABOVE *The rebuilt hospital, used as a museum today. The British barricaded the mission station and linked the house, a storeroom and a stone cattle kraal with bags of maize and boxes of army biscuits.*

ISANDLWANA AND RORKE'S DRIFT 1879

MAP 9
MOVEMENTS 21 TO 23 JANUARY

☞ SEE 3-D TERRAIN MAP ON PAGES 82–83

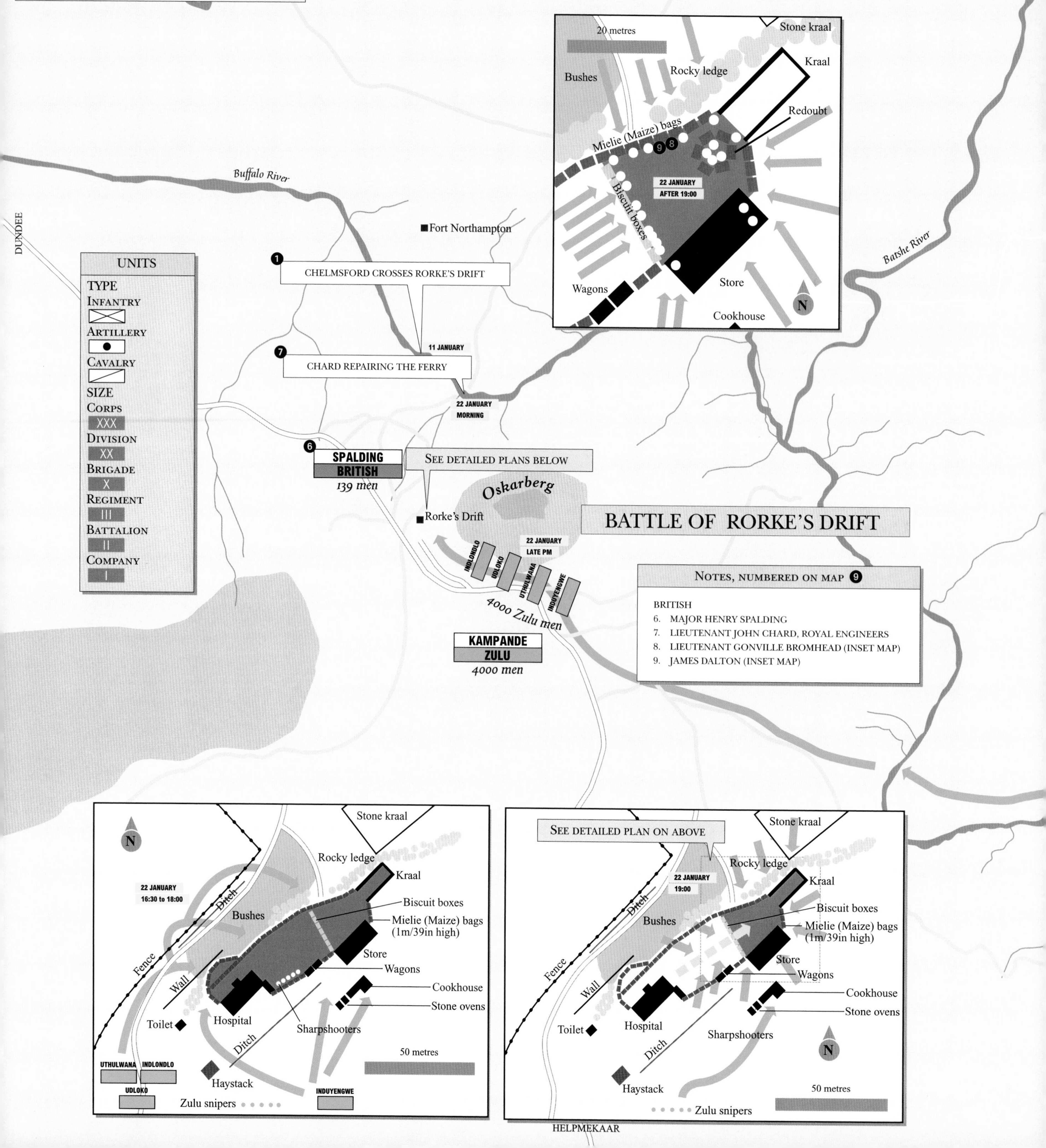

Buffalo River

■ Fort Northampton

Batshe River

DUNDEE

UNITS

TYPE

INFANTRY

ARTILLERY

CAVALRY

SIZE

CORPS — XXX

DIVISION — XX

BRIGADE — X

REGIMENT — III

BATTALION — II

COMPANY — I

1 CHELMSFORD CROSSES RORKE'S DRIFT

11 JANUARY

7 CHARD REPAIRING THE FERRY

22 JANUARY MORNING

6 SPALDING **BRITISH** 139 men

SEE DETAILED PLANS BELOW

Oskarberg

■ Rorke's Drift

BATTLE OF RORKE'S DRIFT

22 JANUARY LATE PM

INDLONDLO
UDLOKO
UTHULWANA
INDUYENGWE

4000 Zulu men

KAMPANDE **ZULU** 4000 men

NOTES, NUMBERED ON MAP **9**

BRITISH
6. MAJOR HENRY SPALDING
7. LIEUTENANT JOHN CHARD, ROYAL ENGINEERS
8. LIEUTENANT GONVILLE BROMHEAD (INSET MAP)
9. JAMES DALTON (INSET MAP)

Inset map (top right)

20 metres

Stone kraal

Bushes

Rocky ledge

Kraal

Redoubt

Mielie (Maize) bags

9 **8**

22 JANUARY AFTER 19:00

Biscuit boxes

Wagons

Store

Cookhouse

N

Detailed plan (bottom left)

N

22 JANUARY 16:30 to 18:00

Stone kraal

Rocky ledge

Kraal

Ditch

Biscuit boxes

Bushes

Mielie (Maize) bags (1m/39in high)

Fence

Store

Wall

Wagons

Cookhouse

Stone ovens

Toilet ◆

Hospital

Sharpshooters

Ditch

50 metres

UTHULWANA | INDLONDLO
UDLOKO | INDUYENGWE

◆ Haystack

Zulu snipers ·····

Detailed plan (bottom right)

SEE DETAILED PLAN ON ABOVE

Stone kraal

Rocky ledge

Kraal

Ditch

Biscuit boxes

Bushes

Mielie (Maize) bags (1m/39in high)

Fence

Store

Wall

Wagons

Cookhouse

Stone ovens

Toilet ◆

Hospital

Sharpshooters

Ditch

22 JANUARY 19:00

N

◆ Haystack

50 metres

····· Zulu snipers

HELPMEKAAR

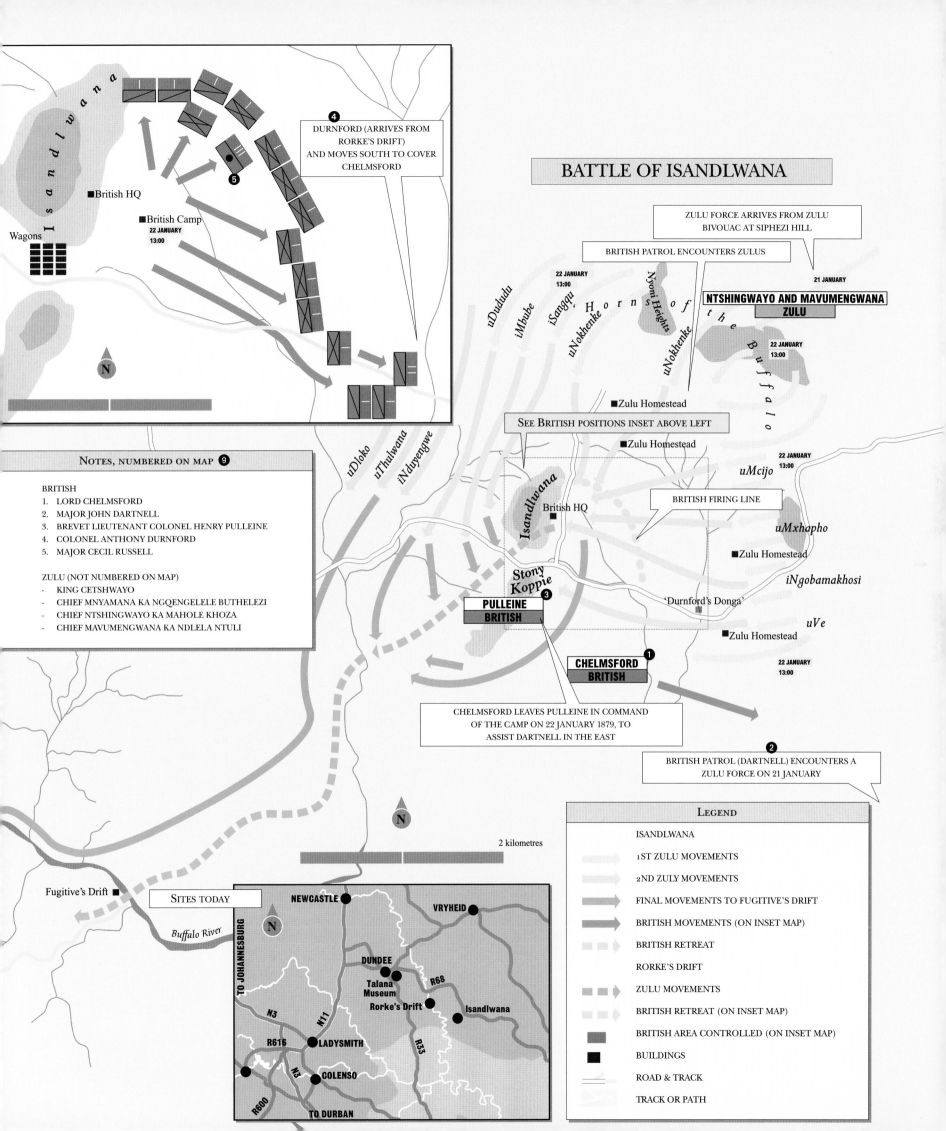

BATTLE OF ISANDLWANA

Isandlwana (inset top left)

British HQ

British Camp
22 JANUARY
13:00

Wagons

4 DURNFORD (ARRIVES FROM RORKE'S DRIFT) AND MOVES SOUTH TO COVER CHELMSFORD

5

N

ZULU FORCE ARRIVES FROM ZULU BIVOUAC AT SIPHEZI HILL

BRITISH PATROL ENCOUNTERS ZULUS

22 JANUARY
13:00

21 JANUARY

NTSHINGWAYO AND MAVUMENGWANA
ZULU

uDududu
iMbube
iSangqu
uNokhenke
Nyoni Heights
uNokhenke
'Horns of the Buffalo'

22 JANUARY
13:00

■ Zulu Homestead

SEE BRITISH POSITIONS INSET ABOVE LEFT

■ Zulu Homestead

uDloko
uThulwana
iNdluyengwe

uMcijo

22 JANUARY
13:00

Isandlwana

BRITISH FIRING LINE

British HQ ■

uMxhapho

■ Zulu Homestead

iNgobamakhosi

Stony Koppie

PULLEINE
BRITISH
3

'Durnford's Donga'

uVe

CHELMSFORD 1
BRITISH

■ Zulu Homestead

22 JANUARY
13:00

CHELMSFORD LEAVES PULLEINE IN COMMAND OF THE CAMP ON 22 JANUARY 1879, TO ASSIST DARTNELL IN THE EAST

2 BRITISH PATROL (DARTNELL) ENCOUNTERS A ZULU FORCE ON 21 JANUARY

SEE BRITISH POSITIONS INSET ABOVE LEFT

NOTES, NUMBERED ON MAP **9**

BRITISH
1. LORD CHELMSFORD
2. MAJOR JOHN DARTNELL
3. BREVET LIEUTENANT COLONEL HENRY PULLEINE
4. COLONEL ANTHONY DURNFORD
5. MAJOR CECIL RUSSELL

ZULU (NOT NUMBERED ON MAP)
- KING CETSHWAYO
- CHIEF MNYAMANA KA NGQENGELELE BUTHELEZI
- CHIEF NTSHINGWAYO KA MAHOLE KHOZA
- CHIEF MAVUMENGWANA KA NDLELA NTULI

N

2 kilometres

Fugitive's Drift ■

SITES TODAY

Buffalo River

N

TO JOHANNESBURG

NEWCASTLE ●

VRYHEID ●

DUNDEE ●
Talana Museum
Rorke's Drift ●
Isandlwana ●

R68

N11

N3

R616
LADYSMITH ●

N3
COLENSO ●

R33

R600

TO DURBAN

LEGEND

ISANDLWANA

1ST ZULU MOVEMENTS

2ND ZULY MOVEMENTS

FINAL MOVEMENTS TO FUGITIVE'S DRIFT

BRITISH MOVEMENTS (ON INSET MAP)

BRITISH RETREAT

RORKE'S DRIFT

ZULU MOVEMENTS

BRITISH RETREAT (ON INSET MAP)

BRITISH AREA CONTROLLED (ON INSET MAP)

BUILDINGS

ROAD & TRACK

TRACK OR PATH

RORKE'S DRIFT 22 JANUARY 1879

Situated at the foot of the Oskarberg near a crossing of the Buffalo River, the little mission station of
Rorke's Drift was an unlikely setting for one of the great epics of heroism of the British Army.
Rorke's Drift was designated as a supply base and hospital facility for the campaign into
Zululand, and as such was manned largely by supply and hospital personnel drawn from the
2nd Battalion of the 24th Regiment of Foot. Faced with imminent attack by the far larger
Zulu army, the little garrison improvised defensive positions using boxes of stores, bags
of *mielies* (maize) and transport wagons. The determined defenders withstood
repeated assaults throughout the night of 22 January until the exhausted attackers
withdrew. The illustration on these pages shows a view, looking southward, of
the defences around the mission station.

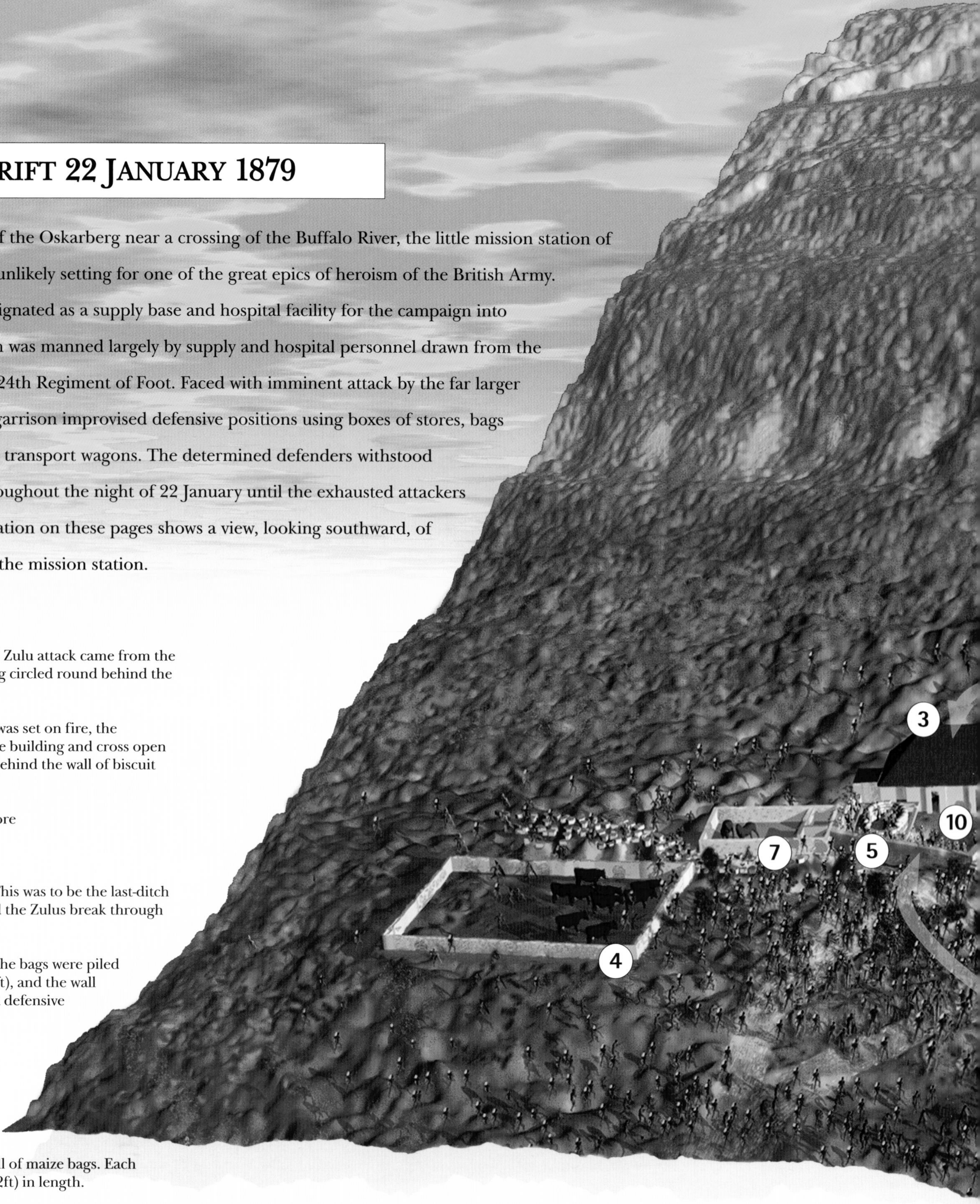

① Zulu impi: The initial Zulu attack came from the
south, the warriors having circled round behind the
bulk of the Oskarberg.

② Hospital: When this was set on fire, the
defenders had to leave the building and cross open
ground to reach shelter behind the wall of biscuit
boxes.

③ Commissariat and store

④ Large cattle kraal

⑤ Maize bag redoubt: This was to be the last-ditch
defensive position should the Zulus break through
the outer defences.

⑥ Wall of maize bags: The bags were piled
to a height of over 1m (4ft), and the wall
consituted the outermost defensive
position.

⑦ Small kraal

⑧ Cookhouse

⑨ Wagons: Two
transport wagons were
incorporated into the wall of maize bags. Each
wagon was about 3½m (12ft) in length.

⑩ Biscuit boxes

⑪ Road

⑫ Oskarberg: Zulu snipers were posted on the
slopes above the fortified mission station.

RORKE'S DRIFT TODAY

VRYHEID

DUNDEE   R68

N11   R33   ①   R68

N11

LADYSMITH   POMEROY

N3   R33

TO DURBAN

① Rorke's Drift

② Isandlwana battlefield

Anglo-Boer War

1899 – 1902

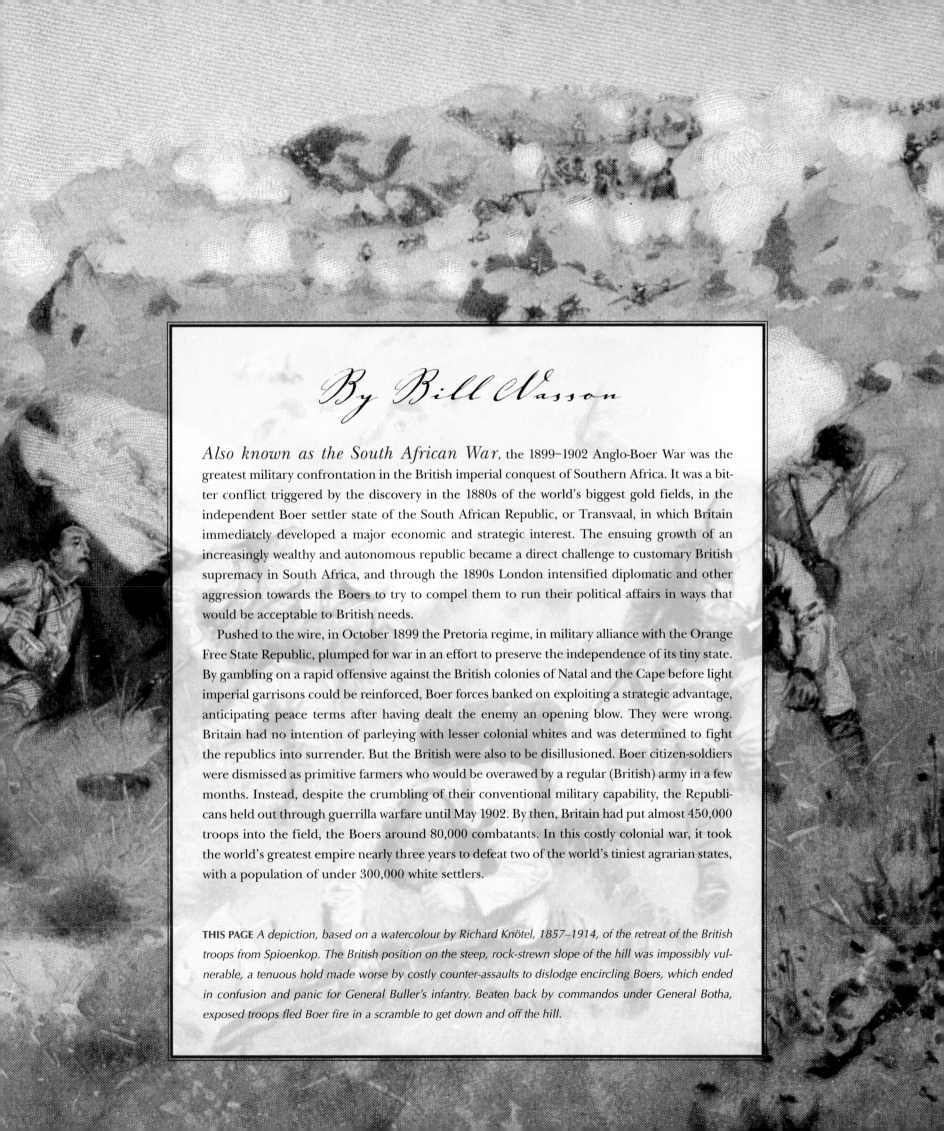

By Bill Nasson

Also known as the South African War, the 1899–1902 Anglo-Boer War was the greatest military confrontation in the British imperial conquest of Southern Africa. It was a bitter conflict triggered by the discovery in the 1880s of the world's biggest gold fields, in the independent Boer settler state of the South African Republic, or Transvaal, in which Britain immediately developed a major economic and strategic interest. The ensuing growth of an increasingly wealthy and autonomous republic became a direct challenge to customary British supremacy in South Africa, and through the 1890s London intensified diplomatic and other aggression towards the Boers to try to compel them to run their political affairs in ways that would be acceptable to British needs.

Pushed to the wire, in October 1899 the Pretoria regime, in military alliance with the Orange Free State Republic, plumped for war in an effort to preserve the independence of its tiny state. By gambling on a rapid offensive against the British colonies of Natal and the Cape before light imperial garrisons could be reinforced, Boer forces banked on exploiting a strategic advantage, anticipating peace terms after having dealt the enemy an opening blow. They were wrong. Britain had no intention of parleying with lesser colonial whites and was determined to fight the republics into surrender. But the British were also to be disillusioned. Boer citizen-soldiers were dismissed as primitive farmers who would be overawed by a regular (British) army in a few months. Instead, despite the crumbling of their conventional military capability, the Republicans held out through guerrilla warfare until May 1902. By then, Britain had put almost 450,000 troops into the field, the Boers around 80,000 combatants. In this costly colonial war, it took the world's greatest empire nearly three years to defeat two of the world's tiniest agrarian states, with a population of under 300,000 white settlers.

THIS PAGE *A depiction, based on a watercolour by Richard Knötel, 1857–1914, of the retreat of the British troops from Spioenkop. The British position on the steep, rock-strewn slope of the hill was impossibly vulnerable, a tenuous hold made worse by costly counter-assaults to dislodge encircling Boers, which ended in confusion and panic for General Buller's infantry. Beaten back by commandos under General Botha, exposed troops fled Boer fire in a scramble to get down and off the hill.*

SPIOENKOP 1900

 By Bill Nasson

At the start of hostilities, the Boers were successful in several set-piece battles. Tactically adept, their generals made skilful use of defensive ground, concealment and superior mounted mobility, exploiting their modern technology of rapid-fire Mauser rifles and smokeless powder to combine fire and movement to ferocious effect. Groping with the illimitable space of a veld environment of long ranges, clear air and wide-open fields of fire, British generals were knocked back in opening battle disasters like Modder River, Stormberg, Magersfontein and Colenso. A casualty of these shock defeats was the commander in chief of the Army Corps in South Africa, General Sir Redvers Buller, a troubled and pessimistic figure criticized for coming close to losing Britain the war. Although the lame-duck Buller was replaced by Field Marshal Lord Roberts immediately after the heavy loss at Colenso in December 1899, he was retained on the eastern front as commander of the Natal Field Force. Here, in a desperate effort to turn the tide in northern Natal, he launched offensives to relieve the besieged town of

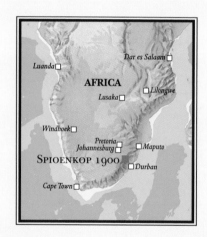

Ladysmith, situated strategically at the junction of the key rail and road routes between the Boer republics and Durban.

On 24 January 1900, one of these offensives led to the disastrous Battle of Spioenkop, sometimes spelt Spion Kop, which means Look-Out or Spy Hill, perhaps the best-known battle name from this war. The heavy casualties suffered by the Lancashire regiments in this Natal engagement made such an impact on popular sentiment in Merseyside that the high terraces of Liverpool Football Clubs ground were dubbed The Kop, and a fan club is still named Spion Kop.

THE SPIOENKOP ACTION

By early January 1900, Buller had assembled substantial forces for his Ladysmith campaign, banking on the effectiveness of a wide, flanking movement to the west of his enemy. Reinforced by the addition of a new 5th Division under General Sir Charles Warren, Buller rumbled out on 10 January with about 24,000 troops, wagons, heavy naval guns and field batteries. This operation entailed propelling the main British force some 30km (18 miles) upstream to cross the Tugela River at Trichardt's Drift; and then gaining command of the open land north of the precipitous hill of Spioenkop for a clear move on Ladysmith. To achieve this penetration, Warren's large division was to be sent on a sweeping left movement

ABOVE *Boer riflemen in makeshift trench lines which provided secure ground cover from which to direct intense fire at confused British infantry, caught stumbling across exposed stony ground.*

around ominous hills and then eastwards to link up with General Neville Lyttelton's brigade, rolling up from the south on the right to hedge in Boer positions on high ground. With these entrenchments flanked by cutting past them through the hills, the combined columns could advance on Ladysmith, 24km (15 miles) from the Tugela bridgehead.

At first, British prospects looked favourable. The Tugela was bridged at both Potgieter's Drift and Trichardt's Drift, and Lord Dundonald's cavalry spurted ahead to the extreme northwestern rise of the hills, Tabanyama, ready to gallop on to Ladysmith. But, to their rear, Buller's progress was an arthritic crawl, hampered by flooded rivers, waterlogged roads and the weight of massive supplies. Alerted to what was coming, General Louis Botha's forces made speedy and thorough defensive preparations, repositioning their front and buttressing steep hill positions, including digging in thickly on Tabanyama. Warren's intended route between the Tabanyama and

MAIN CHARACTERS FEATURED

BRITISH
General Sir Redvers Buller
    Commander of the Natal
    Field Force of the Army
    Corps in South Africa
Field Marshal Lord Roberts
General Sir Charles Warren
    (5th Division)
General Neville Lyttelton

Lord Dundonald (cavalry)
General Edward Woodgate
Lieutenant Colonel Alexander
    Thorneycroft

BOERS
General Louis Botha
General Piet Joubert

General Sir Redvers Buller | *General Louis Botha*

Spioenkop hills was soon packed with Boer defenders, keeping the doings of Buller's lumbering columns under continuous surveillance. Finding it heavy going for his wagons, Warren called back Dundonald's 1500 cavalrymen and authorized ham-fisted frontal attacks on Tabanyama on 20 and 21 January, which broke against fierce resistance.

Buller was enraged by these indecisive assaults, and threatened to withdraw his column across the Tugela unless Warren found a way through. Nervous of another drubbing at Tabanyama, on 23 January he proposed a direct attack to dislodge the Boers from the commanding hills by striking at the highest peak. With the Spioenkop ridge taken and artillery hauled up, surrounding Boer trenches could be battered to cover the British thrust towards Ladysmith.

This whale-like rising had, however, not been a target in British advance planning. Warren did not request, nor was he offered, the use of an observation balloon to survey the spot, pinpoint the summit and fix the strength of enemy positions. He also lacked adequate mapping. British positions to the south and west provided a blinkered view of this formidably steep ground on the Tugela Heights, which rose to almost 460m (1500 feet) above the river line.

At 23:00 on 23 January, in dense mist and very poor visibility, General Edward Woodgate (still lame from a broken leg) took an assault column of 1700 troops, comprising mainly Lancashire infantry, scrambling up the hill. They were guided by Lieutenant-Colonel Alexander Thorneycroft, who had roughly memorized the snaking course of a narrow track up from Trichardt's crossing. Surprising a light Boer picket defence, a rampant bayonet charge disposed of the defence. By 04:00 on 24 January, Spioenkop had seemingly fallen to the British. Still in darkness and thick, drizzling mist, Woodgate ordered his north-facing troops to dig in across the summit as best they could on pitted, stony ground. That amounted to a shallow, 330m-long (300-yard-long) ditch behind a flimsy parapet of small boulders, as sandbags had been left behind and many entrenching tools had been discarded during the ascent. Nor had a telegraph line been spooled up, leaving Woodgate reliant on visual or voice signalling. Before dawn, three cheers to those below signalled a successful occupation.

The immediate Boer reaction was panic that the seizure of Spioenkop spelt a broader British breakthrough. Still, urged on by personal orders from Boer president Paul Kruger, and from his Natal commander, General Piet Joubert, to reclaim the hill at all costs, Botha rallied his edgy commandos, and under early morning mist cover, several hundred Boers wormed their way into attacking positions. To the northwest, the crack Carolina and Pretoria commandos were drafted in to join other riflemen and gun batteries holding positions on the surrounding kopjes of Green Hill, Conical Hill and Aloe Knoll. Gunners on Tabanyama also brought their

Mahatma Gandhi, later peace activist and philosopher, served as the leader of a Natal Indian ambulance corps, which played a crucial role in bearing British troops away from the hill area firing zone.

Winston Churchill later British prime minister, served as a war correspondent for the London `Morning Post`. In the thick of Spioenkop he recorded his distress at British loss and humiliation, which he attributed to incompetent command.

Mahatma Gandhi   *Winston Churchill*

defensive lip were across handy 'dead' terrain, insulated by its angle from effective downward fire. At the same time, the light British entrenchment had left them critically exposed to enemy shelling and close-range rifle volleys and sniper fire from Twin Peaks, Aloe Knoll and adjoining heights from the northwest round to the east.

Fearful of the sloping ground cover for upward Boer movement, at the spread of daylight the British command ran detachments forward to dig in and defend the vital crest. After 08:00, artillery and rifle fire, aided by accurate forward signalling, began to rake the Spioenkop summit, blanketing the huddled British force in a merciless crossfire, particularly from Green Hill on the left flank and Aloe Knoll on the right. In little more than an hour, Lancashire Fusiliers, Scottish Rifles and Thorneycroft's infantry contingent were mowed down, especially by unremitting enfilade fire down the exposed trench, with the hapless troops dying on top of one another. At about 09:00 Woodgate was killed by shrapnel.

Surviving men were soon waving white handkerchiefs or crawling off the ridge in panic; some were delirious from dehydration in the

pom-poms and 75mm guns to bear on Spioenkop to the south, and Botha placed guns on Twin Peaks to fire to the northwest. To complete the prepared onslaught, a Boer assault force was nestled below the northeastern face of Spioenkop, in readiness for an uphill rush. The Republicans were determined to eliminate any threat to their commanding hold on the heights.

REVELATION AT FIRST LIGHT

With the first dipping of the mist at around 07:00 came the sickening realization for the British that they were not where they thought they were. Far from being in control of the summit, their frontal position was on a shallow ridge, well back from the crest line up to 137m (150 yards) away, below which ground fell away steeply to a wide plateau. To the right of their trench position the ridge ground folded into a saddle, ending in a forbidding rise a mere 274m (300 yards) distant. Undetected in the mist, this was the Boer position of Aloe Knoll. Moreover, enemy approaches to their tenuous

ABOVE *Boer officer with characteristic bandolier, slouch hat and well-groomed beard, the universal mark of his patriarchal authority.*

ABOVE *Boer photograph of the British trench taken on the morning after the Battle of Spioenkop. Littered with corpses, it represented a mass grave. Publication in Britain in 1900 provoked public shock and recrimination.*

blazing heat, and already facing sniffing hyenas. Meanwhile, having crammed around the flanks, Botha's commandos stormed up Spioenkop and engaged their enemy at close quarters. At nightfall, Thorneycroft, with Middlesex Regiment and Imperial Light Infantry reinforcements, was still holding the summit amid a continuing muddle among officers over communication lines and operational authority. Having earlier split his command, Buller was left to survey events through a telescope, but without coherent operational control.

Close to, if not beyond, the end of their tether by 20:00, the Spioenkop force decided against another day of terrible casualties and staggered back down the darkening hill. Yet the Boers, too, were at breaking point and itching to disperse after being beaten back continuously. Each side thought that its opponent had prevailed. But the British had yielded first, and the victorious Boers reoccupied a deserted Spioenkop the following morning. Ladysmith remained besieged, and a retreating Buller had to find another forward route. Britain's casualties, in what its Colonial Secretary Joseph Chamberlain called a 'sickening fiasco', numbered 1750 dead, wounded or taken prisoner, while Boer losses numbered about 300 men.

VISITORS' FACT FILE

The Spioenkop site can be reached easily along the scenic N3 dual carriage motorway between Pietermaritzburg and Durban. It winds through high ground, showing the traveller sweeping vistas of largely empty grassland, studded with hills and forbidding rocky outcrops. There is an expansive view of Spioenkop itself from this road. For those wanting a contemporary sense of this war terrain 40km (25 miles) southwest of Ladysmith, it remains little changed from 1900. Since the 1970s, Spioenkop has been a public resort and nature reserve, spread around a dam on the river. There are well-marked walking trails for exploring this hilly area, although walkers need to be mindful of periodic low mist and drizzle, which descends as a chilling reminder of battle conditions. It is very easy to visit Spioenkop independently, and a small museum close to the battlefield provides detailed information on the site and advice on how to get to grips with battle movements across the nearby ground. For those interested in arranging a more specialist guided tour locally, the regional information centre in Dundee, just north of Ladysmith, is reliable and reputable:

• Private Bag 2024, Dundee, Kwazulu-Natal 3000, tel. (341) 22 121 fax (341) 23 856.

SPIOENKOP 1900

MAP 10
POSITIONS AND MOVES 23–25 JANUARY

BRITISH MOVEMENTS AND BOER POSITIONS SHOWN, WITH BRITISH POSITIONS ON SPIOENKOP (SEE INSET), BEFORE LOSING THE HILL TO THE BOERS

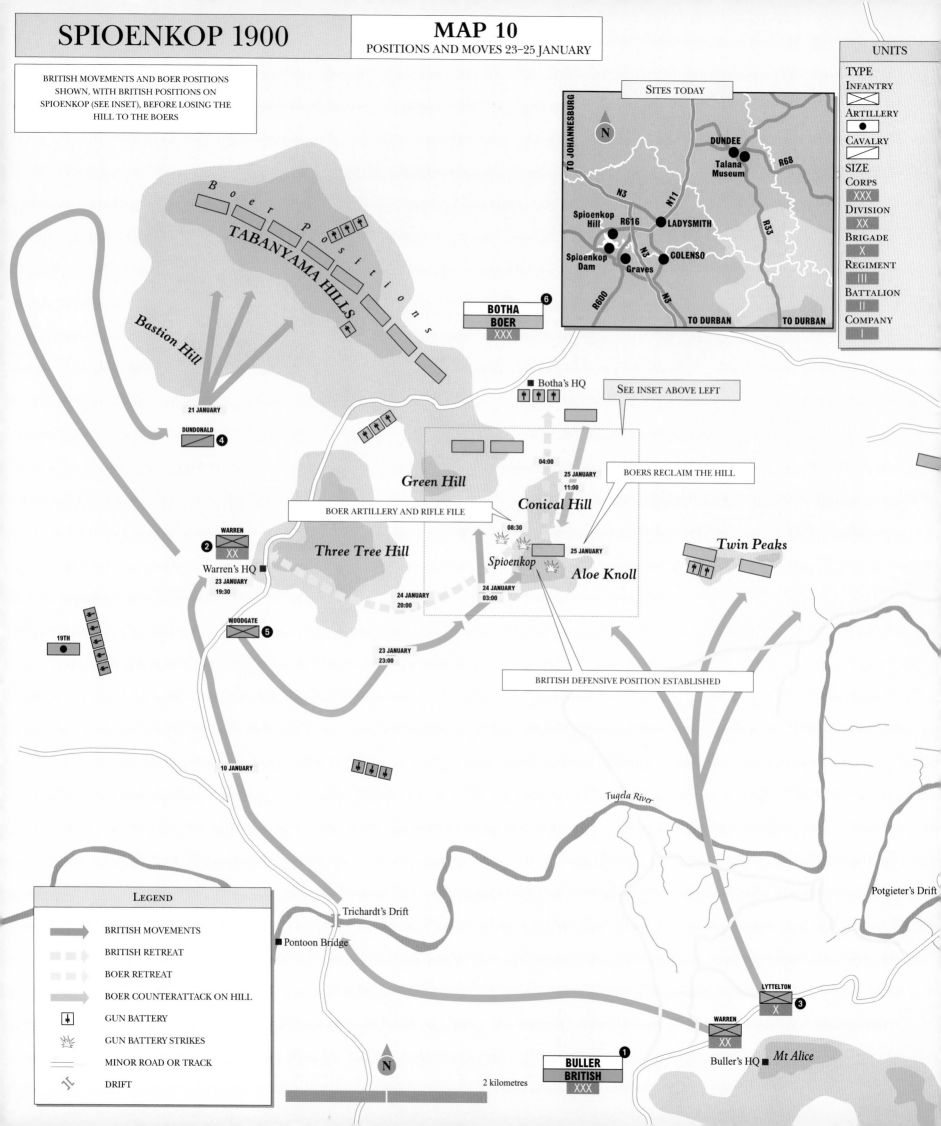

UNITS

TYPE

INFANTRY	
ARTILLERY	
CAVALRY	

SIZE

CORPS	XXX
DIVISION	XX
BRIGADE	X
REGIMENT	III
BATTALION	II
COMPANY	I

Sites Today

N

TO JOHANNESBURG

DUNDEE
Talana Museum

N3
N11
R68

Spioenkop Hill
R616
LADYSMITH

Spioenkop Dam
Graves
COLENSO

N3
N3
R33

R600

TO DURBAN
TO DURBAN

Boer Positions
TABANYAMA HILLS

Bastion Hill

21 JANUARY

DUNDONALD ❹

Botha's HQ

SEE INSET ABOVE LEFT

BOTHA
BOER
XXX ❻

Green Hill

04:00

25 JANUARY 11:00

BOERS RECLAIM THE HILL

Conical Hill

BOER ARTILLERY AND RIFLE FILE

08:30

WARREN
XX ❷

Warren's HQ

23 JANUARY 19:30

Three Tree Hill

Spioenkop
25 JANUARY

Aloe Knoll

Twin Peaks

24 JANUARY 20:00

24 JANUARY 03:00

19TH

WOODGATE
XX ❺

23 JANUARY 23:00

BRITISH DEFENSIVE POSITION ESTABLISHED

10 JANUARY

Tugela River

Potgieter's Drift

LEGEND

➤	BRITISH MOVEMENTS
⇢	BRITISH RETREAT
⇢	BOER RETREAT
➤	BOER COUNTERATTACK ON HILL
♦	GUN BATTERY
✸	GUN BATTERY STRIKES
—	MINOR ROAD OR TRACK
⅃⌐	DRIFT

Trichardt's Drift

Pontoon Bridge

LYTTELTON
X ❸

WARREN
XX

BULLER
BRITISH
XXX ❶

Buller's HQ *Mt Alice*

N

2 kilometres

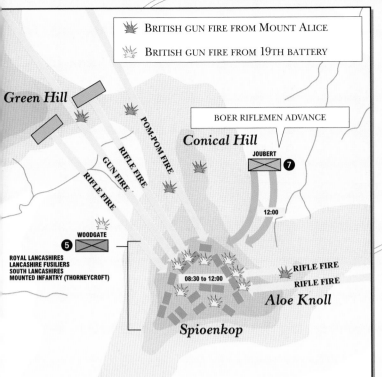

LADYSMITH

BRITISH GUN FIRE FROM MOUNT ALICE

BRITISH GUN FIRE FROM 19TH BATTERY

Green Hill

BOER RIFLEMEN ADVANCE

Conical Hill

POM-POM FIRE

RIFLE FIRE

GUN FIRE

RIFLE FIRE

JOUBERT ⑦

12:00

WOODGATE

⑤

ROYAL LANCASHIRES
LANCASHIRE FUSILIERS
SOUTH LANCASHIRES
MOUNTED INFANTRY (THORNEYCROFT)

08:30 to 12:00

RIFLE FIRE

RIFLE FIRE

Aloe Knoll

Spioenkop

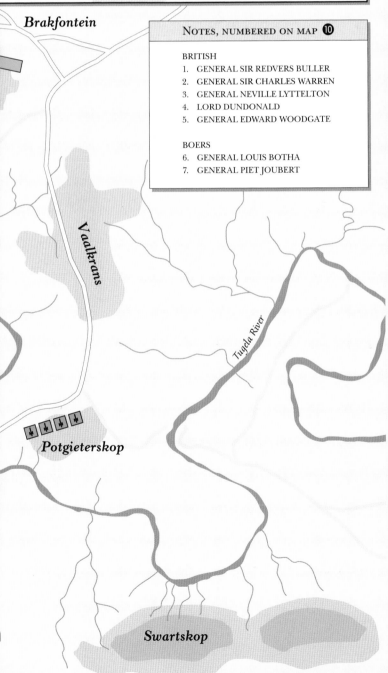

Brakfontein

NOTES, NUMBERED ON MAP ⑩

BRITISH
1. GENERAL SIR REDVERS BULLER
2. GENERAL SIR CHARLES WARREN
3. GENERAL NEVILLE LYTTELTON
4. LORD DUNDONALD
5. GENERAL EDWARD WOODGATE

BOERS
6. GENERAL LOUIS BOTHA
7. GENERAL PIET JOUBERT

Vaalkrans

Tugela River

Potgieterskop

Swartskop

- Well-established KwaZulu-Natal battlefield tours also provide for a day and overnight stay at Spioenkop at Tree Hill Lodge, which overlooks the battlefield. Three Tree Hill Lodge:
  Tel +27 36 448 1171 Fax +27 36 448 1953
  Email: tthl@mweb.co.za
  Website: www.threetreehill.co.za
- Far & Wild Safaris is experienced: 477 Essenwood Road, Durban, KwaZulu-Natal 4001, tel. (31) 208 3684 fax (31) 207 4700 email: farwild@iafrica.com.

SPIOENKOP TIMELINE

Monday 22 January 1900

Ordered by General Sir Redvers Buller to mount a breakthrough, Lieutenant General Sir Charles Warren aims to take the dominating height of Spioenkop, and prepares to lead an attack that night. Other British officers insist on delaying it for a day to reconnoitre unknown terrain.

23 January

19:30   Troops assemble below Three Trees Hill for a night climb up the southern spur.

23:00   Guided by Lieutenant Colonel Alexander Thorneycroft and commanded by Major General Edward Woodgate, the British move off on a well-executed and disciplined uphill march.

24 January

03:00   The British force runs into, and overcomes, a small Boer picket on the summit.

04:00   Infantry prepare a defensive position on the summit plateau while surviving Boer sentries scramble down Spioenkop and alert General Louis Botha, who commits all available forces to the defence of his Tugela line.

07:00   As the mist lifts the British realize that they have positioned themselves on perilously exposed ground. Boers deploy guns to shell the summit.

08.30   Boer artillery and rifle fire begin to sweep the British trench position.

09.00   Woodgate killed by shrapnel.

11:00–12:00   Intensity of Boer shell, pom-pom and rifle fire increases as Botha's commandos approach the British position.

12:00–15:00   Fierce close-quarter fighting for possession of the slopes below the crest line. Neither side is able to dislodge their enemy.

16:00–dusk   Battle becomes static. Holding on tenuously, the British suffer heavy loses from continuous fire, and are unable to push back Republican charges.

20:00   British at breaking point and withdraw from Spioenkop in darkness. Boers also at their limit and begin to disperse in scattered units.

25 January

03:30   Boer scouting party finds the Spioenkop summit deserted and calls up commandos assembled by Botha at the bottom of the hill, in anticipation of an enemy retreat. By daybreak the Boers have taken possession and claimed one of their biggest victories of the war. Buller withdraws across the Tugela.

PAARDEBERG 1900

By Bill Nasson

By early 1900 Lord Roberts, the newly installed British commander in chief, had settled on a broad strategy to turn the war in his favour. He amassed a huge army and used speed and surprise, sweeping through the veld in eastward and westward flanking movements to carry British forces into the Boer states. Buller was flailing on towards Ladysmith in Natal, and in the Cape Colony pressure was brought to bear on invading Boers to abandon their investments of the towns of Kimberley and Mafeking.

In February, General Sir John French's cavalry routed Boer defences on the wide, flat plains between Klip Drift and Kimberley, finally relieving the diamond fields town, which had been besieged for four months. By tearing through to the east of the entrenched Boer position on Magersfontein ridge, some 30km (20 miles) from Kimberley, the British had caught General Piet Cronjé off guard.

By then *laagered* (encamped) in the Magersfontein hills for two months, Cronjé's force had barely stirred for several weeks, well protected from routine British shelling and merely switching position along the Modder River for sanitation needs. During this lull,

he had declined reinforcements, shrugged off pleas from subordinates to attack enemy communications south of the Orange River, and had welcomed into his camp groups of women and children, including his own wife, who had come to visit men or were displaced refugees.

Unsure of the pace, direction and objective of British movements in the surrounding countryside, Cronjé was wrong-footed at Kimberley. Caught napping, the Boers had been outflanked while facing the ominous prospect of the main British force rolling up from the southeast.

Recognizing that his Magersfontein stronghold was in imminent danger of being cracked open, and begged by his officers to devise an escape route before they were trapped, a despondent Cronjé prepared for withdrawal. His situation was serious. The Boers could not push north as French was prowling in and around Kimberley. Southwards there was no chance due to the proximity of General Lord Methuen's forces, which were already regularly bombarding Magersfontein. Ducking west meant moving into barren, waterless countryside and being beyond the reach of potential reinforcements from Bloemfontein.

The only gap was still eastwards, through which a break could be made for the Orange Free State capital, Bloemfontein, 145km (90 miles) away. To cover withdrawal, Cronjé was urged by his commandants to split his army, dispatching his slow wagons and

ABOVE *General Cronje with Lord Roberts's ADC before being led away to captivity after his surrender. Cronjé was treated with consideration.*

MAIN CHARACTERS FEATURED

BRITISH

Lord Roberts (Commander in Chief of the Army Corps in South Africa)

General Sir Redvers Buller

General Sir John French (cavalry, Lancers, Hussars and Royal Horse Artillery)

General Lord Methuen

Lord Kitchener (Roberts's Chief of Staff and deputy)

General Hector MacDonald (3rd – Highland – Brigade)

General Horace Smith-Dorrien (19th Brigade)

General Robert Broadwood (cavalry)

General Thomas Kelly-Kenny (senior British officer at Paardeberg)

Colonel Raymond Hannay (mounted infantry)

Brigadier-General Thomas Stephenson (18th Brigade)

Major-General Sir Henry Colvile (9th Division)

BOERS

General P.A. (Piet) Cronjé

General C.R. (Christiaan) de Wet

Commandant Ignatius Ferreira

President Marthinus Steyn

| *Lord Roberts* | *General P.A. (Piet) Cronjé* |

forward command at Klip Drift spotted their hushed passage. By dawn on 16 February Cronjé was clear of enemy lines. However, he could not avoid churning up dust, and later that morning the column was picked out by British forces to the west. The convoy spent the day on the Modder River behind a protective line of hills, fighting a stiff rearguard action against forces pressed in by Roberts's Chief of Staff and deputy, Lord Kitchener. After dark, the Boers resumed their retreat and by midday on 17 February had reached a *drift* (ford) on the northern river bank. Crossing over to the south would get them to the Bloemfontein road and their line of final escape. In the afternoon, Cronjé halted several miles east of Paardeberg (horse mountain), assuming that he was well away from the enemy. Instead, the British were bearing down on a sitting target.

THE PAARDEBERG ACTION

Roberts had put all available forces in hard pursuit of Cronjé's column. General Hector MacDonald's 3rd (Highland) Brigade and General Horace Smith-Dorrien's 19th Brigade had moved up from the south and, by 17 February infantry from the west were converging on Paardeberg Drift along both river banks. A range of *kopjes* (hillocks) north of the Modder River and east of Paardeberg was being occupied by a cavalry brigade under General Robert Broadwood. French, prodded by an agitated Kitchener to cut off Boer movement to the northeast by blocking all river crossings, had raced up his Lancers, Hussars and Royal Horse Artillery from Kimberley and by late morning had positioned his guns and cavalry formations on the hilly ground of Koedoesrand to the north. Keeping his distance, French began to shell the convoy around noon on 17 February, splintering wagons, gutting oxen and creating panic as terrified commandos and civilians squirmed about in search of shelter.

Increasingly encircled and trapped on the north bank in the vicinity of Vendusie Drift, Cronjé decided to *laager* his force. He placed his main camp among trees above the Vendusie crossing and surrounded it with trenches and well-camouflaged posts. Wagons were trundled down to the dry riverbed to provide a screen for women and children. The Boer command was not entirely without means. It had several thousand commandos for defensive positions, had requested reinforcements, and had the prospect of diversionary assistance from Commandant Ignatius Ferreira and General Christiaan de Wet, whose raiding forces were roaming in the vicinity.

The battleground itself was a crude, stretched oval or amphitheatre, sliced by the Modder River, which coursed for around 16km (10 miles) in a southwesterly direction from Koedoesrand Drift in the northeast (upstream of the Cronjé *laager*) to Paardeberg Drift, 6km (4 miles) downstream from the main Boer position. The river hung between steep, bush-covered banks that tilted onto open ground, sloping upwards for 3–5km (2–3 miles) to a fringe of low

unmounted troops ahead, while mounting a rearguard defence with artillery and horsemen until help could be sent from the Orange Free State. He ignored the advice and kept his convoy intact.

Under cover of darkness on 15 February, the Boers evacuated the Magersfontein hills. About 5000 commandos, accompanied by several dozen women and children, over 400 wagons and several thousand horses, crawled eastwards, keeping parallel to the line of the Modder River. Neither Methuen nor French nor another

ridges with a series of small but prominent *kopjes* on either side. Apart from Koedoesrand and Paardeberg, this higher outcrop encompassed Signal Hill, Gun Hill and a fist of ground that became known as Kitchener's Kopje. In places, *dongas* (deep gullies) extended outwards from the Modder along its banks, furnishing naturally fortified trench locations. Commandos burrowed well down into these high banks, fixing strong positions 3km (2 miles) to the west of their main camp and securing posts stretching 5km (3 miles) eastwards. Entrenched riflemen on both banks faced open ground with virtually no cover for attackers, and had lethally clear fields of fire across a wide arc.

Meanwhile, their enemy closed in. With Roberts ill, Kitchener assumed command at Paardeberg, basing his headquarters about 3km (2 miles) south of the central Boer position. Having cornered an exasperating foe, he was determined to shred Cronjé's army and inflict high losses, finishing off the Boers the next day at all costs. Nervous of enemy capacity in its turn to inflict heavy casualties, General Thomas Kelly-Kenny, the senior British officer at Paardeberg, had favoured throwing a thick cordon around Cronjé, mounting a sustained artillery bombardment, and simply starving him into surrender.

This was all too leisurely for a bristling Kitchener. Following a cursory reconnaissance after his first glimpse of Cronjé's *laager* at daybreak on 18 February, he ordered an immediate early morning assault. Combining a frontal attack from the south and simultaneous charges from east and west along opposite banks of the Modder, he anticipated victory in a few hours and clearance for a British advance upon Bloemfontein. Given the depth of enemy positions, his divisional commanders were rather less sanguine about prospects of an easy victory.

THE MAIN BATTLE

After a devastating artillery barrage laid on by French, Kitchener deployed around 15,000 troops in a concentrated frontal advance from the south and in converging stabs from the east and west, spreading his pincer formations over a wide area and complicating communications and coordination. At 04:00, British mounted infantry under Lieutenant Colonel Raymond Hannay, and Brigadier General Thomas Stephenson's 18th Brigade, pushed up the south bank of the Modder for an attack from the east, but by early morning were stalled by commando rifle fire. With the British soon pinned down by the accuracy and intensity of Boer fire, Kitchener had to acknowledge that he had underestimated the power of Boer resistance, and later in the day the assault ran into the sand.

The offensive also suffered other misfortunes. Afternoon rain and low cloud crippled heliograph communication, and officers were not always sure of orders or who was meant to be making the running. Along ridges to the east they had to contend with a surprise rear incursion by Bloemfontein reinforcements led personally by President Marthinus Steyn, and had later to withdraw troops from their central assault to face down commando charges led by De Wet and Ferreira. Although these were held off, the running Boer seizure of several hill positions, including Stinkfontein farm and the imposing Kitchener's Kopje, some 3km (2 miles) southeast of Cronjé's headquarters, intermittently menaced British backs with gunfire.

Shrugging off soaring casualties by late morning, a remorseless Kitchener continued to hurl units into battle, galloping about in heightened anticipation of the Boer defences being overrun. But attacks along both sides of the river made little progress beyond inching firing lines to within several hundred metres of Boer emplacements. By mid-afternoon, burning to do something to force a victory, Kitchener pushed forward Lieutenant Colonel Raymond Hannay's mounted infantry to link up with the Essex and Welch regiments and to storm Cronjé's main *laager*, still

ABOVE *Bombardment of the Boer camp. Opting for an investment of the Boer position rather than further costly assaults, Lord Roberts settled matters through a sustained artillery bombardment lasting more than a week. Although more fitful than intense, shelling was aided by an overhead observation balloon.*

around 730m (800 yards) away. Forced to traverse open ground in clearing late afternoon light, they, too, were soon turned by heavy fire. Almost in tandem, and to the west, Cornwalls, Royal Canadians and Highland Brigade formations broke assembly cover and struck up the north bank towards the well-insulated Boer *donga* position, but were beaten back by deadly low-trajectory Mauser volleys. There they were grounded as Smith-Dorrien failed to run in support, while he and other commanders bickered over what to do and when to do it.

At 08:00 Major General Sir Henry Colvile's 9th Division was ordered to cross the Modder at Paardeberg to attack from the west. However, fast-moving water delayed their progress and the north bank assault only started after 10:00. Although the unoccupied Gun Hill was taken, infantrymen were again repelled by long-range Boer fire.

The British forces were also distracted by diversionary incursions of mounted Boers and artillery fire from Christiaan de Wet and other Boer commanders operating outside the British trap. Hannay warned Kitchener that his mounted infantry were exhausted and unable to attempt any further advance. However, Kitchener ordered Hannay to charge the enemy in 'a final effort'. Describing his commander as 'a madman blinded by bloodlust', Hannay galloped to his death.

The British command continued to launch further futile infantry charges across open ground. And it was during one of these that Sergeant Albert Atkinson of the Yorkshire Regiment earned the Victoria Cross for gallantry. At 18:00 De Wet attacked from the south and seized ridge positions to fire at British stores and batteries from across the river.

In rapidly fading evening light, even a manic Kitchener was forced to accept that the decisive Paardeberg action was over; his troops began to dig in, leaving their command to brood on wounded hopes. Riding up from the south with several hundred men, De Wet then rubbed in salt by seizing the eastern ridges of Kitchener's Kopje and Stinkfontein, diverting his frustrated opponents into repeated counter-attacks.

The British lost over 1260 killed and wounded (their highest casualty rate of any single day of the war), while the Boer cost was over 300 casualties. But with Cronjé surrounded, and the rising waters of the Modder River a threat to both his supplies and possible flight, the

ABOVE *A convoy of troops, horses and artillery crossing the Modder at Paardeberg Drift to outflank General Cronje during the Boer War.*

looming Paardeberg outcome was never seriously in doubt. Roberts resumed command on 19 February, ringed the Boers with a close cordon of infantry and an outer fence of mounted soldiers, and through a daily siege bombardment throttled them into surrender on 27 February, capturing over 4000 people. It was the first notable British tactical victory of the conflict.

VISITORS' FACT FILE

Situated about 121km (75 miles) southwest of Bloemfontein and 48km (30 miles) north of Kimberley, Perdeberg (Paardeberg) station and its battle site can be reached off the main N12 highway or more directly on the secondary R64 route via Petrusburg. The battlefield is easily accessible, and there are a couple of well-identified and commanding vantage points which expose the extended fighting range along the Modder. One, on Oskoppie (Ox hillock) provides a panoramic view of the whole field. The other, downstream and lower down on the river banks, is on the spot where Cronjé had his main *laager*.

- The bloody chaos of the battle is meticulously documented in the Paardeberg Battlefield Museum, a small branch of the national Anglo-Boer War Museum in Bloemfontein and a local centre through which guided battlefield visits can be arranged: Anglo-Boer War Museum, PO Box 34061, Faunasig 9325. Tel +27 +51 447 0079 fax +27 +51 447 1322. Email: museum@anglo-boer.co.za.

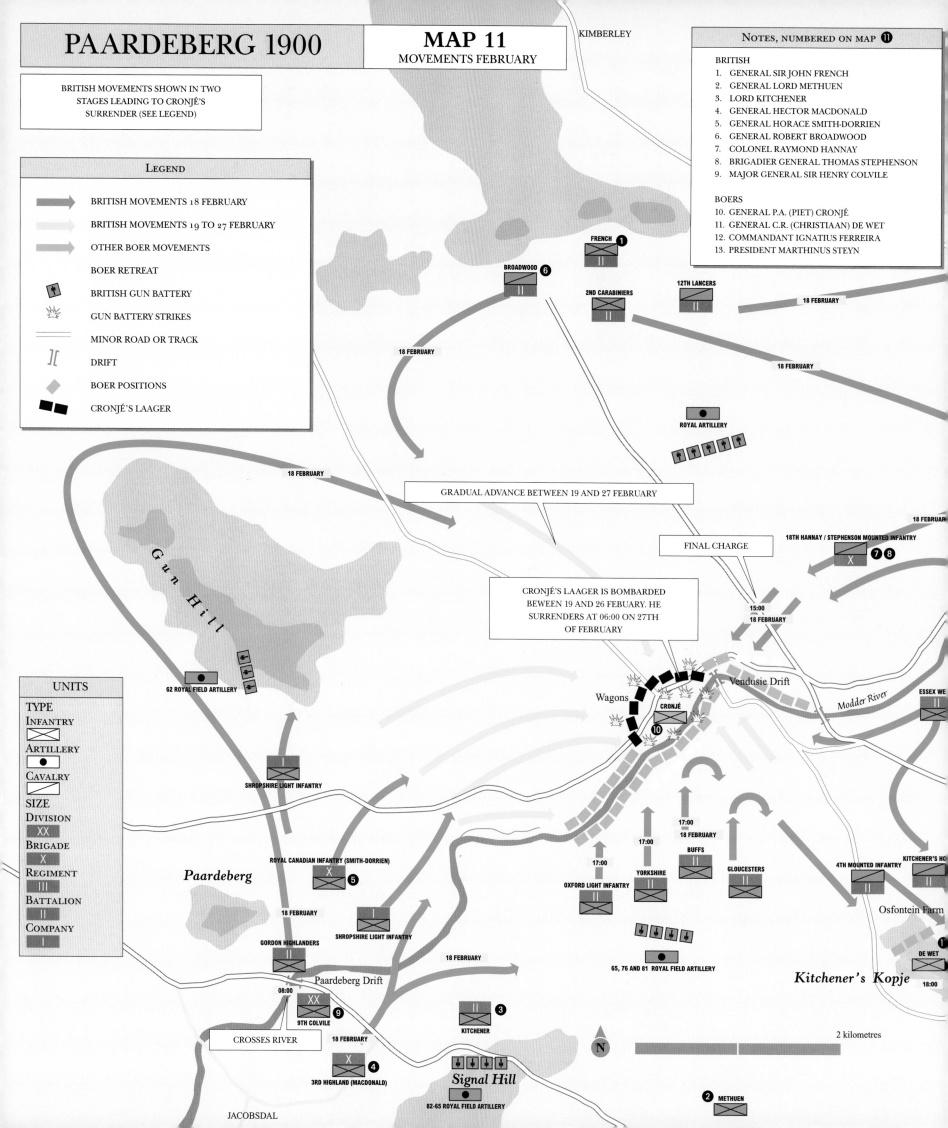

PAARDEBERG 1900

MAP 11
MOVEMENTS FEBRUARY

BRITISH MOVEMENTS SHOWN IN TWO
STAGES LEADING TO CRONJÉ'S
SURRENDER (SEE LEGEND)

KIMBERLEY

NOTES, NUMBERED ON MAP ⑪

BRITISH
1. GENERAL SIR JOHN FRENCH
2. GENERAL LORD METHUEN
3. LORD KITCHENER
4. GENERAL HECTOR MACDONALD
5. GENERAL HORACE SMITH-DORRIEN
6. GENERAL ROBERT BROADWOOD
7. COLONEL RAYMOND HANNAY
8. BRIGADIER GENERAL THOMAS STEPHENSON
9. MAJOR GENERAL SIR HENRY COLVILE

BOERS
10. GENERAL P.A. (PIET) CRONJÉ
11. GENERAL C.R. (CHRISTIAAN) DE WET
12. COMMANDANT IGNATIUS FERREIRA
13. PRESIDENT MARTHINUS STEYN

LEGEND

- BRITISH MOVEMENTS 18 FEBRUARY
- BRITISH MOVEMENTS 19 TO 27 FEBRUARY
- OTHER BOER MOVEMENTS
- BOER RETREAT
- BRITISH GUN BATTERY
- GUN BATTERY STRIKES
- MINOR ROAD OR TRACK
- DRIFT
- BOER POSITIONS
- CRONJÉ'S LAAGER

UNITS

TYPE

INFANTRY

ARTILLERY

CAVALRY

SIZE

Division — XX

Brigade — X

Regiment — |||

Battalion — ||

Company — |

FRENCH ①

BROADWOOD ⑥

2ND CARABINIERS

12TH LANCERS

18 FEBRUARY

18 FEBRUARY

18 FEBRUARY

18 FEBRUARY

ROYAL ARTILLERY

18 FEBRUARY

GRADUAL ADVANCE BETWEEN 19 AND 27 FEBRUARY

FINAL CHARGE

18TH HANNAY / STEPHENSON MOUNTED INFANTRY ⑦ ⑧

CRONJÉ'S LAAGER IS BOMBARDED
BEWEEN 19 AND 26 FEBUARY. HE
SURRENDERS AT 06:00 ON 27TH
OF FEBRUARY

15:00
18 FEBRUARY

G u n   H i l l

62 ROYAL FIELD ARTILLERY

Vendusie Drift

Wagons

CRONJÉ ⑩

Modder River

ESSEX WE

SHROPSHIRE LIGHT INFANTRY

Paardeberg

ROYAL CANADIAN INFANTRY (SMITH-DORRIEN) ⑤

18 FEBRUARY

SHROPSHIRE LIGHT INFANTRY

GORDON HIGHLANDERS

Paardeberg Drift

08:00

9TH COLVILE ⑨

CROSSES RIVER

18 FEBRUARY

3RD HIGHLAND (MACDONALD) ④

18 FEBRUARY

OXFORD LIGHT INFANTRY

17:00

YORKSHIRE

17:00

BUFFS

17:00
18 FEBRUARY

GLOUCESTERS

4TH MOUNTED INFANTRY

KITCHENER'S HO

Osfontein Farm

65, 76 AND 81 ROYAL FIELD ARTILLERY

Kitchener's Kopje

DE WET ⑪

18:00

KITCHENER ③

Signal Hill

82-65 ROYAL FIELD ARTILLERY

METHUEN ②

2 kilometres

N

JACOBSDAL

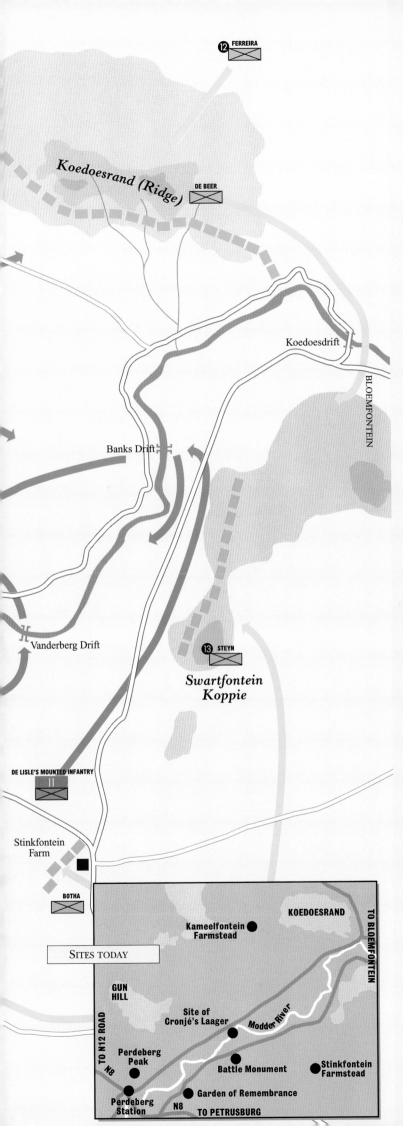

- The full expanse of the Paardeberg site can also be covered imaginatively on guided horseback. Contact Campaign Trails: PO Box 54, Gillits, Kwazulu-Natal 3603, tel/fax +27 +31 767 44166 Email: info@campaigntrails.co.za.

PAARDEBERG TIMELINE

Thursday 15 February 1900
With the Kimberley siege lifted, Cronjé abandons his Magersfontein positions and withdraws eastwards along the right bank of the Modder River. He is spotted and pursued by the British who try to cut off his river line retreat.

17 February

Shortly after midnight, the Boer column halts to rest near Paardeberg Drift. Just before noon, French's artillery batteries open fire on the convoy. Cronjé prepares defensive positions.

18 February

Kitchener arrives in the night to assume command. Rather than await a complete encirclement of the Boer *laager* and its bombardment into submission, he orders an immediate attack.

04:00 British mounted infantry under Hannay and Stephenson's 18th Brigade push up the south bank of the Modder for an attack from the east, but by early morning are stalled by commando rifle fire.

08:00 Colvile's 9th Division ordered to cross the Modder at Paardeberg to attack from the west. Fast-moving water delays progress and the north bank assault only commences after 10:00. Although unoccupied Gun Hill is taken, infantry are again repelled by long-range Boer fire.

11:00 British forces are distracted by diversionary Boer mounted incursions and artillery fire from De Wet and other Boer commanders operating outside the British trap.

14:00 Hannay warns Kitchener that his mounted infantry are exhausted and unable to attempt any further advance.

15:00 Kitchener orders Hannay to charge the enemy in 'a final effort'. Describing his commander as 'a madman blinded by bloodlust', Hannay gallops to his death.

17:00 British command launches further futile infantry charges across open ground. Sergeant Albert Atkinson, Yorkshire Regiment, earns the Victoria Cross for gallantry.

18:00 De Wet attacks from the south and seizes ridge positions to fire at British stores and batteries from across the river.

19:00 As daylight fades the battle loses momentum. Victory having eluded them, both sides wind down.

19th February

10:00 Roberts takes command, consolidates the cordon around Cronje and commences a sustained daily bombardment of the *laager*, while gradually edging trench lines closer to enemy positions.

27 February

06:00 Cronjé surrenders.

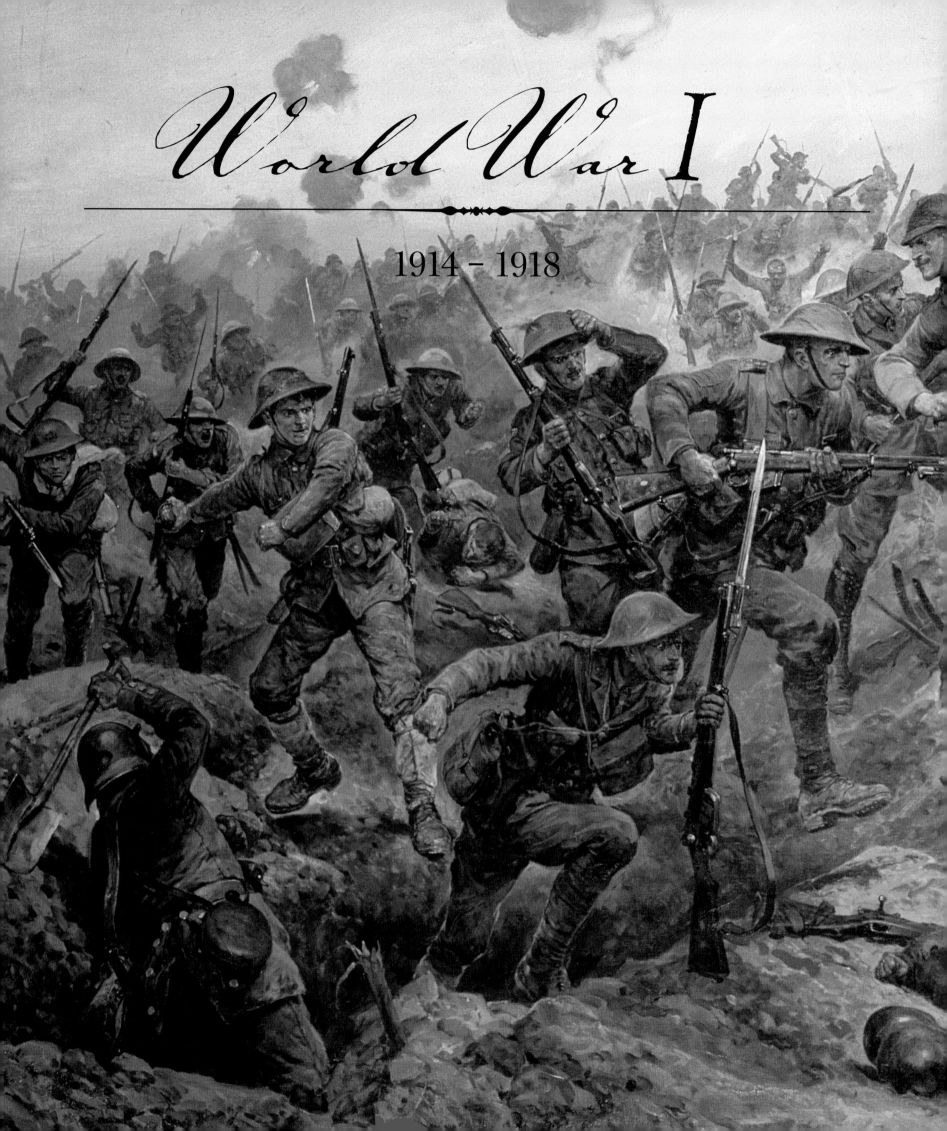

World War I

1914 – 1918

By Martin Marix Evans

The 'Great War' was precipitated by the assassination by Serbian freedom fighters of the heir to the Austro-Hungarian throne on 28 June 1914. The declaration of war on Serbia that followed led to Russia declaring war on Austria, Germany on Russia and France on Germany. The Germans were thus threatened with war on two fronts, a danger long anticipated, and they attempted a knock-out blow on the French by sweeping round through neutral Belgium. This brought the British into the conflict, and by the close of 1914 trenches had formed all the way from the North Sea to the Swiss border; the Western Front had come into being and with it static trench warfare.

The conflict was not limited to the European, Eastern and Western fronts. German naval forces preyed on British commercial shipping worldwide. The Australian warship *Sydney* caught and destroyed the German raider *Emden* in the Indian Ocean and battles were fought in the Pacific, off Coronel, and in the south Atlantic, off the Falkland Islands, with the British eventually victorious. The warring nations had colonies in Africa that were drawn into the war, and the quest for petroleum led to a British landing in Mesopotamia (Iraq) and a German alliance with the Ottoman Empire which declared a jihad on 14 November 1914.

With the Western Front locked solid and a breakthrough unlikely, an Allied attempt to overcome Turkey failed both at Gallipoli and in Mesopotamia in 1915. The fighting on the Russian front and in the Balkans approached stalemate that same year, and both sides had to face the fact that the outcome of the war would be decided in France and Flanders.

The Germans took the initiative with a massive assault on the iconic French fortifications of Verdun. The French held, at great cost, and the Germans were drawn into an attritional fight. On the Somme, the British sought to provide relief by launching a great attack, and in the east a Russian offensive contrived by General Brusilov took some of the pressure off the French, but Allied losses were grievous. The long, hard process of learning how to fight a war in a world dominated by artillery and machine guns had only just started. Both sides studied new theories of attack and new methods of defence. The British and French exploited the potential of tanks, the Germans the possibilities of artillery and gas, and both sides raced for leadership in the air. On the Western Front such ideas were put into action at the cost of thousands of casualties.

Early in 1917, with an increasing possibility of the United States entering the war and pouring thousands of fresh troops into the European theatre, a terrible gamble was taken. The Germans declared unrestricted submarine warfare, certain to incite the USA to fight, but relied on winning in the field before the tiny American army could be expanded to meet the challenge. On the Eastern Front, Riga was taken before Russian power was ended by revolution. The new German artillery and storm-troop tactics were next used in Italy, at Caporetto, and that success was followed by attacks on the Western Front in the spring of 1918. But the cost to Germany was enormous, and the grasp of field operations by the Allies, orchestrating infantry, artillery, armour and air power to overcome entrenched positions, was now supreme. While the Americans took a significant part in the actions leading to victory in 1918 when the German army was beaten in the field, it was their very existence as adversaries that precipitated German defeat. Even the most optimistic and dedicated of Germans could not conceive of victory over the United States.

GALLIPOLI 1915–16

By Christopher Pugsley

The nine-month Gallipoli campaign of 1915–16 grew out of Winston Churchill's scheme of 'knocking Turkey out of the war' by passing a fleet of obsolete pre-Dreadnought British and French battleships through the Narrows of the Dardanelles into the Sea of Marmara and then using the threat of their guns to force the surrender of the Turkish government in what was then the Turkish capital of Constantinople (Istanbul). The idea galvanized Asquith's Liberal administration, which was looking for a way out of the deadlock in which Britain found itself on the Western Front. In France and Belgium more and more resources were being committed with little success, and by 1915 British casualties accounted for 96 per cent of the strength of the original British Expeditionary Force.

Churchill's scheme would use British naval power to open a sea route to the Russian Black Sea ports and threaten Austria-Hungary, the weaker of the two empires with whom Britain and France were

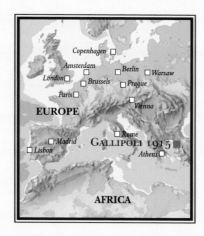

at war. A series of bombardments of the outer forts protecting the Dardanelles Straits began in February 1915. Small landing parties of Royal Marines went ashore unopposed to check the damage. This was a prelude to a naval attack to break through the Straits on 18 March 1915. It failed, with an undetected row of mines sinking three battleships and three others being badly damaged by mines and artillery fire. The ships were expendable, but it was evident that better minesweepers were needed. Moreover, the Gallipoli Peninsula had to be secured on land as far as the Kilitbahir plateau, which dominated the Narrows, before another naval attempt could be made.

HAMILTON'S PLAN

General Sir Ian Hamilton had already been appointed commander in chief of the Mediterranean Expeditionary Force (MEF). This sounded more impressive than the reality of the force of some 70,000 that was available to him. However, on 22 March, Hamilton, who had witnessed the naval failure, agreed to mount a combined amphibious attack on the peninsula which resulted in the Gallipoli landings on 25 April 1915.

Hamilton's force was an ad hoc collection of partly trained, hastily raised British and Dominion forces available in Egypt and England from elements not yet committed to the Western Front.

ABOVE *A 60-pounder heavy field gun in action on a cliff top at Helles Bay, Gallipoli, Turkey.*

PREVIOUS PAGE The Battle of the Somme *by Woodville. The romantic view of war, including an officer brandishing a hunting horn. The reality was very different.*

The backbone was Major General A. G. Hunter-Weston's British 29th Division, consisting of garrison battalions withdrawn from India. Hamilton's plan saw this committed in five landings on a series of small beaches in the south at Cape Helles with the task of advancing north and securing the Kilitbahir plateau. It would be supported by a French Expeditionary Force made up of Foreign Legionnaires and French colonial troops, who would initially feint on the Asiatic shore at Kum Kale before joining the 29th Division in a joint advance up the peninsula. In reserve, offshore, was the 29th Indian Brigade which Hamilton was reluctant to use until victory was assured, as he was not confident how some of its Muslim soldiers would fight against the Turks.

Further north, Lieutenant General Sir William Birdwood's Australia and New Zealand Army Corps (ANZAC) would land north of the Gaba Tepe Peninsula and, once ashore, advance across the Maidos plain to the ferry port of Maidos (Eceabat) thereby cutting Turkish communications and isolating the Kilitbahir plateau. This was a major undertaking for the two hastily raised and barely trained volunteer citizen divisions. Major General W. T. Bridge's 1st Australian Division would land before dawn and seize the coastal Sari Bair range as far as the high ground of Chunuk Bair, while the weaker of the two, the mixed New Zealand and Australian Division commanded by Major General Sir Alexander Godley, would land after them, form up as a reserve and then advance on Maidos.

'It is the general opinion that the Turks will offer an energetic resistance to our landing, but when once we are firmly established on the Peninsula it is thought possible that this opposition might crumble away, and that they may then turn on their German masters. The average Turk has always been most sympathetic to the British Nation, and it is known that many look with envy on the prosperity which Egypt enjoys under British rule.'

Report issued by MEF immediately before landing

ABOVE *Troops land at Anzac Cove during the battle between Allied and Turkish forces at the Gallipoli Peninsula for access to the strategic Sea of Marmara. Six British battleships were either sunk or badly damaged, causing the naval assault on the Dardanelles to stall. A second Allied landing at Gallipoli in August failed and Allied forces evacuated Gallipoli from November 1915 to January 1916.*

Offshore, Hamilton's remaining Royal Naval Division would sail in its transports north to Bulair, the narrowest point of the peninsula, and mount a feint landing. It was a division in name only, consisting of surplus seamen and marines under amateur officers with no artillery support.

THE TURKISH DEFENCE

The failure of the naval attempt on 18 March had stiffened Turkish resolve. The German General Otto Liman von Sanders was placed in command of the Turkish V Army of 70,000 men, equalling the strength of Hamilton's force. Sanders failed to anticipate Hamilton's plan and placed the bulk of his forces at Bulair and on the Asiatic shore. However, the veteran III Corps, which had fought in the Balkan Wars of 1912−13, formed the basis of a series of outposts covering the likely landing points on the peninsula. Wire was laid, counterattack plans practised, and every Turkish soldier exhorted to hold the invader at all costs until reinforcements arrived.

THE LANDINGS AND THE LAND CAMPAIGN

Despite having only five weeks to prepare, Hamilton's landing plan succeeded brilliantly with successful landings at S, X and Y beaches, and despite heavy casualties at W Beach. At V Beach Turkish defenders in the old castle of Seddulbahir poured fire into the ship's boats and onto the gangways of the steamer *River Clyde*, which had been deliberately run aground, as soldiers from the Hampshire, Dublin and Munster Fusilier regiments tried to land. Those who survived sheltered all day under a narrow bank at the edge of the beach that gave protection from Turkish fire, while their comrades died around them, tingeing the waters of the bay red with their blood. Opportunities to advance inland from S, X and Y beaches were not taken, and so the effectiveness of the plan was lost by the inaction of commanders ashore. It was not till the following day that the Turks withdrew on a defended line south of the small village of Krithia (Alcitepe) dominated by the low hill of Achi Baba (Alci Tepe) and, despite some minor gains at heavy cost, this became the front line for the remainder of the campaign.

At Z Beach naval navigation errors saw the leading waves of Australians land around the headland of Ari Burnu, the northern tip of a bay, that became known as Anzac Cove. This was the least expected landing spot, protected by a few Turkish outposts. It was the rugged landscape inland that disorganized the Australians as they came ashore and headed inland. By mid-morning 12,000 Australians had landed and the New Zealanders were just beginning to land, when

BELOW *The first attack on the Dardanelles was a naval bombardment of Turkish artillery positions. Many batteries were destroyed, but others survived and exacted a frightful toll on Allied forces.*

the Turks, led by their divisional commander, Lieutenant Colonel Mustafa Kemal, counterattacked south down the ridge from Chunuk Bair. This hit the ANZAC line at the junction of what became First and Second Ridges on the small hill called Baby 700. Here the ANZAC line was at its weakest. By nightfall they had been driven off and were hanging onto small outposts along both ridges, leaving the critical heights of Baby 700 in Turkish hands. This became the ANZAC front line for the next nine months.

On the advice of his divisional commanders, Birdwood recommended evacuation, but Hamilton assessed that this was impossible and directed them to dig in and hold on. Hamilton then placed all his available resources by landing the Royal Naval Division and the

MAIN CHARACTERS FEATURED

ALLIED

General Sir Ian Hamilton (commander in chief of the Mediterranean Expeditionary Force)

Major General A. G. Hunter-Weston (British 29th Division)

Lieutenant General Sir William Birdwood (ANZAC)

Major General W. T. Bridge (1st Australian Division)

Major General Sir Alexander

Godley

Lieutenant General Sir F. W. Stopford (IX Corps – New Army and Territorial Divisions)

TURKISH

General Otto Liman von Sanders (Turkish V Army)

Lieutenant Colonel Mustafa Kemal (divisional commander)

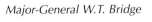

Major-General W.T. Bridge | *Lieutenant-Colonel Mustafa Kemal*

29th Indian Brigade at Helles for a drive north. Despite some gains, the British and French at Helles were unable to take the small hill of Achi Baba that dominated the southern plateau, and with increased numbers of Turkish reinforcements that were better equipped and supplied than the invaders, whose artillery was reduced by shortages to two rounds per gun per day, a stalemate developed.

Turkish attempts to drive the invaders back into the sea failed at Anzac, as the northern bridgehead became known. With the promise of reinforcements, Hamilton planned for an August offensive with a primary aim of breaking out of the Anzac perimeter in a night attack and seizing the high ground of Chunuk Bair. At the same time Lieutenant General Sir F. W. Stopford's IX Corps, consisting of New Army and Territorial divisions, would land at Suvla Bay to secure it as a winter port and base for Hamilton's force. Hamilton's obsessive secrecy and inept planning at every level crippled the offensive, despite the bravery of the troops involved. The veteran Australians were thrown away in a series of fruitless feints out of Anzac, particularly at Lone Pine. The New Zealand Infantry Brigade's success in seizing Chunuk Bair on 8 August was not adequately supported, and the difficulties of supplying water and evacuating men in the searing summer heat saw a collapse of the logistic and medical arrangements.

At Suvla, Stopford got his men ashore, but failed to take advantage of the far inferior Turkish numbers until it was too late. Once again Mustafa Kemal played a critical role in pushing back IX Corps at Suvla and then in retaking Chunuk Bair on 10 August.

By September Hamilton's forces were exhausted and Gallipoli became a stalemate, with Hamilton replaced. There was going to be no easy solution other than to fight and win on the Western Front. Suvla and Anzac were successfully evacuated in December 1915, and a similarly successful evacuation was carried out at Helles in January 1916.

CONCLUSIONS ON THE CAMPAIGN

The Gallipoli campaign determined that there would be no easy short cut to ending the World War I. It destroyed reputations and created legends that are treasured in Australia and New Zealand. It cost the lives of 44,000 Allied soldiers, including 21,000 British and 10,000 French troops, 7594 Australian and 2721 New Zealand dead, out of a total of some 140,000 Allied casualties. The Turks, too, suffered in defending their homeland, with 87,000 dead among estimates of 250,000–300,000 casualties. Today Gallipoli is a place of pilgrimage for every Turk, Australian and New Zealander.

VISITING GALLIPOLI TODAY

The Gallipoli battlefields are 335km (208 miles) from Istanbul. Buses are frequent and inexpensive, and cars can be hired at Eceabat or Canakkale. Despite its name, Gelibolu is too far from the

battlefields and not recommended as a base. The ferry port of Eceabat (formerly Maidos) offers accommodation, as does the provincial capital Canakkale across the Straits. There is also motel accommodation in the south at Cape Helles and at Gaba Tepe. You can do a brief tour encompassing all the battlefields in a day, but allow at least three days or more on site for a full appreciation. A self-drive car or a car and guide, all available locally, are the best ways to visit the battlefields.

THE NAVAL ATTACK OF 18 MARCH 1915

In Canakkale a visit to the Naval Museum in Ottoman Fort Cimenlik offers an insight into the Turkish defences and the naval attack of 18 March, including a replica of the minelayer *Nusrat*, which laid the row of 20 mines that did such damage among the attacking warships. A drive south of the town takes one to Dardanos Battery and a tour of one of the fixed coastal artillery positions. This is only 20km (12 miles) from the purported site of Troy, which offers a view over the plains towards the French landings at Kumkale (still a naval base and out of bounds to visitors).

Take the Canakkale ferry across the Narrows to the impressive Ottoman castle of Kilitbahir, visit the fort and battery, before driving south, skirting the Kilitbahir plateau through Alcitepe (formerly Krithia) which, although visited by British patrols on 25 April, remained in Turkish hands for the campaign.

The Canakkale Martyrs Memorial commemorates the Ottoman soldiers lost in the campaign and which offers a view over the entrance to the Straits and allows you to imagine the rows of battleships belching fire at the batteries and the jubilation of the soldiers viewing from where you stand as they saw the fleet forced to withdraw. This is the site of official Turkish commemorations on 18 March each year.

THE CAPE HELLES LANDINGS AND CAMPAIGN

The French memorial and cemetery is at Morto Bay. This flank was occupied by the French Expeditionary Force, which lost 10,000 dead in this campaign. Below the memorial is the site of S Beach where the British landed against slight opposition, but failed to take advantage of the opportunity to advance on Achi Baba and cut off the Turkish coastal defences.

Cape Helles Memorial dominates the skyline at the site of V Beach. This commemorates all the ships, formations and units of the British Empire that took part in the campaign, and lists the names of 20,763 men who died on land and sea, but who have no known grave. The exceptions to this are the New Zealanders, whose names are listed at specific memorials on each battlefield where they were lost. From the memorial one can see towards W Beach and look down on the Seddulbahir fort and No.1 Battery with its destroyed heavy guns that form the arms of the amphitheatre dominating V Beach. You can see the rocky shoal on which the *River Clyde* grounded and the sandbar behind which the survivors sheltered at the beach edge immediately below the castle. The graves of the men who died here can be visited in V Beach Cemetery at the water's edge. An exploration of the castle and the village brings one to the grave of Lieutenant Colonel C. H. M. Doughty-Wylie, VC, CB, CMG of the Welsh Fusiliers, who was killed on 26 April 1915 leading an attack on the castle. It is the only isolated grave on the peninsula that has been knowingly allowed to remain in its original location.

From the Lancashire Landing Cemetery you can drive through the former military camp to W Beach and the site of the landing itself. Barbed wire barricades blocked this narrow beach. Today you can scramble up the cliffs and explore the Ottoman trenches that cover the beach. At W Beach the Lancashire Fusiliers won six VCs 'before breakfast' for their bravery.

From the site of X Beach a track leads towards the entrance to Gully Ravine, which separated Gully Spur from the main plateau. It can be explored on foot from its entrance up to the barricades marking the final front line to the west of Alcitepe. From Twelve Tree Copse Cemetery one can see the minaret in the village of Alcitepe, which has a small private museum. North of the village is a disused military base, from where a track leads up to the heights of Achi Baba (Alci Tepe). This was Hamilton's objective on the first day. Walk the Ottoman trench lines and marvel at the enormous shellholes made by naval gun fire. South of this is the bridgehead that held the major part of the British and the French Expeditionary forces captive for nine months. Douglas Jerrold wrote in his history of the Royal Naval Division: 'The plain, for all its openness, was a prison, which became a tomb.'

ANZAC COVE AND THE AUGUST OFFENSIVE

The Kabatepe Information Centre offers maps and a museum to introduce you to the area held by the Australia and New Zealand Army Corps (ANZAC). This is the area of the proposed landing site on 25 April, and it was across this low ridge and plain that the Anzacs would advance towards the Narrows, having first sent forces up the ridge to secure Chunuk Bair.

Beach Cemetery and Shrapnel Valley Cemetery shelter under the southern ridge of Plugge's Plateau that encompasses Anzac Cove, a narrow beach, 700m (766 yards) long, with Ari Burnu Point and Ari Burnu Cemetery at its northern end. North Beach is overlooked by the Sphinx feature on Russell's Top that runs up to The Nek, made famous by the attack in Peter Weir's film *Gallipoli*. The outlines of dugouts, terraces and trenches are still visible. Anzac Cove contained all the supply depots, hospitals and headquarters. Under Turkish observation and fire from the open plateaus above, 40,000 men were crammed into these narrow cliffs and gullies. At the landing on 25 April the battle was as much with the landscape as with the Turks and one can retrace the route taken by the Anzacs by clambering over Plugge's Plateau and then down again into Shrapnel Valley and on through the thick bamboo and overgrowth until you reach the head of Monash Gully at the series of spurs running off Baby 700. An easier route is to return to the Chunuk Bair turnoff and drive up Second Ridge; the road marks the front line between the Anzac and Turkish positions. The Lone Pine Memorial and Cemetery commemorates the feint in August by 1st Australian Division, who took this plateau with heavy casualties. It took its name from a popular song of the time 'The Trail of the Lonesome Pine', because a lone pine could be seen from the Anzac trenches. The Memorial to the Missing commemorates 3268 Australians who fought at Gallipoli who have no known graves, together with 465 New Zealanders whose names are not recorded on either Chunuk Bair or Twelve Tree Copse memorials. Also listed are the 960 Australians and 252 New Zealanders who were buried at sea.

I recommend you walk the road from the Pine to Quinn's Post and The Nek. Each side is a myriad of trenches still 2–3m (7–10ft) deep in places; tunnels pass under the road, and each cemetery tells a story of Anzac and Turkish endeavour. Here, barely a road width apart, men fought, died and lived with the smell of death for weeks on end. A Turkish advance of 50m (55 yards) or so would have

thrown the Anzacs into the sea. This is most evident at Quinn's Post, which was separated from its supporting posts at Popes and Russell's Top by Turkish-held territory on the Bloody Angle. What appears to be seashell in the undergrowth, is human bone, both Turk and Anzac, broken down into fragments over the years.

Continue north up the ridge past the memorials and cemeteries on Baby 700, over Battleship Hill to the vital ground of Chunuk Bair. This was seized by the Wellington Battalion of the New Zealand Infantry Brigade on 8 August 1915 and held in an epic struggle until relieved by two British battalions on the night of 9–10 August. The following morning Mustafa Kemal counterattacked and drove the British from the heights, confirming the failure of the August offensive. The New Zealand dead lie on the eastern slopes beneath their memorial on the crest. Alongside stands a statue of Mustafa Kemal whose actions determined the fate of the campaign. One can trace the route of the New Zealand advance in the excellent walking track that snakes up from the New Zealand-held outposts on the beaches below.

Plaques tell the story at each cemetery and there are excellent official Australian, New Zealand and Commonwealth War Graves Commission websites that can be accessed, giving details of walks along the Anzac perimeter and up to Chunuk Bair.

SUVLA BAY

Near the village of Buyukanafarta on Suvla Plain, a series of small hills mark the battle ground of the August offensive and the landing by Stopford's IX Corps – each with its cemetery and memorial: Scimitar Hill, Green and Chocolate Hill and Hill 10. The British forces came ashore with little difficulty at A, B and C beaches, but were poorly briefed and had little idea of their objectives. This

ABOVE *The Canakkale Martyrs Memorial commemorates the Ottoman soldiers lost in the campaign. It is the site of the official Turkish commemorations on 18 March each year.*

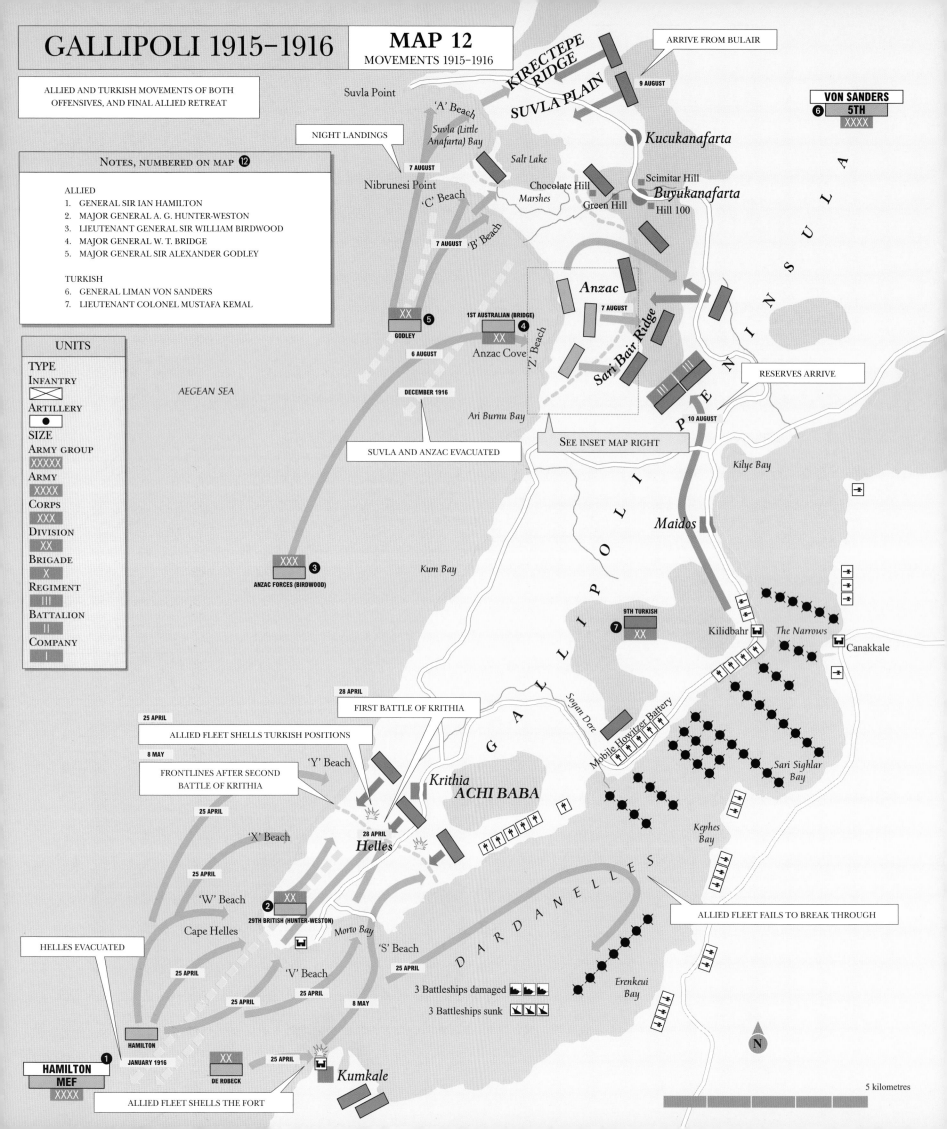

GALLIPOLI 1915-1916

MAP 12
MOVEMENTS 1915-1916

ALLIED AND TURKISH MOVEMENTS OF BOTH
OFFENSIVES, AND FINAL ALLIED RETREAT

NOTES, NUMBERED ON MAP ⑫

ALLIED
1. GENERAL SIR IAN HAMILTON
2. MAJOR GENERAL A. G. HUNTER-WESTON
3. LIEUTENANT GENERAL SIR WILLIAM BIRDWOOD
4. MAJOR GENERAL W. T. BRIDGE
5. MAJOR GENERAL SIR ALEXANDER GODLEY

TURKISH
6. GENERAL LIMAN VON SANDERS
7. LIEUTENANT COLONEL MUSTAFA KEMAL

UNITS

TYPE
INFANTRY
ARTILLERY ●
SIZE
ARMY GROUP XXXXX
ARMY XXXX
CORPS XXX
DIVISION XX
BRIGADE X
REGIMENT III
BATTALION II
COMPANY I

KIRECTEPE RIDGE
SUVLA PLAIN
ARRIVE FROM BULAIR
9 AUGUST

VON SANDERS ⑥ 5TH
XXXX

Suvla Point
'A' Beach
Suvla (Little Anafarta) Bay
Kucukanafarta
NIGHT LANDINGS
Salt Lake
7 AUGUST
Nibrunesi Point
'C' Beach
Chocolate Hill
Marshes
Green Hill
Scimitar Hill
Buyukanafarta
Hill 100
7 AUGUST 'B' Beach

Anzac
7 AUGUST
RESERVES ARRIVE

AEGEAN SEA

1ST AUSTRALIAN (BRIDGE) ④
Anzac Cove
'Z' Beach
Sari Bair Ridge
III III
III III
10 AUGUST
XX ⑤ GODLEY
6 AUGUST
DECEMBER 1916
Ari Burnu Bay
SEE INSET MAP RIGHT

Kilye Bay

SUVLA AND ANZAC EVACUATED

Maidos

XXX ③
ANZAC FORCES (BIRDWOOD)
Kum Bay

9TH TURKISH
⑦ XX
Kilidbahr
The Narrows
Canakkale

FIRST BATTLE OF KRITHIA
28 APRIL
28 APRIL
25 APRIL
ALLIED FLEET SHELLS TURKISH POSITIONS
8 MAY
'Y' Beach
FRONTLINES AFTER SECOND BATTLE OF KRITHIA
Krithia
ACHI BABA
Sogan Dere
Mobile Howitzer Battery

25 APRIL
'X' Beach
25 APRIL
Helles
Sari Sighlar Bay

'W' Beach
② XX
29TH BRITISH (HUNTER-WESTON)
Cape Helles
Morto Bay
'S' Beach
25 APRIL
Kephes Bay

ALLIED FLEET FAILS TO BREAK THROUGH

HELLES EVACUATED
25 APRIL
'V' Beach
25 APRIL
25 APRIL
8 MAY
3 Battleships damaged
3 Battleships sunk
Erenkeui Bay
DARDANELLES

HAMILTON
JANUARY 1916 ①
HAMILTON
MEF
XXXX
XX
DE ROBECK
25 APRIL
Kumkale

ALLIED FLEET SHELLS THE FORT

GALLIPOLI PENINSULA

N

5 kilometres

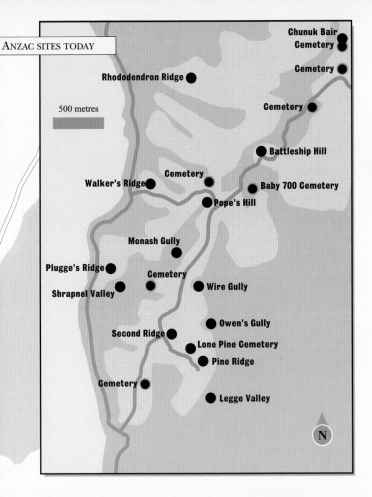

ANZAC SITES TODAY

Chunuk Bair Cemetery
Cemetery
Rhododendron Ridge
500 metres
Battleship Hill
Cemetery
Walker's Ridge
Baby 700 Cemetery
Pope's Hill
Monash Gully
Plugge's Ridge
Cemetery
Shrapnel Valley
Wire Gully
Owen's Gully
Second Ridge
Lone Pine Cemetery
Pine Ridge
Cemetery
Legge Valley
N

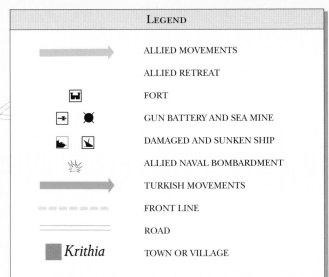

LEGEND

→	ALLIED MOVEMENTS
	ALLIED RETREAT
⌘	FORT
→ ☀	GUN BATTERY AND SEA MINE
◣ ◥	DAMAGED AND SUNKEN SHIP
⁂	ALLIED NAVAL BOMBARDMENT
→	TURKISH MOVEMENTS
– – –	FRONT LINE
——	ROAD
Krithia	TOWN OR VILLAGE

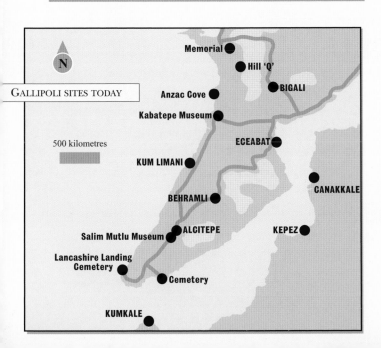

GALLIPOLI SITES TODAY

N
Memorial
Hill 'Q'
BIGALI
Anzac Cove
Kabatepe Museum
ECEABAT
500 kilometres
KUM LIMANI
CANAKKALE
BEHRAMLI
ALCITEPE
KEPEZ
Salim Mutlu Museum
Lancashire Landing Cemetery
Cemetery
KUMKALE

allowed a small force of paramilitary police to hold them until reinforcements could arrive and prevent the British from capturing the high ground that rings the plain. Men fought and died for low hills below the heights, where muzzle flashes set the scrub afire and burned the wounded where they lay.

A Beach is at the foot of Kirectepe (now Kirec), where it is hard to imagine the docks, workshops, stores, dumps and railways that were built here, turning Suvla into a winter base. Little remains. For the fit a scramble up the slopes of Kirectepe gives one a panoramic view of the battlefield, and if you are prepared to walk along the ridge you can explore the front-line trenches hewn into the rock.

GALLIPOLI TIMELINE

February 1915
Bombardment of the forts protecting the Dardanelles. Royal Marines go ashore unopposed to check the damage.

18 March 1915
Failed attempt to break through the Straits. Mines sink three battleships and three are badly damaged.

25 April
Gallipoli Landings:
S, X and Y beaches – successful landings.
W Beach – heavy casualties.
V Beach – Fire from castle of Seddulbahir takes heavy toll of troops trying to land.
S, X, Y beaches – failure to advance inland.
Z Beach – navigation errors land Australians at 'Anzac Cove'.

Mid-morning 12,000 Australians land; New Zealanders start to land. Mustafa Kemal counterattacks down the ridge from Chunuk Bair, hitting the ANZAC line at the junction of First and Second ridges on Baby 700.

Nightfall Heights of Baby 700 are in Turkish hands, becoming the ANZAC front line for the next nine months.

26 April
Turks withdraw to a line south of Krithia, which becomes the front line for the rest of the campaign.
Helles – Royal Naval Division and the 29th Indian Brigade are landed.

August
Series of fruitless feints out of Anzac, particularly at Lone Pine.

8 August
New Zealand Infantry brigade seizes Chunuk Bair, but lacks logistical support.

10 August
Kemal pushes back IX Corps at Suvla and retakes Chunuk Bair.

September
Hamilton's forces are exhausted, Gallipoli is a stalemate and Hamilton is replaced.

December
Suvla and Anzac evacuated.

January 1916
Helles evacuated.

FORT VAUX, VERDUN 1916

By Christina Holstein

When World War I began in August 1914, the city of Verdun in eastern France was an important military stronghold. Situated at a crossing point on the River Meuse close to the border with France's historic enemy, Germany, Verdun was surrounded by a double ring of forts and fieldworks that had been built following the humiliating French defeat in the Franco-Prussian War of 1870–1871. These works controlled the approaches to the city from all sides and were mutually supporting, so that an enemy attacking any one of them came under fire from those on its flanks.

The smallest of these forts was Fort Vaux. It was situated on a ridge on the right (east) bank of the River Meuse, where, at 350m (1148ft) above sea level, it dominated the plain that stretched towards the German border. It also offered flanking protection to a number of other defensive positions. These included Fort

Douaumont, the most important fort in the system, which was situated some 3km (2 miles) to the northwest.

Although small, Fort Vaux was very modern. In 1914 it consisted of a sunken, concrete-covered barrack block, which was connected by underground tunnels to the main defensive elements and surrounded by a ditch. Firepower was provided by two short-barrelled guns under a retractable, rotating steel turret and further guns in two strong bunkers known as Bourges Casemates. Armed concrete bunkers in the outer corners of the ditch provided for ditch defence; and steel-covered observation turrets allowed for safe observation over a wide area. A number of gun batteries situated outside the fort added further strength.

During the first months of World War I the Verdun front was quiet. As a result, in late 1915 the French commander in chief, General Joseph Joffre, ordered the substantial resources of the fortress city to be diverted to more active parts of the line. When, at the end of the same year, the German commander in chief, General Erich von Falkenhayn, decided to attack the Verdun sector in an effort to strike a blow that would bring the war to an end, Verdun's defences had been greatly diminished.

The Battle of Verdun began on 21 February 1916. At first the Germans advanced rapidly, capturing Fort Douaumont on 25 February. However, their advance was soon slowed by fire from French

ABOVE LEFT *Aerial view of Fort Souville (foreground) and external fortifications. It was across such devastation that Buffet made his way on 4 June.*
ABOVE CENTRE *A partial view of Fort Vaux before shelling obliterated the outline of the fort and the trees.*
ABOVE RIGHT *French 75mm field gun in a destroyed position. This construction was not proof against German heavy artillery.*

flanking positions, one of which was Fort Vaux. As further progress was impossible without dealing with the threat from the flanks, an attempt was made to capture Fort Vaux in March 1916. It was unsuccessful, and it was not until 1 June, after weeks of desperate fighting, that the Germans succeeded in reaching positions from which they could try again.

Fort Vaux was by this time seriously damaged. Three months of constant bombardment had brought down the walls of the ditch, damaged the underground tunnels and bunkers and blocked the main entrance. An explosion at the start of the battle had rendered the main gun turret inaccessible, and the other guns had been removed, leaving only machine guns and small weapons for ditch defence. The fort was crowded with frontline troops, runners and wounded, who had swelled the ranks of the garrison to over 600, making hygiene and sanitation impossible. With the telephone lines cut, communication with the outside world depended on the fort's four pigeons. The commander, Major Sylvain-Eugène Raynal, a professional soldier who was recovering from a serious leg wound, had arrived at Fort Vaux only a short time before.

ABOVE *French trench at Verdun. This was the norm in the early days of the battle. Subsequently, heavy artillery reduced these positions to an endless series of interlocking shellholes.*

THE MAIN CHARACTERS FEATURED

CENTRAL POWERS	ALLIED
Crown Prince William	General Joseph Joffre (French commander in chief)
General Erich von Falkenhayn (German commander in chief)	Major Sylvain-Eugène Raynal (Commander, Fort Vaux)
Lieutenant Werner Müller	Officer cadet Leon Buffet

| *Crown Prince William of Germany* | *General Joseph Joffre* |

During the early hours of 2 June the German bombardment of Fort Vaux intensified. At 04:00 the bombardment lifted and German infantry and pioneers rushed forward, some even crossing the damaged ditch to the superstructure. After several hours' fighting, the French defenders of the bunkers in the northern and northeastern corners of the ditch were overcome by the attackers and forced back into the underground tunnels, where they built barricades.

By nightfall the fort was surrounded and German machine guns prevented anyone from entering or leaving. Cut off, the defenders of Fort Vaux now began a period of underground warfare that lasted for five days.

Having gained control of the ditch bunkers, the Germans used smoke projectors, flame-throwers, gas and grenades to force their way along the narrow tunnels that linked the ditch to the barracks. In the darkness the French fought desperately with grenades and machine gun fire to hold the Germans off. As each barricade was destroyed, the French built a new one but gradually

to Fort Vaux. This was vital, as by now there was only one pigeon left to communicate with the outside world.

This pigeon, which had been badly gassed in a recent attack, was sent out on 4 June and died on arrival at Verdun after delivering a desperate appeal for help. Early that morning, a French relief attempt had been destroyed by a German artillery barrage before it had even reached the fort. A further French counterattack on 5 June was also unsuccessful. Against all the odds, Buffet managed to return to the fort with news that another counterattack was to be launched on 6 June, but it too was repelled with terrible casualties.

Although French morale remained high, it was clear to Raynal that the fort could not hold out for long. Seventeen of the defenders had been killed and over 80 were wounded, many of them seriously. None of the dead could be buried or the wounded evacuated.

On 6 June Raynal sent another message to Fort Souville describing the fort's desperate situation and the heroism of the defenders, which he ended with the appeal, 'Send relief before complete exhaustion.' Touring the fort, Raynal was dismayed to see the effect of exhaustion and thirst on his men. The water cisterns were by now completely empty. Since 4 June each man had received the equiva-

the Germans pushed them back. The number of wounded rose. In the barracks, sleep was impossible. Smoke filled the air, making breathing difficult and putting out the lights. On 4 June Major Raynal discovered to his horror that the water cisterns were almost empty. To save water he ordered non-vital units to leave the fort during the night. Led by a young officer cadet named Leon Buffet, some men did manage to escape. They included two signallers who succeeded in reaching the nearby Fort Souville, where they managed to re-establish the optical link

lent of only one glass of water, and by 6 June some were licking moisture off the walls or drinking their own urine. The Germans had only succeeded in advancing some 60m (66 yards) during the four days of the siege, but with immediate relief impossible, further resistance was hopeless.

In the early hours of 7 June Raynal flashed a final message to Fort Souville but only a few words were picked up. Receiving no reply, he ordered the machine guns to be put out of action and a white flag was pushed through the barricade in one of the underground tunnels. An

LEFT *The façade of Fort Vaux today.*
BELOW LEFT *A view of the damaged gun turret (rebuilt after the battle).*

Germany, who congratulated him on the fort's brave resistance. Raynal accepted the sword and left for captivity.

Raynal was made a Commander of the Legion of Honour for his part in the defence of Fort Vaux and returned to the army after the war, retiring in 1929 with the rank of Colonel.

The capture of Fort Vaux in June 1916 reduced the threat to the German left flank at Verdun, but it did not win the battle. During the summer of 1916 the German lines were pushed slowly forward but eventually the demands of other fronts drained their resources and forced them on the defensive. Fort Vaux remained in German hands for five months, during which time it served as a vital infantry support point for the frontlines and was under constant bombardment. A French counteroffensive in October 1916 failed to retake the fort but made it clear that the Germans could not hold it for much longer. The main gun turret and other vital sectors were blown up and the fort was evacuated on 2 November 1916. When the first French patrols arrived on 3 November 1916, Fort Vaux had been empty for 24 hours.

TOURING THE SITE TODAY

The battlefield of Verdun lies in eastern France approximately 250km (155 miles) from Paris. The train service to Verdun is limited but the area is well served by motor-

officer from a German machine gun unit, Lieutenant Werner Müller, entered the barracks and Raynal signed the capitulation.

Later that morning, the exhausted defenders left the shattered fort. Their path to captivity led them to the mill pond at the foot of the ridge on which the fort stood, where they threw themselves down to drink the muddy water.

Major Raynal left the fort at 10:00. Since he had arrived at Fort Vaux with only a walking stick for support, he was offered a French officer's sword when he was taken to meet Crown Prince William of

ways. It is not difficult to self-tour, and the city tourist office also organizes short tours of the battlefield, although there are few English-language guides. There is no accommodation on the battlefield, but the city offers accommodation ranging from three-star hotels to campsites, and a large number of restaurants.

There are various monuments and sights to visit in Verdun, but the battlefield lies about 5km (3 miles) outside the city and you need private transport to get there. The main sites are signposted from the city and further signposting on the battlefield will help the

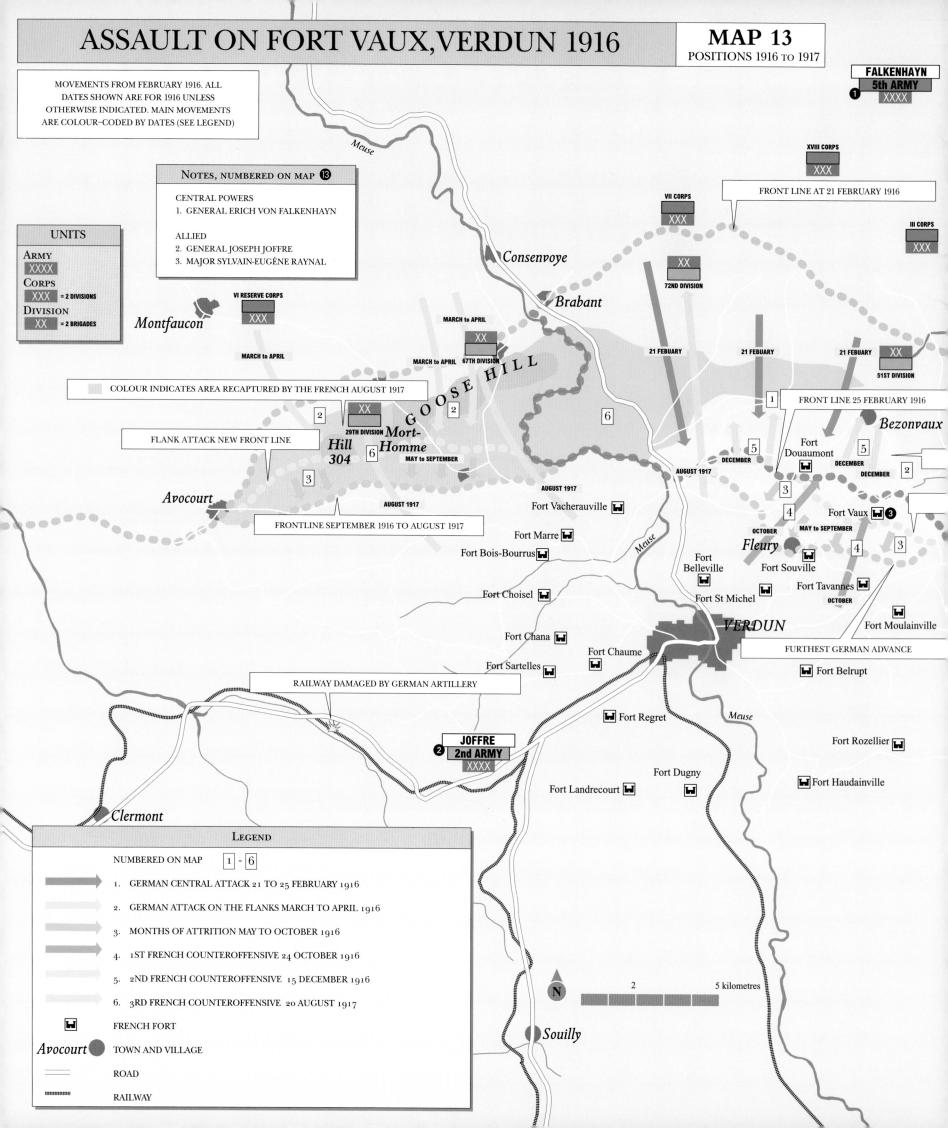

ASSAULT ON FORT VAUX, VERDUN 1916

MAP 13
POSITIONS 1916 TO 1917

MOVEMENTS FROM FEBRUARY 1916. ALL
DATES SHOWN ARE FOR 1916 UNLESS
OTHERWISE INDICATED. MAIN MOVEMENTS
ARE COLOUR–CODED BY DATES (SEE LEGEND)

FALKENHAYN
5th ARMY
XXXX
1

NOTES, NUMBERED ON MAP 13

CENTRAL POWERS
1. GENERAL ERICH VON FALKENHAYN

ALLIED
2. GENERAL JOSEPH JOFFRE
3. MAJOR SYLVAIN-EUGÈNE RAYNAL

XVIII CORPS
XXX

FRONT LINE AT 21 FEBRUARY 1916

VII CORPS
XXX

III CORPS
XXX

UNITS

ARMY
XXXX
CORPS
XXX = 2 DIVISIONS
DIVISION
XX = 2 BRIGADES

72ND DIVISION
XX

Consenvoye

VI RESERVE CORPS
XXX

Montfaucon

Brabant

MARCH to APRIL

MARCH to APRIL

MARCH to APRIL
67TH DIVISION
XX

MARCH to APRIL

21 FEBRUARY
21 FEBRUARY
21 FEBRUARY

51ST DIVISION
XX

COLOUR INDICATES AREA RECAPTURED BY THE FRENCH AUGUST 1917

2

29TH DIVISION
XX

FLANK ATTACK NEW FRONT LINE

Hill
304

Mort-
Homme

6

GOOSE HILL

2

6

5

1

FRONT LINE 25 FEBRUARY 1916

Bezonvaux

Fort
Douaumont

5

3

2

MAY to SEPTEMBER

3

AUGUST 1917

AUGUST 1917

DECEMBER

DECEMBER

DECEMBER

Avocourt

AUGUST 1917

FRONTLINE SEPTEMBER 1916 TO AUGUST 1917

Fort Vacherauville

Fort Marre

Fort Bois-Bourrus

Meuse

4

OCTOBER

Fleury

Fort Vaux 3

MAY to SEPTEMBER

4

3

Fort
Belleville

Fort Souville

Fort Tavannes

Fort Choisel

OCTOBER

Fort St Michel

Fort Moulainville

Fort Chana

VERDUN

FURTHEST GERMAN ADVANCE

Fort Belrupt

Fort Sartelles

Fort Chaume

RAILWAY DAMAGED BY GERMAN ARTILLERY

Fort Regret

Meuse

Fort Rozellier

JOFFRE
2nd ARMY
XXXX
2

Fort Dugny

Fort Haudainville

Clermont

Fort Landrecourt

LEGEND

NUMBERED ON MAP 1 - 6

1. GERMAN CENTRAL ATTACK 21 TO 25 FEBRUARY 1916

2. GERMAN ATTACK ON THE FLANKS MARCH TO APRIL 1916

3. MONTHS OF ATTRITION MAY TO OCTOBER 1916

4. 1ST FRENCH COUNTEROFFENSIVE 24 OCTOBER 1916

5. 2ND FRENCH COUNTEROFFENSIVE 15 DECEMBER 1916

6. 3RD FRENCH COUNTEROFFENSIVE 20 AUGUST 1917

N

2   5 kilometres

FRENCH FORT

Avocourt TOWN AND VILLAGE

ROAD

RAILWAY

Souilly

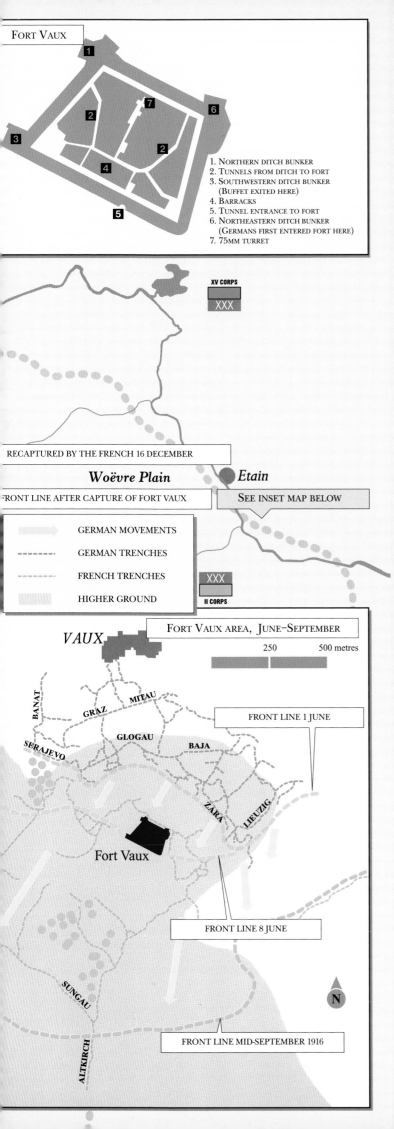

FORT VAUX

1. NORTHERN DITCH BUNKER
2. TUNNELS FROM DITCH TO FORT
3. SOUTHWESTERN DITCH BUNKER
   (BUFFET EXITED HERE)
4. BARRACKS
5. TUNNEL ENTRANCE TO FORT
6. NORTHEASTERN DITCH BUNKER
   (GERMANS FIRST ENTERED FORT HERE)
7. 75MM TURRET

XV CORPS
XXX

RECAPTURED BY THE FRENCH 16 DECEMBER

Woëvre Plain

Etain

FRONT LINE AFTER CAPTURE OF FORT VAUX

SEE INSET MAP BELOW

→ GERMAN MOVEMENTS

----- GERMAN TRENCHES

----- FRENCH TRENCHES

HIGHER GROUND

II CORPS
XXX

VAUX

FORT VAUX AREA, JUNE–SEPTEMBER

250   500 metres

BANAT

GRAZ   MITAU

GLOGAU

SERAJEVO   BAJA

ZARA   LIEUZIG

FRONT LINE 1 JUNE

Fort Vaux

FRONT LINE 8 JUNE

SUNGAU

N

ALTKIRCH

FRONT LINE MID-SEPTEMBER 1916

visitor to get around. However, the important sites are some distance apart and the thick forest that covers the battlefield today does not make it easy to understand the lie of the land. To help visitors, a special battlefield map, IGN No 3112 ET, entitled *Forêts de Verdun et du Mort-Homme: Champ de Bataille de Verdun*, is on sale at various outlets. A list of walking tours is also available. On the battlefield, several important sites relating to the Battle of Verdun are open to the public. These are the Fleury Memorial Museum, the Ossuary, which houses the bones of the men who received no formal burial, Fort Douaumont and Fort Vaux. Other sites that are signposted and accessible by car or on foot include destroyed villages, gun turrets, infantry shelters and fieldworks. Refreshment and toilet facilities are very limited. A selection of books, mostly in French, is on sale at several sites. Short films about the battle are on view at the memorial museum and the Ossuary.

Fort Vaux was so damaged during the Battle of Verdun that only a small part of the interior can be visited. The underground tunnels and main gun turret are not accessible but visitors may inspect the main gallery and various other features, including one of the Bourges Casemates. The superstructure and ditch are accessible and a walk down any of the nearby forest paths will reveal numerous traces of the devastating bombardment to which the fort was subject between February and December 1916.

VISITORS' FACT FILE

- Verdun Tourist Office, Place de la Nation, Tel. +33 3 29 86 14 18, fax +33 3 29 84 22 42; email: verduntourisme@wanadoo.fr; www.verdun-tourisme.com.
- Contact the tourist office for information about opening times at Fort Douaumont, Fort Vaux and the Citadel.
- Douaumont Ossuary, Tel. + 33 3 29 84 54 81.
- Fleury Memorial Museum, Tel. + 33 3 29 84 35 34.
- Visitors should note that for most of the year the above sites close for up to two hours at lunchtime.

FORT VAUX TIMELINE 1916

2 June

    04:00   German troops begin assault on Fort Vaux.

4 June

    Major Raynal discovers the lack of water; last pigeon sent out by Buffet leaves the fort.

5 June

    Unsuccessful French attempt to relieve the fort.

6 June

    Major Raynal asks for immediate relief.

7 June

    Fort Vaux surrenders.

2 November

    German troops abandon Fort Vaux.

3 November

    French troops re-enter the fort.

SOMME 1916

By Martin Marix Evans

The Somme front was formed, as was the entire line of trenches from the North Sea to the Swiss border, in the closing months of 1914. As winter came, both sides consolidated their positions. The Germans were determined to retain their gains and, having captured positions of advantage such as ridges and hills, built solidly. The Allies intended to roll the invaders back, and saw their trenches as temporary shelter.

By spring 1916 the German commander, Erich von Falkenhayn, had made up his mind to strike a decisive blow against the French by attacking a place they would be bound to defend to the last: Verdun. An Anglo-French offensive on the Somme had already been planned and now that the French were hard pressed, the obligation on General Sir Douglas Haig to hit the Germans was irresistible.

The small British regular army had suffered fearful losses at the outset of the war. British Minister of War Lord Kitchener's appeal had attracted 2,500,000 volunteers. These men were new to soldiering and, in the spring of 1916, the newly arrived battalions of Kitchener's 'New Army' were lacking experienced officers and

non-commissioned officers. Volunteers were formed into comradely units from particular towns, called Pal's Battalions, which became the cause of terrible misery when heavy casualties imposed bereavement on entire communities.

The main attack was to be made by Lieutenant General Sir Henry Rawlinson's 4th Army, comprising 16 divisions (some 500,000 men) of which 11 divisions would be engaged on the first day. Of those, three were formed of regular soldiers, three were part regulars and part Territorial (reserves), or New Army, and five were entirely formed of New Army units. To the left of the 4th Army, the 3rd Army, under Lieutenant General Sir Edmund Allenby, was to make a diversionary attack at Gommecourt; and to the right the French Sixth Army, commanded by General Émile Fayolle, was to attack astride the river Somme.

Assembly of the forces was carried out with remarkable concealment, given that the artillery, for example, amounted to hundreds of guns. The British deployed 808 18-pounders, 202 4.5-inch howitzers, 182 heavy guns, 245 heavy howitzers, 28 heavy mortars and 288 medium trench mortars. The French supplied 16 220mm howitzers, 24 120mm guns and 60 75mm field guns. British aircraft patrolled to prevent German reconnaissance and much was done by night. Nonetheless, Allied intentions did not go entirely undetected and the Germans strengthened and improved their defences.

ABOVE *In the Newfoundland Memorial Park, Beaumont Hamel, the trenches of the Allies face the German defences near Y Ravine, softened by the regeneration of grass, but otherwise unaltered.*

THE FIRST DAY – 1 JULY 1916

The plan was to destroy as much as possible of the German defence works before the attack. The artillery bombardment began at 06:00 on 24 June and by 1 July 71 shells had been fired for every metre of front. Reports of the effect were inconsistent: in some places the barbed wire was said to have been destroyed and in others it was uncut, but overall the burning German installations and shattered trenches suggested the result was satisfactory. At 06:30 in the morning of 1 July men moved forward from the British trenches and lay down to await the order to advance, while shells deluged the German front line. Just before 07:30 ten British mines beneath German positions were blown and the men advanced. The barrage lifted to fall on the Germans' second line and avoid hitting its own side.

At the northern end of the 3rd Army's front, near Serre, was the 31st Division with, in official terminology, the 12th York and Lancashires on the left, the 11th East Lancashires in the centre and the 15th West Yorkshire Regiment on the right; these were the Sheffield City, the Accrington and the 1st Leeds Pals. At 07:20 they passed through their own wire and lay down in no-man's-land. Ten minutes later they stood up and started forward. As they did so the Germans emerged from their deep shelters with machine guns and opened fire. Few of the Pals covered more than 100m (110 yards) before being struck down. Some of the Accrington men got as far as Serre itself where they were killed or captured. The Barnsley Pals and the Bradford Pals came forward in support and met the same fate as previously ranged German artillery turned no-man's-land into a maelstrom of shellbursts. Kitchener's New Army, and the towns from which its men came, suffered terribly.

West of Beaumont Hamel the Germans had fortified the ridge with a position the British called Hawthorn Redoubt, and under which they had tunnelled to install 40,000 pounds (18,000kg) of ammonal explosive. At 07:20 it was blown and the artillery bombardment lifted to allow the 2nd Royal Fusiliers to charge forward unharmed to take it. The cessation of the bombardment permitted the Germans to do the same, neither side securing the objective, and German machine guns were free to fire on the other attackers. The 1st Lancashire Fusiliers advanced no more than 50m (55 yards) from the Sunken Lane on the northern side of the New Beaumont Road. A little to the south, Y Ravine gave the Germans concealed access to Hawthorn Ridge where the 1st Royal Inniskilling Fusiliers and 2nd South Wales Borderers faced uncut wire and the attack was stopped. At 08:05am 1st King's Own Scottish Borders and 1st Border Regiment tried to attack, but they, too, were cut down. Eager to go to their comrades' aid, 1st Newfoundland left the communication trenches, jammed as they were with wounded, and hurled themselves forward through narrow gaps in the wire. An infantry battalion's full establishment in 1914 was about 1000 men. The Newfoundlanders attacked with 801 men and sustained 733 casualties.

Further southeast, on the other side of the marshy valley of the River Ancre, the 36th (Ulster) Division rushed forward from the northeastern edge of Thiepval Wood and, finding the wire cut, smashed through the German front line to enter the massive position of the Schwaben Redoubt and penetrate to trenches beyond; in an hour they advanced almost a mile. Further south again, where the Leipzig Redoubt jutted out north of Authille Wood, the 17th Highland Light Infantry had crept forward before the attack close to the German lines, and their rush took them into the position before resistance could form. On either side of these gains the attack stalled. Close to the river in the north, fire from St Pierre Division stopped the Irish. Just west of Thiepval the survivors of 16th Northumberland Fusiliers and 15th Lancashire Fusiliers were pinned down in no-man's-land by machine-gun fire and efforts to reinforce them failed as men of the 32nd Division were pushed back into Thiepval Wood. The long, thin penetration of the German line

MAIN CHARACTERS FEATURED

GERMAN
General Erich von Falkenhayn (German commander)

ALLIED
General Sir Douglas Haig
Lieutenant General Sir Henry Rawlinson (4th Army)

Lieutenant General Sir Edward Allenby (3rd Army)
General Émile Fayolle, (French Sixth Army)
Lieutenant General Walter N. Congreve, VC (commander of XIII Corps)

General Erich von Falkenhayn   *General Sir Douglas Haig*

achieved by the Ulster Division could not be sustained and, worse, having gone so far forward they fell victim to their own artillery fire, for the British observers could not see them.

On the Roman road climbing the ridge between Albert and Bapaume the story was again one of heroic failure. The Tyneside Scottish and Tyneside Irish of the 34th Division attacked immediately after two mines, one north and one south of La Boiselle, had blown. Within ten minutes 80 per cent of the leading battalion had become casualties. By the end of the day a small gain on the division's right was all they had to balance the loss of 6392 men, of whom 1927 had been killed.

Only at the extreme right of the British line, where XIII Corps was alongside the French 39th Division, was the day a success. The 30th Division, with the Liverpool Pals and the Manchester Pals leading the way, took all its objectives, seizing Montauban, and the 18th Division on their left benefited from this, although their progress was slower. In front of Mametz the 7th Division had a hard time, but the village was in British hands by 15:00. Five kilometres (three miles) of the German front had fallen to the British and a further 5km (3 miles) to the French. The commander of XIII Corps, Lieutenant General Walter N. Congreve, VC, reported to Rawlinson, asking for permission to release the cavalry into the open country before him. It was denied.

The Battle of the Somme continued until November when Beaumont Hamel fell to the British. What had started as an attempt to take pressure off the French at Verdun had turned into a long, bloody battle of attrition. On 2 July Von Falkenhayn ordered the cessation of attacks at Verdun and the transfer of men and guns to the Somme. It would be some time before commanders learnt when to stop.

ABOVE *Shattered ruins are all that remain of Mametz after the capture of the village on 1 July.*

THE MACHINE GUN AT MAMETZ

On 8 December 1914 Marcel Riser, by then an auxiliary medic in the French 329th Regiment of Infantry, wrote to his father, Albert. He apologized for the rarity of his letters, but offered as excuse the fact that, when he was still a private soldier, his regiment had fought on the Marne and eventually had come to the Somme front. He said:

'On the Somme we had no rest for three weeks, fighting hard. The whole 53rd Division was moved by motor car via Compiègne. We went to the Albert-Fricourt-Mametz sector. We did 14 days in the front line trenches without a break. The food was cold because the cook-house was four kilometres [2½ miles] to the rear, at Meault. We had rain and fog, maybe not because of the time of the year but of the proximity of the marshes of the Somme. We twice attacked the village of Mametz and twice we were met with tough resistance. The 'Caïsonette' [pillbox] at the cemetery was occupied by German machine-gunners we thought we had destroyed. We hadn't. The phone lines were broken and the attack of the 7th did not take place. Shelling with high explosive and shrapnel erupted on the flat approach to the position…

(Historial de la Grande Guere, Péronne, Somme, #22553)
As winter set in, Riser's only comfort was his promotion to auxiliary medic with some improvement in his accommodation, but he still asked for warm clothes to be sent.

In 1916, as the British were making their preparations for the 'Big Push', as the assault on the Somme was named in the popular press, Captain D. L. Martin of the 9th Devonshire Regiment, a New Army unit, was lucky enough to go home on leave. With him went the map of the sector his men were to attack, Mametz. While at home he made a plasticine model of the front and came to the conclusion that as they passed Mansel Copse and came down the slope, the machine-gun post at the cemetery, behind the German front line trenches, would do terrible damage to them.

On the morning of 1 July Martin led the Devons forward as planned, heading down the slope into the coincidentally named Vallée Martin. His report of the danger had gone unheeded, and no one knew of the experiences of the French 329th Regiment of Infantry. The machine gun did, indeed, open up from a range of some 365m (400 yards). Captain Martin and many more fell. The morning's attack failed.

CASUALTIES

ALLIED		GERMAN CASUALTIES
British casualties 1 July 1916		**(ESTIMATED)**
Killed/died of wounds	19,240	
Wounded	35,493	5800 (killed,
Missing	2152	wounded and missing)
Taken prisoner	585	2200
Total	57,470	8000
Total 1 July–18 November 419,654		**419,989**
French casualties (total) 204,253		

VISITING THE SOMME

For those with limited time making an independent visit, the Newfoundland Memorial Park, the Ulster Tower and the Thiepval Visitor Centre provide information and the opportunity to appreciate the terrain which bestowed such advantage on the defenders. Guided day and half-day tours are also available from the towns mentioned below. The trenches from which the British attacked and positions at Y Ravine can be seen at the Memorial Park, where there is also an excellent museum devoted to the Royal Newfoundland Regiment. Guided tours in French or English are available here. The peaceful landscape can be filled with the terror of battle in the imagination of the sensitive visitor.

The Ulster Tower, near Thiepval village, has been built next to the site of the Schwaben Redoubt and the Redoubt itself is now the property of the owners, the Somme Association, as well. At the time of writing the Redoubt is not ready for visiting.

RIGHT *The ancient town of Péronne, on the invasion routes of both the Napoleonic and Franco-Prussian wars, was devastated in the fighting of 1916–1918.*

From the grounds of the Tower in springtime and after harvest, the pale chalk scars of the trenches of 1916 can be seen on the hillside beneath Newfoundland Park.

Thiepval is the site of the huge memorial by Lutyens that commemorates those with no known grave – more than 73,000 of them. In 2004 a new visitor centre opened near the memorial to provide information on the history of the Battle of the Somme as a whole and on the wartime history of Thiepval in particular.

Thiepval can be approached or left by way of Pozières, where a German command post called Gibraltar is now open to visitors. There is also a viewing platform from which an excellent impression of the approaches to this key position on the ridge can be had. The area can also be entered by way of the town of Albert, where the Somme 1916 Museum offers an impressive vision of trench life and warfare. All these sites are part of the more extensive Circuit du Souvenir (Circuit of Remembrance) which drivers can take by following the poppy-marked signposts. The route has one extremity at Albert and the other in the town of Péronne, both good places to stay. Péronne also has, in its ancient castle, the magnificent Historial de la Grande Guerre, an outstanding museum of the Great War which should not be missed. Ideally it should be visited before moving on to the battlefields themselves; a tour will be enormously enhanced by the knowledge gained.

One of the less conventional attractions is the light railway built to carry supplies and munitions up to the front. Le P'tit Train de la Haute Somme museum is at Froissy, to the south of Bray-sur-Somme, and trips can be taken on the narrow-gauge railway.

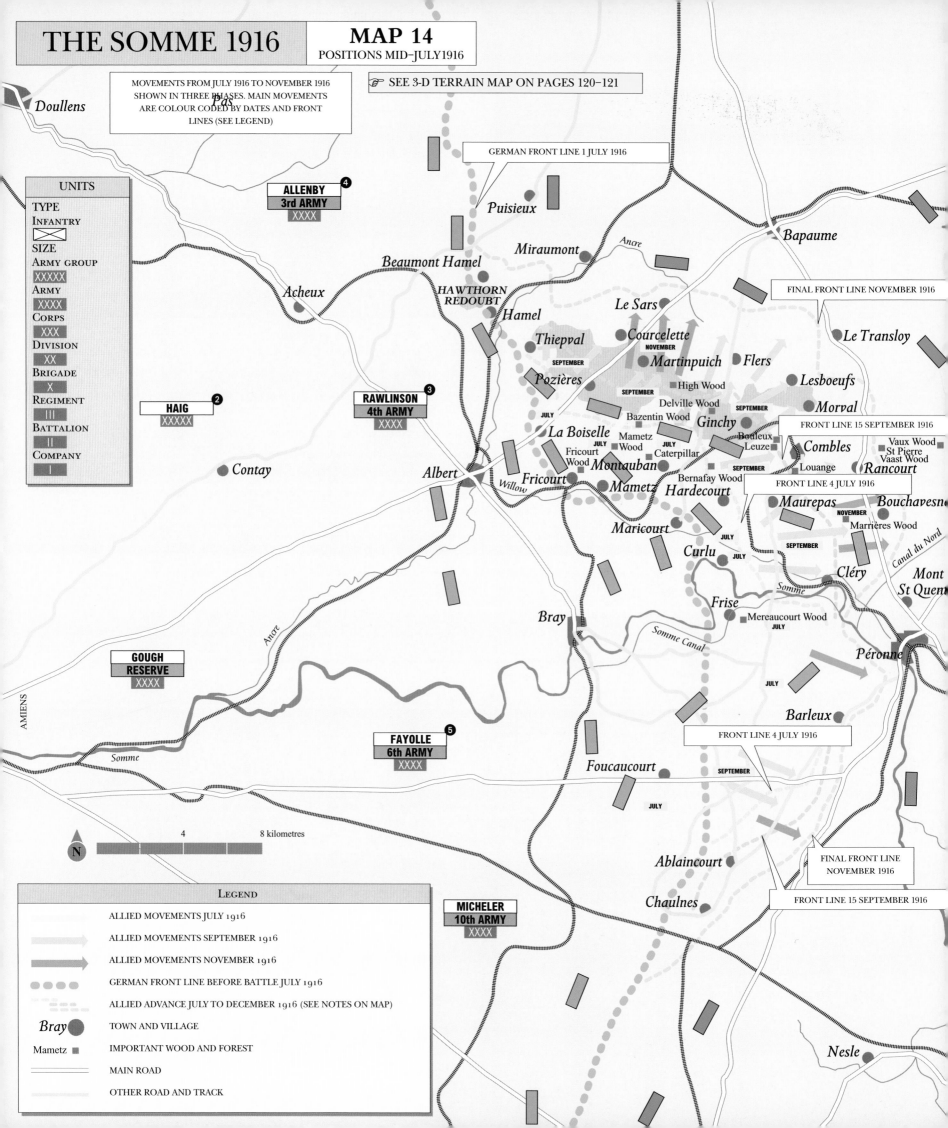

THE SOMME 1916

MAP 14
POSITIONS MID–JULY 1916

MOVEMENTS FROM JULY 1916 TO NOVEMBER 1916 SHOWN IN THREE PHASES. MAIN MOVEMENTS ARE COLOUR CODED BY DATES AND FRONT LINES (SEE LEGEND)

☞ SEE 3-D TERRAIN MAP ON PAGES 120–121

GERMAN FRONT LINE 1 JULY 1916

FINAL FRONT LINE NOVEMBER 1916

FRONT LINE 15 SEPTEMBER 1916

FRONT LINE 4 JULY 1916

FRONT LINE 4 JULY 1916

FINAL FRONT LINE NOVEMBER 1916

FRONT LINE 15 SEPTEMBER 1916

UNITS

TYPE

INFANTRY ⊠

SIZE

ARMY GROUP
XXXXX

ARMY
XXXX

CORPS
XXX

DIVISION
XX

BRIGADE
X

REGIMENT
III

BATTALION
II

COMPANY
I

ALLENBY
3rd ARMY
XXXX ④

HAIG
XXXXX ②

RAWLINSON
4th ARMY
XXXX ③

GOUGH
RESERVE
XXXX

FAYOLLE
6th ARMY
XXXX ⑤

MICHELER
10th ARMY
XXXX

Place names

Doullens
Pas
Puisieux
Miraumont
Bapaume
Beaumont Hamel
HAWTHORN REDOUBT
Acheux
Hamel
Le Sars
Le Transloy
Thiepval
Courcelette
NOVEMBER
SEPTEMBER
Martinpuich
Flers
Lesboeufs
Pozières
SEPTEMBER
High Wood
Morval
SEPTEMBER
Delville Wood
Combles
JULY
Bazentin Wood
Ginchy
St Pierre
Vaux Wood
La Boiselle
Mametz Wood
Boileux Leuze
Vaast Wood
Contay
Fricourt Wood
JULY
Caterpillar
Louange
Rancourt
Albert
Fricourt
Montauban
SEPTEMBER
Willow
Mametz
Bernafay Wood
Maurepas
Bouchavesne
Hardecourt
NOVEMBER
Marrières Wood
Maricourt
JULY
Ancre
Curlu
JULY
SEPTEMBER
Cléry
Canal du Nord
Frise
Mont St Quentin
Bray
Mereaucourt Wood
JULY
Somme
Somme Canal
Péronne
AMIENS
Ancre
JULY
Barleux
Somme
Foucaucourt
SEPTEMBER
JULY
Ablaincourt
Chaulnes
Nesle

N — compass
4 — 8 kilometres

LEGEND

→ ALLIED MOVEMENTS JULY 1916

→ ALLIED MOVEMENTS SEPTEMBER 1916

→ ALLIED MOVEMENTS NOVEMBER 1916

•••• GERMAN FRONT LINE BEFORE BATTLE JULY 1916

---- ALLIED ADVANCE JULY TO DECEMBER 1916 (SEE NOTES ON MAP)

Bray ● TOWN AND VILLAGE

Mametz ■ IMPORTANT WOOD AND FOREST

—— MAIN ROAD

··· OTHER ROAD AND TRACK

GERMAN
1. GENERAL FRITZ VON BELOW

ALLIED
2. GENERAL SIR DOUGLAS HAIG
3. LIEUTENANT GENERAL SIR HENRY RAWLINSON
4. LIEUTENANT GENERAL SIR EDMUND ALLENBY
5. GENERAL ÉMILE FAYOLLE

Cambrai

Pas

Marcoing

BELOW
2nd ARMY ❶
XXXX

Roisel

Vermand

ST QUENTIN

Athies

Beauvois

Somme

Ham

St Simon

VISITORS' FACT FILE

- Historial de la Grande Guerre, Péronne: Tel ++33 (0)3-22-83-14-18. Fax ++33 (0)3-22-83-54-18. www.historial.org/us/home/htm
- Le P'tit Train de la Haute Somme museum: Tel ++33 (0)3-22-44-55-40. www.appeva.org
- Newfoundland Memorial Park: Tel ++33 (0)3-22-76-70-86.
- Somme 1916 Museum, Albert: Tel ++33 (0)3-22-75-16-17.
- Thiepval Visitor Centre: Tel ++33 (0)3-22-74-60-47. fax: ++33 (0)3-22-74-65-44.
- Ulster Tower: Tel ++33 (0)3-22-74-81-11.
- Information on the whole area can be had from the Somme tourist board (Tel: ++33 (0)3 22 71 22 71, and www.somme-tourisme.com) and on the battlefields themselves on www.somme-battlefields.com.

SOMME TIMELINE

24 June	Allies open barrage along 40km (25-mile) front.
29 June	Planned Allied attack postponed.
1 July	British and French attack – British capture Fricourt; French advance further, taking Herbecourt.
10 July	British capture Contalmaison.
15 July	South African brigade takes Delville Wood but forced to abandon it on 20th. British reach High Wood but forced to withdraw on 16th.
20 July	British attack for possession of High Wood; not finally captured until 15 September.
23 July	Australians involved in fighting for Pozières; finally captured on 5 August.
28 July	British recapture Delville Wood.
12 August	French gain the German third line of trenches from the Somme to Hardecourt.
28 August	Falkenhayn replaced by Hindenburg.
3 September	Guillemont captured by British.
9 September	Ginchy taken.
13 September	French mount successful attack southeast of Combles.
15 September	British offensive in which tanks used for first time in advance towards Flers.
25 September	British begin attack in Morval area; French attack against Bouchavesnes.
26 September	British capture Thiepval, a 1 July objective.
28 September	Capture of Combles and Morval.
30 September	Thiepval Ridge occupied except for part of Schwaben Redoubt.
October	Heavy rain makes battlefield a quagmire. Allied attacks continue.
7 October	British secure Le Sars, but further progress in this sector halted on slopes of Butte de Warlencourt. Butte finally taken 5 November.
13 November	British attack at Beaumont Hamel and along north bank of the Ancre. Beaumont Hamel and Beaucourt captured.
17/18 November	Overnight snow brings battle to an end.

HAWTHORN CRATER AND BEAUMONT HAMEL

After the initial phases of movement in 1914, warfare on the Western Front settled into near-immobility, a stalemate dominated by trench warfare. The opposing armies, dug into complex and ingenious systems of trenches and protected by barbed wire entanglements and machine-gun emplacements, faced each other across the bleak, shell-torn landscape of no-man's-land. The Germans occupied the high ground, and remained on the defensive for much of the war. The 1916 offensive north of the Somme River was intended to draw German strength away from the battle of Verdun, being waged to the east, thus taking the pressure off the French army. The Somme offensive was thought of as 'the big push'; the overwhelming attack that would splinter the German defences and allow the Allied armies to break out. The illustration on these pages shows a section of the front line around the village of Beaumont Hamel, which lay just behind the German front line, around 07:30, when the British assault began.

① Hawthorn Crater: This was the largest of 17 mines set off by the British on 1 July. British Royal Engineers tunnelled under a German strongpoint, known as Hawthorn Redoubt, on Hawthorn Ridge. The tunnellers packed the tunnel with 18,000kg (40,000 lb) of high explosive. Detonation of the mine, at 07:20, left a crater 24m (80ft) deep and 137 x 92m (150 x 100yd) wide. Troops from the 2nd Royal Fusiliers and Middlesex Regiment, supported by the Royal Dublin Fusiliers, were assigned the task of capturing Hawthorn Ridge.

② No-man's-land: The unoccupied zone that separated the opposing armies varied greatly in width, depending on the particular sector of the battlefront. In places, only a few hundred metres separated the combatants. In this sector of the battlefield, the British and German front-line trenches were about 500m (550yd) apart.

③ Bombardment: The attack was preceded by eight days of preliminary bombardment of the German positions by artillery dug in behind the trench lines. Allied commanders believed bombardment was essential to 'soften up' the German defences and to destroy the barbed wire

obstacles in front of the trenches. In reality, the bombardment achieved its objective only in part, and also tore up the terrain, making it difficult for the attackers to reach their objectives.

④ Beaumont Hamel

⑤ New Beaumont Road

⑥ Sunken Lane

⑦ Y Ravine

⑧ Front-line trenches: From here, the men of the Royal Inniskilling Fusiliers, the South Wales Borders, Royal Fusiliers, Lancashire Fusiliers and other regiments went 'over the top', beginning their advance on the German lines.

⑨ Communication trenches: these zigzagged back from the front-line positions, allowed reinforcements and supplies to be moved up to the front and the wounded to be ferried back to aid posts and evacuation.

⑩ Barbed wire entanglements: both armies' trench systems were protected by elaborate networks of barbed wire. In many places the preliminary bombardment failed to destroy the German wire, as Allied commanders had hoped.

⑪ St John's Road: The Newfoundland Regiment began their advance from this support trench, 230m

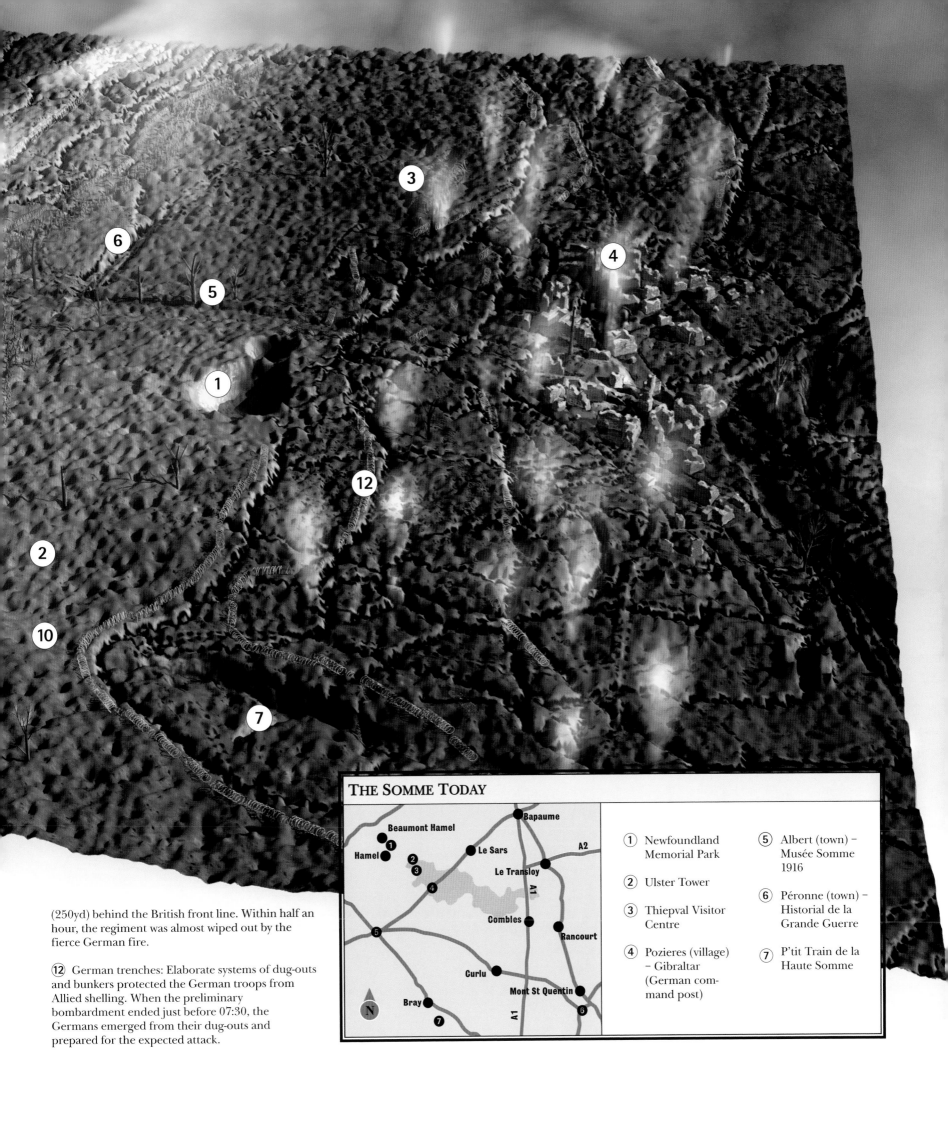

(250yd) behind the British front line. Within half an hour, the regiment was almost wiped out by the fierce German fire.

⑫ German trenches: Elaborate systems of dug-outs and bunkers protected the German troops from Allied shelling. When the preliminary bombardment ended just before 07:30, the Germans emerged from their dug-outs and prepared for the expected attack.

THE SOMME TODAY

① Newfoundland Memorial Park

② Ulster Tower

③ Thiepval Visitor Centre

④ Pozieres (village) – Gibraltar (German command post)

⑤ Albert (town) – Musée Somme 1916

⑥ Péronne (town) – Historial de la Grande Guerre

⑦ P'tit Train de la Haute Somme

VIMY RIDGE 1917

By Martin Marix Evans

After the battles of Verdun and the Somme, General Erich von Falkenhayn was replaced as German commander in chief by Field Marshal Paul von Hindenburg and his Chief of Staff General Erich Ludendorff, the heroes of the Eastern Front. In order to pursue their plans in the east they decided to adopt a defensive posture in the west and, in Operation Alberich, withdrew to prepared positions that the British called the Hindenburg Line. A new approach to defence was being adopted, rejecting the idea of a stubbornly held front line in favour of a more flexible system of defence in depth. On 21 February 1917 the Germans pulled back, leaving looted, burnt and dynamited towns and villages behind them, as well as a vast number of mines and booby-traps. By 19 March, virtually unhindered by the Allies, they had completed the withdrawal. The Allies had planned renewed assaults for 1917 but now had to think again. The

French commander was now General Robert Nivelle. He proposed a massive attack through the hills north of the River Aisne, topped by the old road called the Chemin des Dames, to St Quentin and the Oise valley. This was to be supported by the British and their Dominion forces striking near Arras for Vimy Ridge and for the new German line, the Wotan-Stellung, between Drocourt and Quéant, astride the River Scarpe. It was timed for 9 April, Easter Monday, and the French attack for a week later.

THE CANADIANS AT VIMY RIDGE

North of Arras one of the most important physical features of the Western Front, the 14.5-km (9-mile) long Vimy Ridge, rises gently from the west to overlook Lens and the Douai plain in the east, beyond a steep drop. The crest is marked by two heights known by their altitude in metres, Hill 145 in the north and Hill 135 some 3km (2 miles) southeast. Between them is La Folie Farm, and at the extreme northern end of the ridge is the last summit, which they called The Pimple.

The task of capturing these heights was given to the Canadian Corps under the command of Lieutenant General Sir Julian Byng. The Corps was four divisions strong, each with an establishment of 21,000 men, as opposed to the British manpower of 15,000. They had taken over this part of the line the previous October and, since

ABOVE Today, on Vimy Ridge, trees grow in fields pitted with craters from World War I artillery bombardment. A park surrounds the Canadian National Vimy Memorial, which marks the site of the battle. It commemmorates not only those who gave their lives to seize this key position, but also all Canadian servicemen who died in this war. The trenches of the opposing forces and the Canadian tunnels are also preserved.

this. Beyond the ridge a third line ran south from Lens, and numerous additional fortifications contributed to the strength of the German positions.

The first and second lines formed the Canadian objective, but the extra depth in the south added two stages to the plan that suited the north. The front line was designated the Black Line, and the second line was marked as the Red Line, the final objective, in the north. The additional objectives needed in the south were called the Blue Line and the Brown Line. The artillery assembled for the two-week-long preliminary bombardment was three times more concentrated in heavy guns than it had been on the Somme – at one for every 18m (20 yards) of front – and the field guns were twice as dense – at one for every 9m (10 yards). A new fuse was used in the high-explosive shells, specially designed to give above-ground shell-burst and ensure, in contrast to the Somme, effective cutting of the barbed wire. Immense support works of rail lines, plank roads and deeply buried telephone lines were carried out. Most remarkable of all were the 11 tunnels, totalling about 6.5km (4 miles), and running more than 7.5m (25 feet) below ground. Chambers dug off them formed headquarters, ammunition stores and first-aid stations, while more ancient caves would shelter up to a complete battalion.

The men received equally thorough preparation. The overall activity was evidence of a forthcoming attack to the most negligent of observers, so no attempt was made to impose secrecy except about the timing of the assault. It was therefore possible to brief the men in detail and organize practical rehearsals.

On 20 March the bombardment began, using only half the guns. On 2 April the intensity was increased, steadily destroying the villages of Thélus, Farbus and Givenchy. The German trenches were remorselessly smashed, so that parties bringing

MAIN CHARACTERS FEATURED

GERMAN
Field Marshal Paul von Hindenburg (commander in chief)
Chief of Staff General Erich Ludendorff

ALLIED
General Robert Nivelle (French commander)
Lieutenant General Sir Julian Byng (Canadian Corps)

Field Marshal Paul von Hindenburg

Lieutenant General Sir Julian Byng (Canadian Corps)

January, had been making raids with increasing frequency on the German lines. It was a costly business. Nightly raids in the two weeks before the attack incurred 1400 casualties, but yielded invaluable understanding of the enemy defences. The front line consisted of a mass of barbed wire interspersed with machine-gun posts and deep dug-outs and tunnels; the area was some 550m (500 yards) deep across the whole frontage. The second line trench became further away as it thrust southeastwards because the ridge itself is wedge-shaped, narrowing to the north. An intermediate trench line compensated for

RIGHT *Canadian troops dig a machine-gun pit to consolidate their hold on Vimy Ridge.*

food, a task formerly taking a quarter of an hour, now took as long as six hours – if they arrived at all. Cold food and no food added to what the Germans described as 'the week of misery'. In the skies above, the Royal Flying Corps sought out German gun positions to guide counter-battery fire. The weather turned colder and frost hardened the ground. On the evening of Easter Sunday 15,000 men were assembled to form the first wave of the attack.

THE BATTLE OF VIMY RIDGE, 9 APRIL

By 04:00 the attackers were in position. Some had emerged from the tunnels to conceal themselves in the shellholes of no-man's-land and some had filed through the gaps in their own wire to creep forward, close to the enemy line. Just before dawn a cold northwest wind brought sleet and snow showers across the hill, prolonging the darkness. At 05.30 nearly a thousand mortars and guns blazed out and 150 machine guns poured their fire into a belt about 360m (400 yards) in front of the Canadians. Both German

defences and German artillery were targets; alarm rockets (signal rockets colour-coded, in this case, calling for defensive artillery bombardment) from their front line brought no supporting, defensive fire from the rear.

There had been nothing to distinguish this morning from the horror and suffering of previous mornings, so many Germans were still in their dug-outs when Canadian troops poured into their trenches. The attackers slipped and struggled across the tortured terrain, but for much of the time were spared defensive fire. The tanks with the 1st Division (Mark I veterans of 1916 and Mark II training machines lacking combat armour) could get no grip, having dropped through the frosty crust over the mud, and fell behind. Nonetheless the 1st and 2nd Divisions had taken their Black Line objectives by 06:15 and the 3rd took theirs only ten minutes later. Stubborn machine-gunners were overcome by individual courage on the way and two posthumous awards of the Victoria Cross were made in consequence. At 06:45, after a planned pause, the advance resumed.

ABOVE *Canadian troops demonstrate 'going over the top' for the benefit of a photographer. This is almost certainly one of many pictures made during training to give the folks back home some idea of what their men were required to do.*

ABOVE *Although the restored trenches are neater and more permanent than the muddy diggings of 1917, a little imagination recreates the Vimy Ridge of the time in the mind's eye.*

In front of Hill 145 the 4th Division was not so fortunate. Here, more thoroughly overlooked than elsewhere, preparation was hardest. Six subways had been excavated and from them the men took position only 140m (153 yards) from the Germans, but at the northern end of the sector a part of the German trench had been spared shelling because it was considered essential to the Canadians once it had been taken. From it the Germans poured machine-gun fire on their attackers. The slow progress allowed the second line's defenders to man their trenches. It was dark before grenades, Stokes mortars and machine guns gave the Canadians the position.

The 1st Division's renewed attack on 10 April had the advantage of having the wind behind it, carrying a snowstorm into the faces of the Bavarians manning the Zwischen-Stellung (intermediate trench line). They were nearly to grips with them before the Bavarians even saw them. On their left the 2nd Division moved almost as fast and by 08:00 they had the Red line. The 3rd Division were over the crest by 07:30 and into the edge of the woods. Soon La Folie Farm was also in their hands. On the left flank they came under fire from Hill 145, still German, and had to establish a line facing that danger, but they had achieved their day's objectives. The Blue and Brown Lines fell to the 1st and 2nd Divisions before dark, in part because, when the weather cleared briefly, the Canadian possession of Hill 135 could be seen and the Germans knew their position was hopeless.

The next day the Canadians held off a German attempt to retake trenches on Hill 145, but the weather cleared enough for their enemy to lay down fire from the Pimple. The previous evening the commander of the 12th Brigade had asked for help from the 11th. Thus reinforced, Hill 145 was secured and the rest of the objective taken by mid-afternoon on 11 April. Vimy Ridge was Canadian.

The Pimple was attacked in driving snow at 05:00 on 12 April. Again surprise was achieved, but on the left stubborn resistance had to be overcome. It was not enough to prevent the Pimple becoming a Canadian position by daybreak.

On 13 April the Canadians advanced to the line of the Lens–Arras railway and on 14 April the 1st Army, including the Canadians, went forward another 1000m (1094 yards) as the Germans retreated to new positions.

Canadian losses during the six days of 9–14 April amounted to a total of 10,602, of which 3598 were killed and 7004 wounded. They gained 4100 metres (4500 yards), 54 guns, 104 trench mortars, 124 machine guns and over 4000 German prisoners. German losses were not recorded.

VISITING VIMY RIDGE

Thousands of travellers speed past Vimy Ridge on their way south and east from Calais or Lille on the A1 and A26 autoroutes. It takes little time to visit.

The trees and grass have softened the scars of 1917, but on the summit of Hill 145 the twin pylons of the Canadian Memorial stand in honour of all the Canadians who died or risked their lives in World War I. The names of 11,285 who died (not only at Vimy Ridge) and have no known grave are carved on the walls. The monument stands in a park still marked by shellholes. Preserved trenches can be seen and there are guided visits to the underground tunnels. Places can be reserved at the Interpretation Centre by phoning ahead; in the holiday season a reservation is vital. The Centre itself, located some 200m (220 yards) from the monument, offers a five-part display covering not only the attack of 9 April 1917, but the Canadian part in the war as a whole. It includes a multimedia audio-visual presentation.

The French had been fighting on this front since the early months of the war; the Battle of Lorette lasted from October 1914 to October 1915, claiming 100,000 casualties. Their memory is preserved in the National Military Cemetery, Notre Dame de Lorette, northwest of Vimy Ridge. It is a massive graveyard and ossuary.

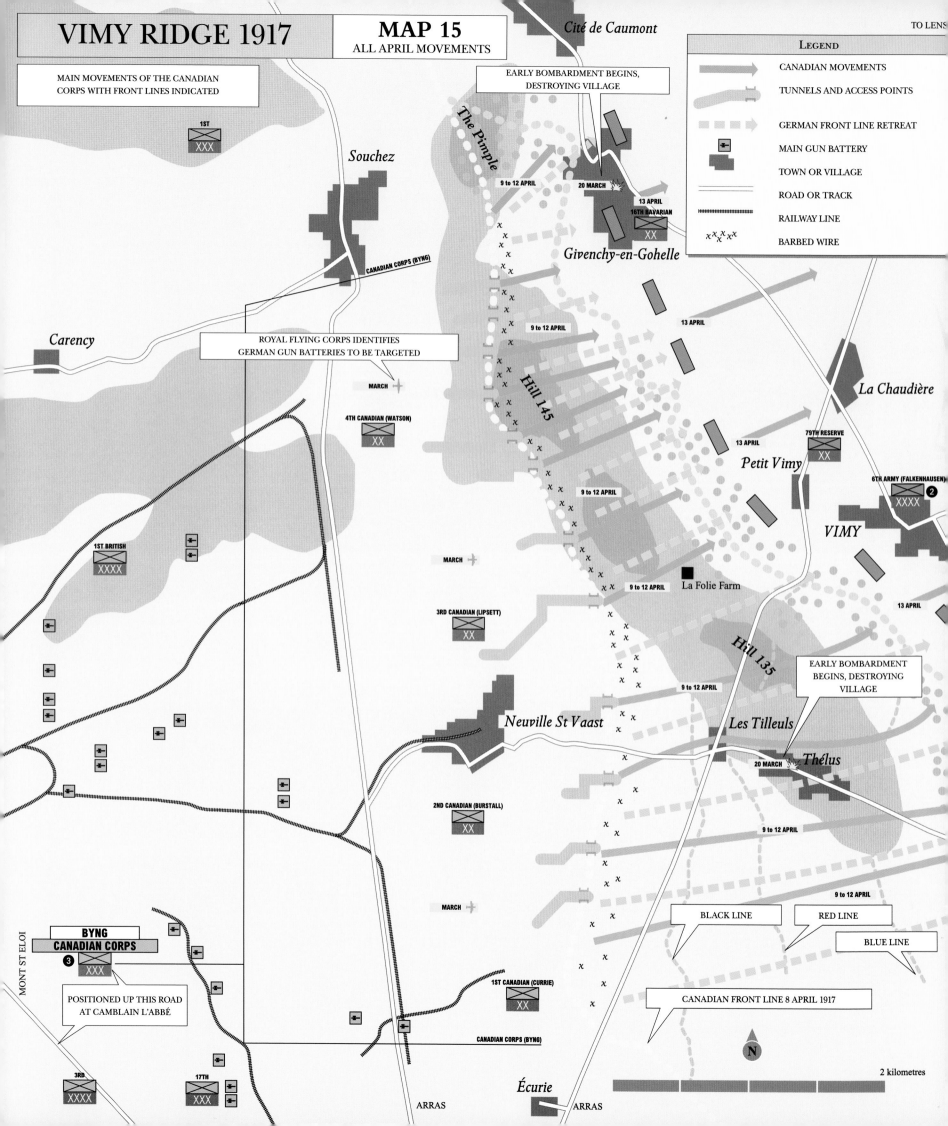

VIMY RIDGE 1917

MAP 15
ALL APRIL MOVEMENTS

TO LENS

MAIN MOVEMENTS OF THE CANADIAN CORPS WITH FRONT LINES INDICATED

Cité de Caumont

EARLY BOMBARDMENT BEGINS, DESTROYING VILLAGE

LEGEND

→	CANADIAN MOVEMENTS
	TUNNELS AND ACCESS POINTS
- - →	GERMAN FRONT LINE RETREAT
	MAIN GUN BATTERY
	TOWN OR VILLAGE
	ROAD OR TRACK
	RAILWAY LINE
x x x	BARBED WIRE

1ST
XXX

The Pimple

Souchez

9 to 12 APRIL

20 MARCH

13 APRIL

16TH BAVARIAN
XX

Givenchy-en-Gohelle

13 APRIL

CANADIAN CORPS (BYNG)

Carency

ROYAL FLYING CORPS IDENTIFIES GERMAN GUN BATTERIES TO BE TARGETED

9 to 12 APRIL

MARCH

Hill 145

13 APRIL

La Chaudière

4TH CANADIAN (WATSON)
XX

13 APRIL

79TH RESERVE
XX

Petit Vimy

9 to 12 APRIL

6TH ARMY (FALKENHAUSEN) ②
XXXX

1ST BRITISH
XXXX

VIMY

MARCH

9 to 12 APRIL

La Folie Farm

13 APRIL

3RD CANADIAN (LIPSETT)
XX

Hill 135

EARLY BOMBARDMENT BEGINS, DESTROYING VILLAGE

9 to 12 APRIL

Neuville St Vaast

Les Tilleuls

Thélus

20 MARCH

2ND CANADIAN (BURSTALL)
XX

9 to 12 APRIL

9 to 12 APRIL

BYNG
CANADIAN CORPS ③
XXX

BLACK LINE

RED LINE

BLUE LINE

POSITIONED UP THIS ROAD AT CAMBLAIN L'ABBÉ

MONT ST ELOI

1ST CANADIAN (CURRIE)
XX

CANADIAN FRONT LINE 8 APRIL 1917

CANADIAN CORPS (BYNG)

N

3RD
XXXX

17TH
XXX

Écurie

ARRAS

ARRAS

2 kilometres

SITES TODAY

SOUCHEZ
GIVENCHY-EN-GOHELLE
A26
Craters
Cemetery
Moroccan Monument
Canadian National Vimy Memorial (see below)
D937
A26
D55
Information Centre, Tunnels and Trenches
LA TARGETTE
NEUVILLE ST VAAST
Museum
D49

Canadian Monument
Interpretive Centre
Moroccan Monument
D55
Subways & restored trenches

UNITS

TYPE	
INFANTRY	⊠

SIZE	
ARMY GROUP	XXXX
ARMY	XXXX
CORPS	XXX
DIVISION	XX
BRIGADE	X
REGIMENT	III
BATTALION	II
COMPANY	I

20 MARCH

13 APRIL

RUPPRECHT
GERMAN ❶
XXXX

NOTES, NUMBERED ON MAP ⓯

GERMAN
1. RUPPRECHT, CROWN PRINCE OF BAVARIA
2. GENERAL FREIHERR VON FALKENHAUSEN

ALLIED
3. LIEUTENANT GENERAL SIR JULIAN BYNG

13 APRIL

EARLY BOMBARDMENT BEGINS, DESTROYING VILLAGE

Farbus
Arleux-en-Gohelle
1ST BAVARIAN RESERVE
XX
Willerval

20 MARCH

13 APRIL

13 APRIL

CANADIAN FRONT LINE 12 APRIL 1917

BROWN LINE

OPPY

Bailleul

There is an orientation table near the entrance to the cemetery which explains the strategic importance of the Hill of Notre-Dame-de-Lorette and a 1914–1918 Living Museum.

Arras was in the front line throughout the war. It is a good centre from which to tour the battlefields of northern France. The medieval buildings were constructed of stone quarried from beneath the town itself, leaving a maze of tunnels (Les Bôves) that were put to use as shelters, hospitals, offices and headquarters to evade the shellfire above. Guided tours start from the Tourist Information Office in the Place des Héros.

VISITORS' FACT FILE

- Interpretive Centre, Canadian National Vimy Memorial:
  Tel: ++ 33 (0)3-21-50-68-68
  www.vac-acc.gc.ca/general/sub.cfm?source=memorials/ww1mem/vimy
Notre Dame de Lorette:
- National Military Cemetery, Tel: ++ 33 (0)3-21-29-30-62
- 1914-1918 Living Museum, Tel: ++ 33 (0)3-21-45-15-80
  Open daily, 9am to 8pm.
- Arras: Tourist Office, Place des Héros, Tel: ++ 33 (0)3-21-51-26-95

VIMY RIDGE TIMELINE

9 April

04:00	Attackers are in position (Some had emerged from the tunnels to conceal themselves in the shellholes of no-man's-land and some had filed through the gaps in their own wire to creep forward, close to the enemy line).
05.30	Nearly a thousand mortars and guns blaze out and 150 machine guns pour their fire into a belt about 360m (400 yards) in front of the Canadians.
06:15	1st and 2nd Divisions had taken their Black Line objectives.
06:25	The 3rd takes its objective.
06.45	After a planned pause, the advance begins again.
Evening	4th Division takes Hill 145.

10 April

Morning	Renewed attack by the 1st Division on the Zwischen-Stellung.
08:00	The 2nd Division takes the Red line.
07:00	The 3rd Division are over the crest and into the edge of the woods. Soon La Folie Farm is also in their hands.
Evening	Commander of 12th Brigade asks for help from the 11th.

11 April

Morning	Canadians hold off a German attempt to retake trenches on Hill 145.
Mid-afternoon	Hill 145 is secured and the rest of the objective taken by mid-afternoon. Vimy Ridge is Canadian.
Before dark	The Blue and Brown Lines fall to the 1st and 2nd Divisions.

12 April

05:00	The Pimple is attacked in driving snow.
Daybreak	Pimple becomes a Canadian position.

World War II

1939 – 1945

By Martin Marix Evans

World War II, an agglomeration of a series of smaller conflicts from 1939 onwards, affected almost every country on the globe. Poland was invaded on 1 September 1939, after the German leader Adolf Hitler had formed a non-aggression pact with his only rival for European dominance, the USSR. As guarantors of Poland's freedom, France and Britain declared war, but could not prevent her defeat. The Allies made ready for a long war of attrition. What hit them in May 1940 was a short, sharp attack by mobile forces on narrow fronts that cut their forces in two and isolated the British and many of the French on the Channel coast near Dunkirk. Nearly 340,000 troops, 59 per cent of which were British, had to be evacuated. France surrendered on 20 June. Germany's plans to invade England were frustrated by failure to destroy the RAF in the Battle of Britain and Hitler's attentions turned towards the USSR.

Italy had made an alliance with Germany in June 1940, and Britain fought her in the Mediterranean and in Africa. By February 1941 the Italians had been ejected from Libya and by May they were defeated utterly in East Africa. The Germans were obliged to become involved in this arena, and the British were pushed back towards the Suez Canal. In November 1942, the battle at Alamein marked the start of an advance by the Allies, now including the Americans, to be concluded in Tunisia where an Axis surrender was forced in May 1943.

In June 1941 Hitler unleashed a massive assault on the USSR in Operation Barbarossa. His forces swept to the shores of the Black Sea and the outskirts of Moscow where winter halted them. In 1942 they attempted to secure the oilfields of the Caucasus, but the Soviet army cut off General Paulus's 6th Army in Stalingrad and, by the end of January 1943, defeated it.

In the Far East the Japanese Empire had been expanding since the 1930s, constrained only by American and European power. The war in Europe and the USSR distracted Japan's adversaries. Although not a combatant, the USA was rendering immense aid to the Allies. On 7 December 1941 the Japanese hit the US Pacific Fleet in Pearl Harbor, invaded Malaya and began operations against the USA in the Philippines. The first of these attacks was intended to immobilize the greatest of Japan's enemies to buy time for conquest in Asia. However, it stirred the reluctant giant of the USA into sustained effort that would bring her, island by island, to the Japanese homeland.

By common agreement among the Allies the defeat of Hitler was the priority. Sicily was invaded in July 1943 and, as the Germans defended lines in northern Italy in June 1944, the D-Day landings in Normandy opened a front in France. The Soviets pressed from the east while the British and Americans advanced to the western borders of Germany. The bold thrust to outflank Hitler's defensive line, by seizing the bridges in the Netherlands, failed at Arnhem in September. A dramatic but futile German attempt to counterattack in the Ardennes in the winter, led to the fighting known to history as the Battle of the Bulge. With spring the defences on the Rhine and on the Elbe melted away and by May 1945 Germany was entirely destroyed. The war in the Far East now had the full attention and power of the Allies, but the long fight anticipated was cut short by the unleashing in August of the most fearsome weapon of all time, the atomic bomb.

THIS PAGE *An American landing party lend helping hands to others whose landing craft was sunk by enemy action off the coast of France. These survivors reached Utah Beach by using a life raft.*

PEARL HARBOR 1941

By John Hughes-Wilson

For many of an older generation the defining memory will always be of exactly where they were on 7 December 1941, the date of the Japanese surprise attack on the US naval base at Pearl Harbor in Hawaii.

Japan's primary motive for war was economic. In 1931 she had invaded Manchuria to seize the raw materials her economy needed, and the western powers, led by the USA, reacted with economic sanctions. Blocked at every turn, Japan then looked north towards the mineral potential of Siberia. That invasion ended in disaster as the Soviet Army, under an obscure general called Zhukov, threw the Japanese back at Khalkin Ghol in August 1939.

The result was inevitable. By the autumn of 1941 Japan was faced with a stark political choice: economic ruin or war. Japan's new hard-line military rulers were in fact left with no real alternative: the only way that they could get the oil, tin and rubber their economy so desperately needed was to seize it by force. Only the colonial

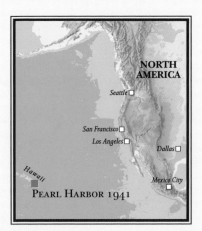

PEARL HARBOR 1941

riches of Malaya and the Dutch East Indies were left undefended for the taking. Purely as a flank protection operation – nothing more – and to stop the American fleet interfering with their real assault, the cabinet of Japanese premier and war minister Hideki Tojo then decided to attack the US Pacific base at Pearl Harbor. Pearl Harbor – astonishing as it may seem from its consequences – was never more than a sideshow to the Japanese strategic planners.

Planning for the attack had begun in January 1941. Admiral Yamamoto, the Imperial Japanese Navy's (IJN) Chief of Staff, had been impressed by the British Royal Navy's successful attack by torpedo aircraft on the Italian fleet at Taranto. Now he directed his staff to incorporate these new tactics into the IJN's contingency plans for Pearl Harbor. Finally, after prolonged and unsuccessful negotiations with the US government, on 29 November the Imperial Cabinet voted for war. The die was cast.

Much has been made of 'the mystery of Pearl Harbor'. Just how much did US President Franklin D. Roosevelt (FDR) and the US administration really know of the Japanese war plans? The FBI knew that the Japanese were collecting intelligence on Pearl Harbor; Naval Intelligence knew that an IJN carrier task force was at sea in the Pacific heading east; the State Department knew that Japanese invasion fleets were at sea heading for Malaya and the Dutch East Indies; and the services' codebreakers were reading Japan's top

ABOVE *Huge columns of smoke go up from the USS* West Virginia *and the USS* Tennessee, *crippled in their berths at Pearl Harbor, Hawaii, by a Japanese surprise attack. The* West Virginia *sank soon afterwards. The early morning attack on 7 December 1941 prompted the United States to enter World War II.*

MAIN CHARACTERS FEATURED

AMERICAN
Rear Admiral Patrick Bellinger
Admiral Husband E. Kimmel
   (commander in chief, Pacific)
Lt Commander Francis J.
   Thomas

JAPANESE
Commander Mitsuo Fuchida

Lieutenant Commander
   Shigekazu Shimazaki
Admiral Isoruko Yamamoto
   (Imperial Japanese Navy
   Chief of Staff)
Vice Admiral Chuichi
   Nagumo

Admiral Isoruko Yamamoto   *Admiral Husband E. Kimmel*

Hawaiian time. Secondly, a new US radar station picked up incoming planes at a range of 258km (160 miles). Both warnings failed. The news of the diplomatic rupture was sent from Washington by a normal, civilian RCA telegram to Pearl Harbor and arrived too late. Secondly, the operator who reported radar blips was told to 'ignore it' as it was 'a flight of incoming US B-17s from the States'.

A possible third chance to warn the base was taking place off the mouth of the harbour where the destroyer *Ward* had depth-charged an unidentified midget submarine. At 06:55 she alerted the Commander in Chief Pacific: 'Attacked ... and sunk submarine in defensive area ...' HQ reacted slowly, alerting the commander in chief Admiral Husband E. Kimmel at 07:40. Even as they did, early risers pointed at a huge cloud of planes sweeping in from the southwest. Pearl Harbor lay naked to the rising sun.

THE ATTACK

Commander Mitsuo Fuchida, leading the first attack wave, tried to marshal his forces. Not all the squadrons saw his signals and most Japanese aircraft just piled into the attack as they arrived. At 07:53, ignoring protocol, Fuchida signalled '*Tora, Tora, Tora!*', the signal for success, even as the first bomb crashed down on Ford Island. Seconds later his torpedo bombers bored in on the berth normally reserved for the Pacific Fleet's carriers northwest of Ford Island. The cruisers *Raleigh* and *Helena* took torpedo hits, as did the battleship *Utah*, despite orders for the pilots to ignore the old training battleship. One stunned naval observer, believing that he was seeing an exercise, thought that the United States Army Air Force would really get into trouble this time, as 'their practice attack had been mistakenly armed with real bombs...'

secret naval and diplomatic messages. The trouble was, no-one was putting all this intelligence together. By dawn on 7 December Admiral Nagumo's Combined Striking Fleet of six attack carriers, two battleships, three heavy cruisers and ten destroyers, was only 160km (200 miles) northwest of Hawaii and undetected.

THE PLAN

The Japanese plan called for 353 aircraft to hit Pearl Harbor in two waves. The first, consisting of 100 bombers and 40 torpedo planes escorted by 43 fighters, took off at dawn on Sunday 7 December 1941 at 06:00 to attack a sleepy, peacetime Pearl Harbor. At 07:15 the second wave thundered off the carriers' decks to head south for the islands.

However, the unsuspecting American base still had two last chances. During the night Washington had suddenly realized the significance of an intercepted 14-part Japanese diplomatic telegram about the intention to break off diplomatic relations – at dawn

ABOVE *A ball of flame erupts from gasoline stores or aircraft at the Naval Air Station at Pearl Harbor. Base personnel can only watch helplessly as the Japanese surprise attack destroys much of the area.*

ABOVE *US battleships Lined up on Battleship Row lie helpless as air-dropped torpedoes streak across Pearl Harbor.*

As the attackers swept in over Ford Island and Hickam Field, sleepy US sailors assembling in the harbour for the morning flag-raising ceremony could only stand and stare. One called out, 'Chaplain, those planes look like Japs!' Another replied, 'Hell I didn't even know they was sore at us!' as the explosions started.

On the far side of Ford Island the USS *Nevada* was moored at the north end of Battleship Row. The ceremony of the raising of the colours was met by a hail of bullets as machine-gunning Japanese torpedo bombers roared low overhead. Their torpedoes were already tracing white lines towards the helpless battleships as dive bombers swooped down.

As the stalagmites of torpedo splashes subsided, bombs sliced into *Arizona* to blow out the battleship's bottom. Burning fiercely, she began to settle on the sea bed. Three torpedoes ripped open *Oklahoma*, moored outboard of *Tennessee*. The great battleship slowly turned turtle, trapping over 400 men in her upturned hull.

West Virginia and *California* were both hit and began to flood as blazing oil leaked into the sea around them. *Nevada* was hit by two bombs and a torpedo as the crew struggled to get the ship under way. At 08:10 a one-ton bomb dropped from 3000m (10,000ft) blew the *Arizona*'s forward magazine apart, taking over 1100 sailors to their doom and blowing the on-deck crew of the repair ship *Vestal*, moored alongside, into the water.

The inboard battleships were luckier. Although they were trapped by their crippled neighbours outboard, *Maryland* and *Tennessee* were safe from torpedoes, but not from bombs. Now the Japanese bombers concentrated on them.

Suddenly, to everyone's surprise, the *Nevada* slowly left her moorings and began to head towards the harbour mouth. A diligent watch officer had kept steam up and a determined damage control officer had taken over the bridge. To the embattled Americans the battleship was an inspiring sight as she sailed past her stricken sisters, Stars and Stripes fluttering on the fantail, bright against the pall of smoke over Ford Island. Men paused at their guns to watch the great battleship glide majestically down the channel, guns spitting defiance. But her passage attracted every remaining Japanese plane. In a welter of explosions, spray and smoke, *Nevada* fought for her life until her temporary skipper, Lt Commander Francis J. Thomas, was finally forced to run his shortlived command aground off Hospital Point.

The attackers now turned their attention to the *Pennsylvania*, immobile and helpless in dry dock, before turning north to rejoin their carriers. Commander Fuchida, leader of the first Japanese strike wave, signalled the aircraft carrier *Akagi*: 'Attack successful.' Even as he did so, Rear Admiral Patrick Bellinger, ashore on Ford Island, flashed a plain text message to the world: 'Air raid, Pearl Harbor. This is no drill!'

North of Ford Island, *Utah* had finally capsized. Despite the Japanese fire raining down around them, a working party began cutting a hole in her upturned hull to free trapped sailors, one of the many heroic deeds performed that day.

From the dockside frantic officers and ratings, who had left their berths for a Saturday night ashore, tried desperately to rejoin their embattled ships. Now they could only watch in horror as Nagumo's second strike bore in, this time concentrating on the remaining ships and on the lines of fighters and flying boats ranged wing tip to wing tip on the airfields. At 09:30 a spectacular explosion blew the destroyer *Shaw* apart as her magazine detonated, showering fragments into Honolulu itself.

By 09:35 it was all over. Lieutenant Commander Shigekazu Shimazaki's 130 attack aircraft had completed the work of the first wave, leaving 2273 US servicemen dead and another 1119 wounded. Three battleships were sunk, three more seriously damaged and another dozen warships put into the dockyard for months. On land 188 aircraft were written off. Burnt and wounded men filled the hospitals. Dead and wounded civilians added to the casualty list as spent shells from the Americans' own guns fell onto downtown Honolulu, adding insult to injury. Offshore, another abortive attack by Japanese

midget submarines added confusion to panicky reports of Japanese parachute landings. Pearl Harbor was in chaos, the Governor whisked off by security men and terrified Japanese workers fled into the cane plantations to avoid American wrath.

As Nagumo's elated airmen, chased by a few straggling US fighters and still being tracked by US radar, began to recover to their carriers northwest of Hawaii they brought a clear message: 'Let's go back and finish the job!' However, despite minimal casualties (only 29 Japanese planes and 55 aircrew had been lost), and fearful of a retaliatory airstrike against his ships, the cautious admiral refused the airmen's request for a third wave. Instead he headed northwest at flank speed, anxious to put as much range as possible between his carriers and the islands, leaving the airmen to celebrate their victory. It was a mistake.

AFTERMATH

The Japanese triumph was illusory. Not only had Nagumo's strike, despite its deadly success, failed to catch the US carriers – who were at sea on a training exercise that Sunday morning – but the Japanese attacks had also failed to hit Pearl Harbor's vital fuel supplies. The oil tank farm on Ford Island held six months' supply of fuel oil and aviation spirit. It was a key target. Without it the Pacific Fleet really would have been crippled for months. In reality, Pearl Harbor was a job unfinished. The Japanese attack on the US Pacific Fleet's base did, however, have an impact out of all proportion to its military results.

RIGHT *Captured Japanese photograph of the bombing of the United States Army Air Force airfield on Oahu, Hawaii.*

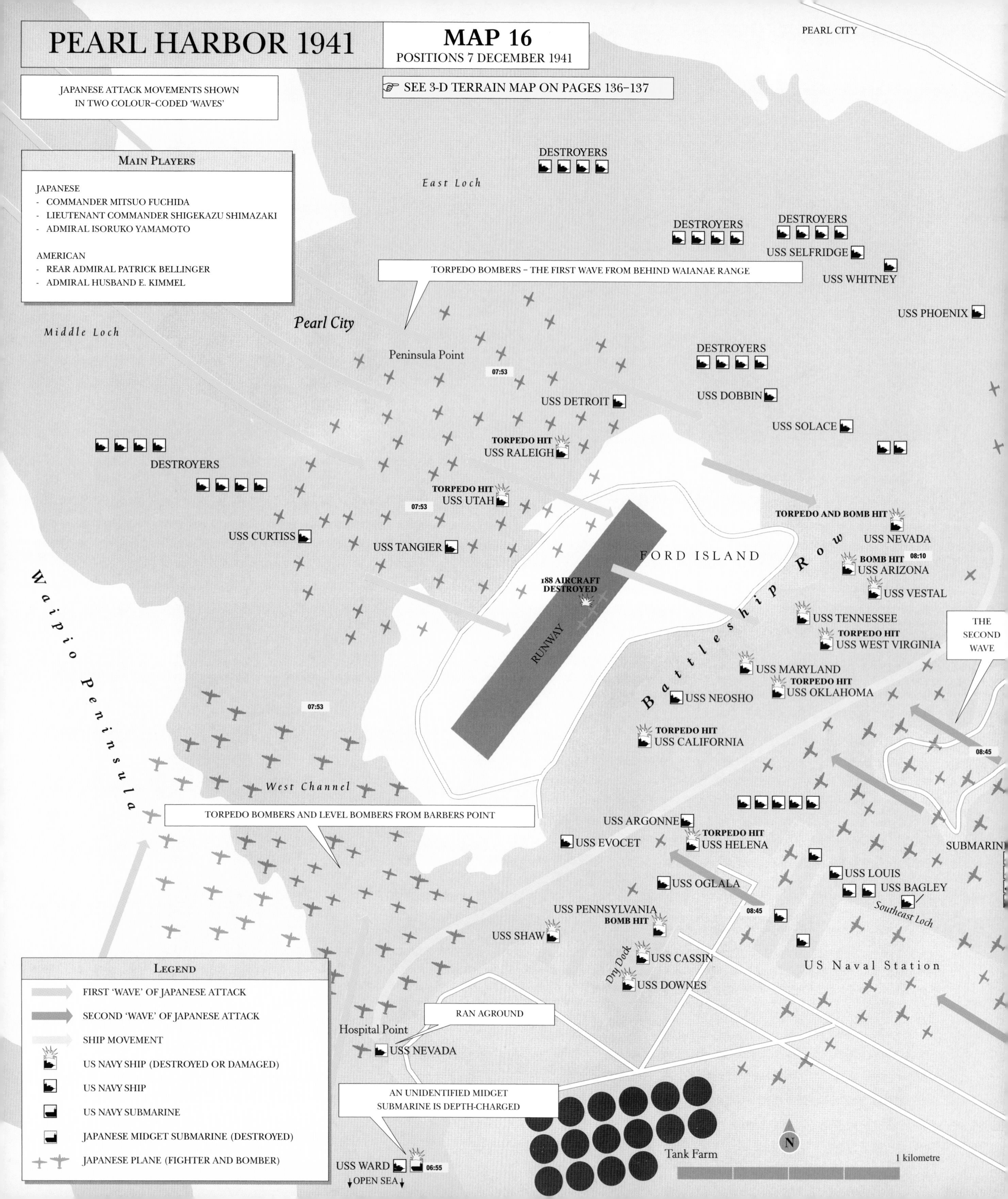

PEARL HARBOR 1941

MAP 16
POSITIONS 7 DECEMBER 1941

PEARL CITY

JAPANESE ATTACK MOVEMENTS SHOWN
IN TWO COLOUR-CODED 'WAVES'

☞ SEE 3-D TERRAIN MAP ON PAGES 136–137

Main Players

JAPANESE
- COMMANDER MITSUO FUCHIDA
- LIEUTENANT COMMANDER SHIGEKAZU SHIMAZAKI
- ADMIRAL ISORUKO YAMAMOTO

AMERICAN
- REAR ADMIRAL PATRICK BELLINGER
- ADMIRAL HUSBAND E. KIMMEL

East Loch

DESTROYERS

DESTROYERS

DESTROYERS

USS SELFRIDGE

USS WHITNEY

TORPEDO BOMBERS – THE FIRST WAVE FROM BEHIND WAIANAE RANGE

Middle Loch

USS PHOENIX

Pearl City

Peninsula Point

DESTROYERS

07:53

USS DETROIT

USS DOBBIN

USS SOLACE

TORPEDO HIT
USS RALEIGH

DESTROYERS

TORPEDO HIT
USS UTAH

07:53

DESTROYERS

TORPEDO AND BOMB HIT
USS NEVADA

USS CURTISS

07:53

USS TANGIER

FORD ISLAND

BOMB HIT 08:10
USS ARIZONA

188 AIRCRAFT
DESTROYED

USS VESTAL

B a t t l e s h i p   R o w

USS TENNESSEE

RUNWAY

TORPEDO HIT
USS WEST VIRGINIA

THE
SECOND
WAVE

USS MARYLAND

TORPEDO HIT
USS OKLAHOMA

W a i p i o   P e n i n s u l a

USS NEOSHO

07:53

TORPEDO HIT
USS CALIFORNIA

08:45

West Channel

TORPEDO BOMBERS AND LEVEL BOMBERS FROM BARBERS POINT

USS ARGONNE

TORPEDO HIT
USS HELENA

SUBMARIN

USS EVOCET

USS LOUIS

USS OGLALA

USS BAGLEY

Southeast Loch

USS PENNSYLVANIA
BOMB HIT

08:45

USS SHAW

US Naval Station

Dry Dock

USS CASSIN

RAN AGROUND

USS DOWNES

Hospital Point

USS NEVADA

Legend

FIRST 'WAVE' OF JAPANESE ATTACK

SECOND 'WAVE' OF JAPANESE ATTACK

SHIP MOVEMENT

US NAVY SHIP (DESTROYED OR DAMAGED)

US NAVY SHIP

US NAVY SUBMARINE

JAPANESE MIDGET SUBMARINE (DESTROYED)

JAPANESE PLANE (FIGHTER AND BOMBER)

AN UNIDENTIFIED MIDGET
SUBMARINE IS DEPTH-CHARGED

USS WARD 06:55

↓OPEN SEA↓

Tank Farm

N

1 kilometre

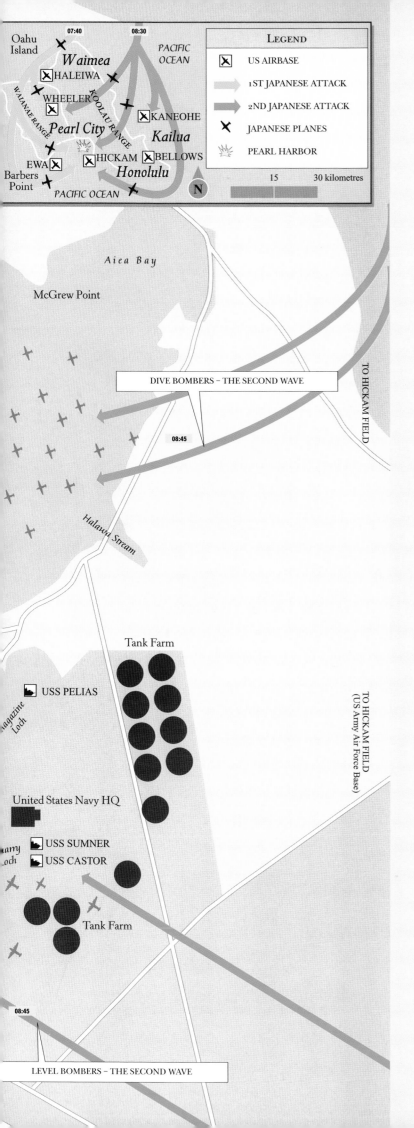

Pearl Harbor brought the United States into the war. A livid Franklin D. Roosevelt demanded reprisals from the US Congress for what was quite clearly an unprovoked attack on sleeping sailors in peacetime. An enraged America prepared for war: 'Remember Pearl Harbor!' was the cry as the queues lengthened outside the recruiting offices and American industry geared up for war.

Hitler added to the political fallout by rashly declaring war on the USA, telling an old Nazi party crony, Walther Hewell: 'At last, we have an ally who has not been vanquished in 3000 years!' In London, a delighted Churchill heaved a sigh of relief: at last, his long-sought goal of bringing America to join in Britain's struggle had been achieved – thanks to the Japanese.

Far away in Japan, the victorious airmen of the Imperial Navy were fêted for their stunning victory. Even as they did so, the architect of that victory, Admiral Isoruko Yamamoto, was warning that his masterstroke remained incomplete. Early in 1942 he wrote: 'In the last analysis, the success of our strategy ... will be determined by whether or not we succeed in destroying the United States fleet and particularly its carrier task force...'

Japan's course to Midway, and her ultimate defeat, was charted.

MEMORIALS

The best known are the USS *Arizona* Visitor Center (see www.nps.gov/usar and also www.arizonamemorial.org); the USS *Utah* Memorial (see www.ussutah.org) and the Hickam Field memorial.

PEARL HARBOR TIMELINE

January 1941
　　　　Planning for the attack begins.

29 November
　　　　Imperial Cabinet votes for war.

7 December

Dawn Admiral Nagumo's Combined Striking Fleet of six attack carriers, two battleships, three heavy cruisers and ten destroyers, is only 160 kilometres (200 miles) northwest of Hawaii and undetected.

06:00 The first wave of 100 bombers and 40 torpedo planes escorted by 43 fighters, takes off.

07:15 The second wave takes off.

06:55 The destroyer *Ward* alerts CinCPac that she had sunk a submarine in defensive area.

07:40 Commander in Chief Admiral Kimmel is alerted.

07:53 Fuchida signals 'Tora, Tora, Tora!', the signal for success, as the first bomb crashes down on Ford Island.

08:10 A one-ton bomb dropped from 10,000 feet blows the *Arizona*'s forward magazine apart.

09:30 The destroyer *Shaw* is blown apart as her magazine is detonated, showering fragments into Honolulu itself.

09:35 It is all over.

PEARL HARBOR 7 DECEMBER 1941

DAY OF INFAMY

Pearl Harbor was the US Navy's main Pacific base, a magnificent natural harbour located on the southern coast of the Hawaiian island of Oahu. Pearl Harbor was the fleet anchorage and command centre, and housed storage, fuelling, dry-docks and repair facilities. On Ford Island, in the centre of the harbour, lay the hangars and runways of Pearl Harbor Naval Air Station.

Launched from carriers approximately 145km (230 miles) north of Oahu, the Japanese torpedo and dive bombers struck in waves, coming in from the southwest, northwest and east, and taking the Americans by surprise. The mighty but ageing battleships, lined up two abreast along Battleship Row, presented the Japanese pilots with easy targets. However, the absence of the American aircraft carriers – away on a training exercise – meant that Japan's successful surprise attack was not a complete victory.

① Ford Island: The island housed Pearl Harbor Naval Air Station, which included a seaplane base, as well as important fuel storage facilities. The Japanese attack destroyed many American aircraft, which were parked wingtip to wingtip as if on parade, but failed to destroy the fuel storage areas.

② Battleship Row

③ USS *Nevada*

④ USS *Arizona*

⑤ USS *Vestal* (repair ship)

⑥ USS *Tennessee*

⑦ USS *West Virginia*

⑧ USS *Maryland*

⑨ USS *Oklahoma*

⑩ USS *Pennsylvania* (in drydock)

⑪ USS *Utah*

⑫ USS *Tangier*

⑬ USS *Raleigh*

⑭ USS *Detroit*

⑮ USS *Neosho*

⑯ USS *Shaw*

⑰ USS *Oglala*

⑱ USS *Helena*

⑲ Ford Island Command Center

⑳ CinCPac Headquarters

㉑ Drydocks and repair facilities

㉒ Oil storage tanks

㉓ Middle Loch

㉔ Pearl Harbor

㉕ Southeast Loch

㉖ To Mamala Bay and Pacific Ocean

㉗ Pearl City

28 **1st wave (07:55)** The first wave of Japanese planes consisted of 40 B5N2 Kate torpedo bombers, 51 Aichi D3A1 Val dive-bombers, 49 Kate high-level bombers and an escort of 43 Zero fighters. The first wave reached Oahu at 07:53, and began to hit their targets just after 07:55.

29 **2nd wave (09:07)** The second wave of attacking planes consisted of 170 dive and high-level bombers, with an escort of Zero fighters.

PEARL HARBOR TODAY

PEARL HARBOR

USS UTAH MEMORIAL

FORD ISLAND

HICKAM FIELD MEMORIAL

N

5000 metres

1 USS *Arizona* Memorial

2 USS *Arizona* Memorial Visitor Center

3 USS *Bowfin* Submarine Museum and Park

EL ALAMEIN 1942

By Christopher Pugsley

The turning point in the campaign for North Africa was the battle of El Alamein (23 October – 4 November 1942). It pitted the veteran desert campaigner General Erwin Rommel, 'The Desert Fox' whose Panzer Army Africa had defeated the best that British generalship had to offer, against Lieutenant General Bernard Law Montgomery, the new boy to desert warfare, a brash, confident officer whose arrival had reinvigorated the 8th Army largely made up of Commonwealth forces. Montgomery, or 'Monty' as he became known to his citizen soldiers, frustrated Rommel's attempt to mount an offensive on Cairo at the Battle of Alam Halfa (30 August – 7 September 1942). Now he was determined to break through and destroy Rommel's Axis army of German and Italian forces at El Alamein.

Today El Alamein is sometimes described as a battle that Montgomery could not lose because of overwhelming logistic superiority. It is also seen as a solely political battle, a victory that Churchill needed before the Anglo-American Torch landings in Algeria condemned Britain to a minor role. The latter is true, but war is a

political act and Alamein was a necessary victory both in tactical and strategic terms. It was also a battle that Montgomery could lose because he faced a skilled enemy and a very cleverly sited defensive position. It incorporated all the strengths gained from German defensive doctrine of the First World War in a position that was impossible to bypass. Montgomery had no choice but to break through and he had an army that was ill-trained and lacking in morale. They also had little experience in coordinating infantry, armour and artillery in the combined arms role that was the particular strength of Rommel's Afrika Korps. Under its previous commanders the 8th Army had managed to lose its battles despite a superiority of resources. Montgomery had broken that pattern at Alam Halfa and was about to do so again.

THE PLAN

The principal problem facing Montgomery at Alamein was how to break through Rommel's defences. It was a three-layered sponge cake, with the sponge made up of interspersed Italian and German formations and the thick creamy icing being the minefields in between. The minefields provided a depth of some 4–5km (2–3 miles) through which the British infantry would have to fight before the engineers could clear minefield gaps big enough for the armour to get through. This cream filling was called 'mine (or devil's) gardens'

ABOVE *The second Battle of El Alamein on 26 October 1942. Italian troops run for cover as British bombs rain down during an RAF attack on Axis positions.*

by the German defenders, who saw the open areas as killing fields surrounded by hedges enclosing rows of mines. A total of 445,358 mines, anti-tank and anti-personnel, were laid in these mine gardens.

Montgomery's plan was to feint in the south with Lieutenant General Brian Horrocks' 13th Corps, while breaking through the defences and seizing Miteiriya Ridge with the infantry of Lieutenant General Oliver Leese's 30th Corps on the night of 23–24 October in Operation Lightfoot. The two armoured divisions of Lieutenant-General Herbert Lumsden's 10th Corps would pass through the secured line on Miteiriya Ridge and establish themselves forward of the infantry positions. There they would destroy the German armoured counterattacks, while behind them the infantry would deal with the German and Italian strongpoints.

MAIN CHARACTERS

GERMAN/ITALIAN

General Erwin Rommel (Panzer Army Africa)

Lieutenant General Wilhelm Ritter von Thoma

General Guisepe di Stefanis

ALLIED

Lieutenant General Bernard Law Montgomery, 'Monty' (8th Army)

Lieutenant General Brian Horrocks (13th Corps)

Lieutenant General Oliver Leese (30th Corps) Infantry

Lieutenant General Herbert Lumsden (10th Corps)

Lieutenant Colonel Victor Turner

Major General Bernard Freyberg (2 New Zealand Division)

Major General Leslie Morshead (9 Australian Division)

Brigadier John Currie (9th Armoured Brigade)

General Erwin Rommel

Lieutenant General Bernard Law Montgomery

> 'There will be no tip and run tactics in this battle; it will be a killing match; the German is a good soldier and the only way to beat him is to kill him in battle.'
> Lieutenant General Bernard L Montgomery

THE ACTION

Supported by a concentrated artillery barrage of 882 guns that pounded known strongpoints and which laid down a creeping barrage in front of the advancing soldiers, the infantry attack of Operation Lightfoot was largely successful, with gaps being made for armour in 2 NZ Division's and 51 Highland Division's sectors on the night of 23–24 October. The 9th Armoured Brigade, equipped with Grant and Sherman tanks, got through in the New Zealand sector and was in position at first light. However, behind them the armoured columns of 10 Corps, consisting of 1 and 10 Armoured Divisions, were held up in an enormous traffic jam in the minefields and at daybreak were still behind the leading infantry. Attempts to break through by armour the next night, 24–25 October, failed. During this fighting Lieutenant Colonel Victor Turner fought a brilliant defensive anti-tank battle with 2nd Battalion Rifle Brigade at Snipe, on the Kidney feature – a hard, shallow, limestone-based depression – despite a total lack of support. He was awarded a VC for his actions.

Montgomery now found himself with his experienced infantry largely exhausted and his armour still stuck in the minefield. He was like a tennis player having lost the first set in the tie-breaker and having to come up with another plan before the next set.

Lightfoot confirmed to Montgomery that his two most capable generals were Major General Bernard Freyberg, commanding 2 New Zealand Division, and Major General Leslie Morshead, commanding 9 Australian Division. This became the partnership that he used to win his battle. Having stretched, but not broken, the defences on Miteiriya Ridge, Montgomery switched the pressure to the north, with the Australians conducting a series of mini-encirclements along the railway line. This became the focus of Rommel's counterattacks in a series of savage battles around Barrel Hill in what became known as the 'Cauldron' from 28 October on.

Meanwhile Montgomery withdrew his armour to regroup. He took brigades from 13th Corps and from the less capable British divisions and gave them to 2 New Zealand Division, which was tasked with mounting another infantry night attack, codenamed Supercharge, which involved 151 Brigade (from 50 Division, 13th Corps) and 152 Brigade (from 51 Highland Division), together

RIGHT *Scots Guards fire at enemy positions during the battles at El Alamein.*

with 9 Armoured Brigade under command of Freyberg's headquarters, while the two weak New Zealand infantry brigades would conduct the breakout with the armour. Signal intercept showed that Rommel had massed his reserves in the north, where Operation Supercharge was originally planned, and so Montgomery adjusted it to strike in the centre on the night of 1–2 November 1942. Once again it was not a complete success, but it drew in the last reserves of 21 Panzer and had reduced Rommel's German infantry and anti-tank gun strength to a third of what was available at the start of the battle. Unlike Montgomery, Rommel had no reserves to call upon. The Axis defensive dyke had crumbled, and over the next 24 hours it fell apart, with first armoured cars and then armour fighting their way through with heavy losses against a gritty, but diminished, Axis defence. To save his Afrika Korps, Rommel sacrificed his Italian formations and withdrew on 4 November in what became a retreat that would end with the final surrender of German and Italian forces in Tunisia in May 1943. Montgomery had his victory.

THE IMPORTANCE OF EL ALAMEIN

Alamein is seen as a traditional set-piece battle lacking any claim to manoeuvre. This does Montgomery an injustice. He wanted to manoeuvre, but had to fight the battle with the army he had, rather than the one he wanted. He had to adjust his plans to its capabilities. Even then he was over-optimistic and misjudged the capabilities of British armour. However, he was the first British general of World War II to fight a coordinated battle to an operational design and one where he insisted that his infantry and armour follow his plan. In seeking to achieve manoeuvre, it became a bloody attritional dogfight, but he adjusted to match Rommel's response, and won.

EL ALAMEIN TODAY

Today El Alamein is a road junction and a cluster of war memorials 106km (66 miles) west of Alexandria. The museum offers an overview of the campaign, and of the weapons and equipment used in the battle. South from the road junction a tarred road runs through the sprawl of houses and shop fronts towards the railway line and the desert beyond. Over the railway line, immediately west of a shining new marble and limestone station, is the original El Alamein station. The building has holes in the roof, and its two rooms are filled with rubbish, yet this is where every tour should start. In 1942 this station was El Alamein, a lonely spot in the desert, strategically important because the Qattara Depression some 64km (40 miles) to the south turned this into the most defensible position available to harried British commanders in the summer of 1942. There is famous newsreel footage dating from mid-July 1942 of an Australian 'digger' carving the word HEAVEN on the side of the building.

THE BATTLEFIELD

South of the railway line the desert opens out into a vast open plain imperceptibly rising from north to south away from the coast on what is a hard limestone plateau covered by scattered camel thorn and shifting sands. This area was riddled with minefields, and even today it is important to keep to the tarred roads or well-used vehicle tracks; and not to pick up any ammunition or battle debris.

OPERATION LIGHTFOOT START LINE

Drive south down what was the Springbok Track past the barracks of the Egyptian mine-clearing unit to the junction of the new east-west road and turn right. This was in 30th Corps area and the road runs diagonally across what was the axis of advance of 1 South African, 2 New Zealand and 51 Highland divisions for Operation Lightfoot. Stop at the cluster of maintenance buildings where the underground pipeline intersects the road. This is the inter-divisional boundary between the New Zealanders and the Highland Division just into no-man's-land in front of what would have been the British protective minefields. There is a good view towards Miteiriya Ridge on the skyline to the southwest. This low ridge provided ideal protection for Rommel's antitank guns and hid the movement of his vehicles. It was Montgomery's objective for Lightfoot. Picture infantry filing through and shaking out in battle formation for the night advance towards the ridge in the distance. Apart from the coastal ridge to the north and the almost imperceptible Miteiriya Ridge about 4km (2–3 miles) away, there are no distinguishing features. At night the attackers would have had to rely on compass bearings and paces to negotiate the minefields surrounding the German and Italian strongpoints. The South African, New Zealand and Scots' battalions had some 5300–6400m (5800–7000 yards) to advance and fight through, while behind them engineers cleared lanes in the minefields for the armour of 10 Corps. Montgomery was straining the bounds of what was possible in a single night. Although the infantry took the ridge, the armoured divisions could not break through the antitank gun screen before daylight and so Lightfoot failed. However, it drew in Rommel's reserves.

SNIPE

Continue west along the central road to a canal culvert. Some distance beyond this is an obvious bend in the road to the northwest, marked by a loose pile of road rubble. About 400m (440 yards) beyond this is the small square ruined building. This marks the general area of the Kidney feature. It is a hard limestone-based depression, perhaps a metre or so below the surrounding sand. This shallow depression, an area of some 650m by 300m (710 by 330 yards), is where Lieutenant Colonel Turner and 2nd Battalion (The Rifle Brigade) fought the battle for Snipe. It is marked on its northern and eastern flanks by two mounds of spoil, possibly ancient wells, one of which is next to a vehicle track that turns off the tarred road. Do not venture off the hardpan of the track. This was a mined area. The surrounding sand walls became perfect positions for Turner's 6-pounder anti-tank guns.

THE RAHMAN TRACK AND MARSEILLES CAIRN

Continue west along the tarred road to where a line of telegraph poles cross the road in a north–south direction. A prominent stone pyramid can be seen inside a marked-out perimeter south of the road. This is the Marseilles Cairn, where the highest-scoring German fighter ace crashed and was killed. Follow with your eyes the line of telegraph poles north to the town of Sidi Abdul el Rahman on the main coastal highway. The telegraph poles mark Rommel's final anti-tank gun line and the area of deployment of his last panzer reserves. The immediate 2–3km (1–2 miles) of telegraph line from the cairn marks the objectives for Operation Supercharge, which was the break-in battle orchestrated by Freyberg's New Zealand Divisional Headquarters, using two British brigades in the night attack. Its success allowed Currie's 9th Armoured Brigade to reach Rommel's antitank gun line. It is also in this vicinity that British armour, at great loss, finally stretched Rommel's defences to breaking point. It is immediately south of the cairn where British armoured cars commenced the breakthrough.

BARREL HILL AND THE BLOCKHOUSE

Soft sand prevents further progress and you have to retrace your route back by road through Alamein. Past Alamein you should turn left and drive west past the memorials on the coast road to the area of Morshead's 9th Australian Division's epic battles at Barrel Hill.

Today Barrel Hill is being quarried away to provide building material for the growing spread of coastal condominiums, but it can be identified by the blockhouse and railway accommodation barracks that feature at regular intervals along the railway line. This in 1942 became hospital facilities used by both the Axis and Australians during the October/November fighting. In the area of Barrel Hill and the Cauldron, as it was known, Australian attacks forced Rommel to commit his reserves. It burnt up what was left of 164 Light and then, in turn, 15 Panzer and 90 Light Divisions. It stretched the Axis defences to the point that when Supercharge was mounted against the Rahman track, defences there were too thin to prevent a breakthrough.

THE MEMORIALS

Return to El Alamein by driving east. The first memorial on the left is the Italian memorial, the marble tower of which can be seen from all points on the battlefield. The forecourt has 40mm tank guns set at the base of each supporting pillar, with the walls inset with memorial tablets to the various regiments and divisions. Inside is a vast echoing chamber where the slightest whisper

ABOVE *The graves of the El Alamein cemetery through an arch of the cloisters. In the background is the Cross of Sacrifice found in British Commonwealth cemeteries all over the world.*

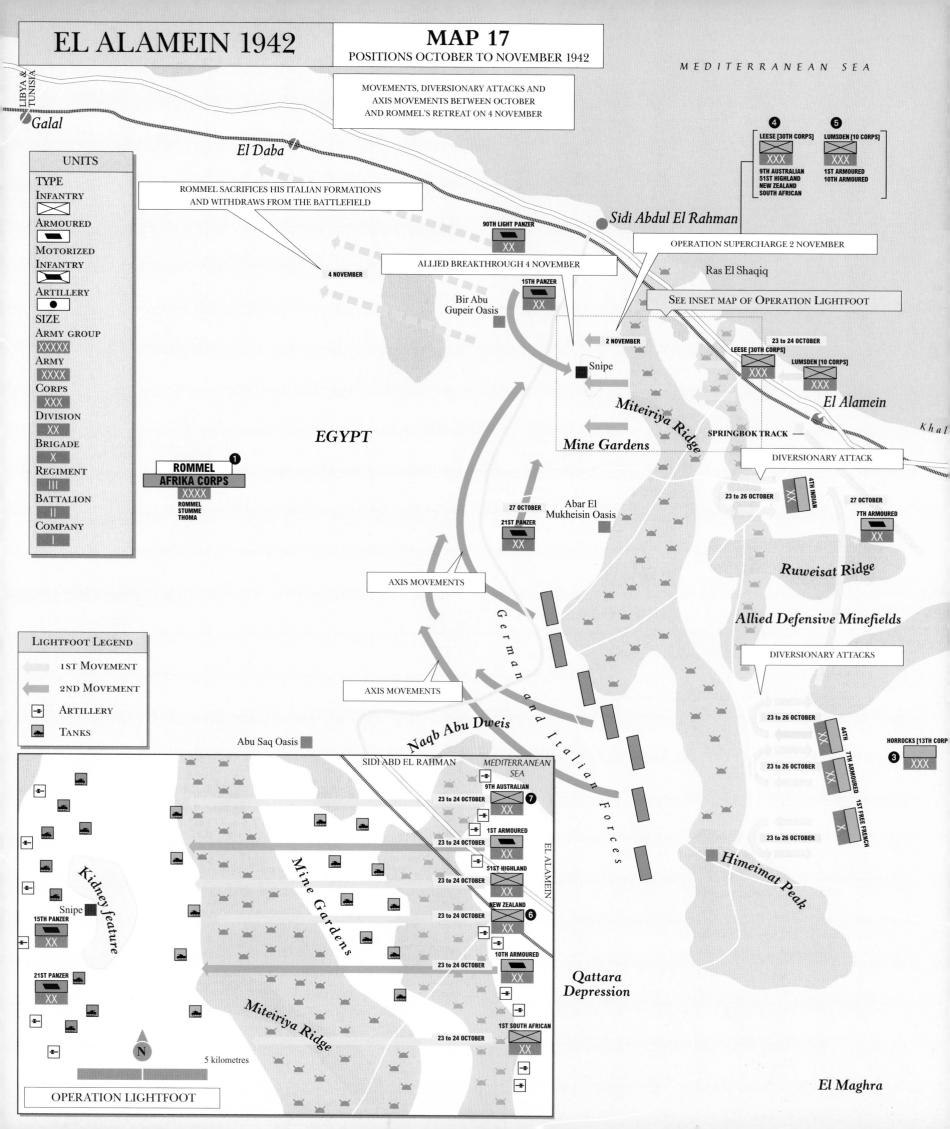

EL ALAMEIN 1942

MAP 17
POSITIONS OCTOBER TO NOVEMBER 1942

MOVEMENTS, DIVERSIONARY ATTACKS AND
AXIS MOVEMENTS BETWEEN OCTOBER
AND ROMMEL'S RETREAT ON 4 NOVEMBER

MEDITERRANEAN SEA

Galal

LIBYA &
TUNISIA

El Daba

4 LEESE [30TH CORPS]
XXX
9TH AUSTRALIAN
51ST HIGHLAND
NEW ZEALAND
SOUTH AFRICAN

5 LUMSDEN [10 CORPS]
XXX
1ST ARMOURED
10TH ARMOURED

Sidi Abdul El Rahman

UNITS

TYPE
INFANTRY
ARMOURED
MOTORIZED
INFANTRY
ARTILLERY

SIZE
ARMY GROUP — XXXX
ARMY — XXXX
CORPS — XXX
DIVISION — XX
BRIGADE — X
REGIMENT — III
BATTALION — II
COMPANY — I

90TH LIGHT PANZER
XX

OPERATION SUPERCHARGE 2 NOVEMBER

ROMMEL SACRIFICES HIS ITALIAN FORMATIONS
AND WITHDRAWS FROM THE BATTLEFIELD

ALLIED BREAKTHROUGH 4 NOVEMBER

Ras El Shaqiq

4 NOVEMBER

15TH PANZER
XX

SEE INSET MAP OF OPERATION LIGHTFOOT

Bir Abu
Gupeir Oasis

2 NOVEMBER

23 to 24 OCTOBER

LEESE [30TH CORPS]
XXX

El Alamein

Snipe

LUMSDEN [10 CORPS]
XXX

Khal

EGYPT

Miteiriya Ridge

Mine Gardens

SPRINGBOK TRACK —

DIVERSIONARY ATTACK

ROMMEL **1**
AFRIKA CORPS
XXXX
ROMMEL
STUMME
THOMA

23 to 26 OCTOBER

4TH INDIAN
XX

27 OCTOBER

7TH ARMOURED
XX

27 OCTOBER
21ST PANZER
XX

Abar El
Mukheisin Oasis

Ruweisat Ridge

AXIS MOVEMENTS

Allied Defensive Minefields

DIVERSIONARY ATTACKS

AXIS MOVEMENTS

23 to 26 OCTOBER

44TH
XX

HORROCKS [13TH CORP]
XXX
3

Naqb Abu Dweis

7TH ARMOURED
XX
23 to 26 OCTOBER

Abu Saq Oasis

SIDI ABD EL RAHMAN

MEDITERRANEAN
SEA

1ST FREE FRENCH
X
23 to 26 OCTOBER

LIGHTFOOT LEGEND

1ST MOVEMENT
2ND MOVEMENT
ARTILLERY
TANKS

9TH AUSTRALIAN **7**
XX
23 to 24 OCTOBER

Himeimat Peak

1ST ARMOURED
XX
23 to 24 OCTOBER

Kidney feature

51ST HIGHLAND
XX
23 to 24 OCTOBER

Snipe

15TH PANZER
XX

Mine Gardens

NEW ZEALAND **6**
XX
23 to 24 OCTOBER

German and Italian Forces

21ST PANZER
XX

10TH ARMOURED
XX
23 to 24 OCTOBER

EL ALAMEIN

*Qattara
Depression*

Miteiriya Ridge

N

5 kilometres

1ST SOUTH AFRICAN
XX
23 to 24 OCTOBER

OPERATION LIGHTFOOT

El Maghra

N

reverberates. The sea provides a backdrop to the marble-walled catacombs of the Italian dead, which are set into alcoves like private post boxes.

Further east is the German memorial, the design of which is based on an early Norman castle at Apulia in southern Italy. It was built in the 1950s. Inside, it has the feel of a cloistered monastery with alcoves, each of which contains three sepulchres carved with the regions from which the soldiers came. In a small side chapel there is a plaque to Erwin Rommel.

A signpost shows the way to the Commonwealth war graves. It is like walking into a desert garden through an inviting archway into which are engraved the names of the missing. The graves are ordered and edged with bushes in purple and crimson. The Commonwealth dead are buried chronologically in the various national groups. It is a beautiful setting with the battlefield beyond, spoilt only by the encroaching pylons and buildings from the Alamein sprawl.

EL ALAMEIN TIMELINE

23–24 October
Night
- Infantry attack (Lightfoot), supported by a creeping artillery barrage of 882 guns in front of advancing soldiers and pounding known strongpoints.
- Gaps are made for armour in 2 NZ Division's and 51 Highland Division's sectors.

24 October
First light
- The 9th Armoured Brigade, equipped with Grant and Sherman tanks, gets through in the New Zealand sector and is in position.
- 10 Corps (1 and 10 Armoured Divisions) are held up in a traffic jam in the minefields.

24–25 October
Attempts to break through by armour fails Lieutenant-Colonel Turner fights a defensive anti-tank battle with 2nd Battalion Rifle Brigade at Snipe, on the Kidney feature despite lack of support.

28 October onward
Montgomery switches the pressure to the north: a series of mini-encirclements by the Australians along the axis of the railway line. This becomes the focus of Rommel's counterattacks in a series of battles around Barrel Hill, the 'Cauldron'.

1–2 November
- Signal intercept informs Montgomery that Rommel has massed his reserves in the north, where originally planned. Montgomery strikes in the centre (Supercharge), drawing in the last reserves of 21 Panzer and reduces Rommel's German infantry and anti-tank gun strength to a third of what it was at the start of the battle.
- The Axis defensive dyke crumbles.
- To save his Afrika Korps, Rommel sacrifices his Italian formations.

4 November Rommel withdraws.

D-DAY 1944

By Martin Marix Evans

The remaining troops at Dunkirk, the French who had held the last perimeter to allow their British comrades-in-arms to get away, surrendered on 4 June 1940 to the German Army and on 20 June the last British unit left France on a Welsh collier out of Marseilles. On 19 August 1942 the 2nd Canadian Division attempted a landing at Dieppe that ended in bloody failure and demonstrated how little the British knew then about the conduct of opposed invasions on enemy shores. However, if the Germans were to be ejected from France and their other conquests on the mainland of Europe, a landing sometime was mandatory. In 1943 it was decided that the Allies would land somewhere between Le Havre and Cherbourg.

The target area had only one harbour, at Cherbourg. It was strongly defended and would have to be taken by land from the south, so the supply of food, ammunition and fuel to the landing force had to be achieved in unconventional ways. Two huge artificial harbours, code-named Mulberries, were made from obsolete

ships, concrete caissons and floating jetties for sea-borne supplies. Fuel was to be pumped through a Pipe Line Under The Ocean: PLUTO. There were new weapons as well: a number of specialized tanks were created. The Duplex-Drive, or D-D, was fitted with a propeller and flotation devices; American Shermans were converted to this type. 'Crabs' were Churchills fitted with flails to detonate landmines, 'Crocodiles' had flame-throwers and 'Petards' carried 290mm mortars for smashing bunkers. Armoured Vehicles, Royal Engineers (AVREs) were equipped with various devices for bridging streams and filling in ditches. The Americans at first declined to use any of the 'Funnies' except the D-Ds. They later invented one of their own, the 'Rhino', which was fitted with a spiked bar to crash through the unique earth-and-hedge field boundaries of the bocage country (characterized by small fields, high hedgerows and sunken lanes).

THE BEACHES OF NORMANDY

The chosen landing area was varied in its terrain. In the west the eastern side of the Cotentin peninsula is largely sandy, with dunes between the shore and a marshy, poorly drained strip of land that separates it from the firm ground inland. Utah Beach is here. The coast turns east at the foot of the peninsula, and there the delta of the rivers Douve, Taute, Vire and Aure was flooded around

ABOVE *Once Omaha Beach and the bluffs above it were secured, the larger landing craft could bring in the troops and supplies vital to the drive inland. The beach was to have been the site of a 'Mulberry Harbour' – a prefabricated port – but the storm of 19 June destroyed it before completion.*

Copenhagen
Amsterdam *Berlin*
London *Brussels* *Prague*
D-DAY 1944 *Paris*
EUROPE *Vienna*

Madrid *Rome*
Lisbon
Athens

AFRICA

Carentan, while inland the bocage country provided defenders with ready-made parapets. Cliffs run eastwards with a threatening gun battery at the Pointe de Hoc, west of the next beach, Omaha. The cliffs rise again until, on the other side of Arromanches, they give way to sandy beaches again; Gold, Juno and Sword. East of these the River Orne comes down from the town of Caen and the land rises briefly before falling once more to the valley of the River Dives, which was also flooded. The beaches are all different in their character and aspect, each presenting different challenges.

The operation for the invasion of Europe, code-named Overlord, was under the command of the American General Dwight D. Eisenhower, to whom the commanders of the navy, army and air forces reported. For the assault on Normandy, named Neptune, the army was assigned to General Sir Bernard Law Montgomery. Under him was the 1st US Army (Lieutenant General Omar N. Bradley) and the British 2nd Army (Lieutenant General Sir Miles Dempsey). The Americans were to land on Utah and Omaha beaches, while the British were allocated Gold and Sword and the Canadian forces were to land between them at Juno. To hold the flanks, the US 82nd and 101st Airborne Divisons were to land between Ste Mère Église and Carentan, while the British 6th Airborne Division was to secure the bridges over the Caen Canal and the Orne, as well as the high ground to the east.

D-DAY

The landings were planned for 5 June, but the weather made that impossible. Courageously seizing a short interval of better weather, Eisenhower gave the order for the operation to begin the next day. Soon after midnight the British airborne forces landed close to the bridge over the Caen Canal, abruptly waking the Gondrée family asleep in the café next to it. After a brief fight the canal bridge was

taken, followed by the river bridge next to it. The American parachutists started their drop on the opposite flank within the hour. Both forces were beset with adverse winds, navigational problems and enemy action, and suffered accordingly. But their objectives were achieved before the huge armada of warships, transports, landing craft and amphibious vehicles went into action soon after dawn.

The German troops overlooking Utah Beach were jolted into the alert as dawn broke and the bombardment by the warships began. The landing craft had already been in the water for some two hours and as they approached it became clear that they were being pushed southeastwards by the current. Brigadier General Theodore Roosevelt, a veteran of the previous war, decided that it was more important to get ashore somewhere than to battle the sea in an attempt to stick to the plan. On they went, providentially being swept away from the principal German defence works. The causeways over the marshland had been taken by their airborne buddies and they were able to proceed inland swiftly. Over 23,000 men landed there that day, suffering no more than some 200 casualties.

To the east, on the cliff-top at Pointe du Hoc, a bloody battle was being fought. The American 2nd Ranger Battalion under

ABOVE *At about 08:45 hours on 6 June, still under intermittent enemy fire, heavily laden members of 50th (Northumbrian) Division and British second-wave troops land on Sword Beach.*

MAIN CHARACTERS FEATURED

GERMANY
Field Marshal Karl von
 Rundstedt, Supreme
 Commander West
Field Marshal Erwin Rommel,
 Army Group B (Normandy)

ALLIED
General Dwight D.
 Eisenhower (army, navy and
 air forces)
General Sir Bernard Law
 Montgomery (army assault
 on Normandy)
Lieutenant General Omar N.
 Bradley (1st US Army)
Lieutenant General Sir Miles
 Dempsey) (British 2nd
 Army)
Brigadier General Theodore
 Roosevelt

Brigadier General Norman D.
 Cota (29th Division)
Lieutenant Colonel James E.
 Rudder (American 2nd
 Ranger Battalion)

General Dwight D Eisenhower

The heaviest casualties were sustained on Omaha Beach. The shore is dominated on the west by a great cliff, in which the German gun emplacements can still be seen, peering along the length of the strand. Facing the sea is a line of only slightly less daunting cliffs, topped with defensive entrenchments, through which five gullies (or draws) gave access to the flat land above. The beach was peppered with obstacles that had landmines fastened on top. Then there was the challenge of the sea. First, the decision was taken to launch the landing craft and D-D tanks almost 19km (12 miles) offshore rather than the 11km (7 miles) chosen for the British beaches. Second, the wind was driving the seas from west to east, forcing the incoming vessels off course. Unlike Roosevelt, the commanders tried to regain their planned positions and the D-D tanks, in particular, paid for it. They were not designed to claw their way at an angle across the waves and, of the 32 machines launched, 27 sank. Finally, the Germans were here in force. Intelligence had reported, correctly, that the 716th Coastal Defence Division (made up both of older and of inexperienced men) was here. What they did not know was that the front-line 352nd Infantry Division was here too, on exercise.

As the landing craft lowered their ramps to pour the men of the 1st Infantry Division (the Big Red One) into the water, the Germans opened fire. The 29th Division was sent in next.

To those on the beach the impression was one of absolute and lethal chaos. By noon they were still on the beach, either huddled under the seawall, or wounded, or dead. Three companies of the 2nd Ranger Battalion were off the western end of the beach, waiting for orders to join Colonel Rudder, but no signal came. They went instead for the cliffs overlooking the end of the beach. About half of them made it. While other units were shattered by similar casualties, they proceeded to scale the cliffs and take on the defensive positions one by one.

At 07:30 Brigadier-General Norman D. Cota of the 29th Division came ashore to find the beach jammed with dead and wounded and, with a few notable exceptions, by troops sheltering. It was vital to get off the beach and he moved from group to group ordering, cajoling, cursing. More landing craft were bringing more men all the time; slowly the pressure from seaward and the courage of individuals and small squads propelled men up the gullies and cliffs. By 11:00 the village of Vierville had been taken. As the afternoon drew on, the high ground fell into American hands and by evening the beachhead was secure. The cost had been high. More than 2000 men were killed and at least as many wounded on this beach alone. The 1st and 2nd Divisions were regular soldiers and they found it

ABOVE *American assault troops of the 16th Regimental Combat Team, 1st Division, wounded in the taking of Omaha Beach, wait by the Chalk Cliffs for evacuation to a field hospital.*

Lieutenant Colonel James E. Rudder had been given the task of taking the position and destroying the heavy artillery believed to be there. They came ashore further east than they had planned and then had to scale the cliffs. Their grapnels fell back, dragged down by sodden ropes, and the Germans above rolled grenades down on them. Air and warship fire gave them the cover they needed to clamber up the cliffs at last. They found the guns, not yet mounted, further inland and destroyed them, but now they were counterattacked and driven back to the cliff where friendly fire – their own side's shelling – hit them. The Stars and Stripes was pegged out to identify them from the air and there they held on until relieved two days later. Sixty per cent casualties had been inflicted on the Rangers by then.

The American sector ended at Port-en-Bessin, a fishing port sheltered in a deep inlet in the cliffs that continued to Arromanches, the eventual site of the British Mulberry harbour, and the western end of Gold Beach. Between the two towns, near Longues, was the four-gun battery of Le Chaos. It was put out of action by shells from HMS *Ajax* and then, in the afternoon, it had to be silenced a second time by the French cruiser *Georges Leygues*. It was vital to suppress it because here the seas were so rough that it was decided to run the D-D tanks all the way in on the landing craft. The 'Funnies' earned their keep here, both through the use of their flails, exploding mines to clear paths through the minefields, and by using their guns conventionally to take out enemy positions. Compared to the American experience to the west, the British found they advanced relatively quickly and by evening they were approaching Bayeux, almost 10km (6 miles) inland.

The Canadian landing ground on Juno Beach proved difficult to approach because the storms had resulted in a tide higher than anticipated, concealing the mine-topped 'hedgehog' obstacles, but the D-Ds ran well and supported the troops as they fought their way through the coastal townships. To the western end of Juno the seas precluded the launch of the tanks and the defensive bunkers imposed a heavy cost on the landing force; the tanks were arriving after the infantry and the foot-soldiers suffered as they held on,

'Fire rained down on us, machine-gun, rifle, rockets from the bunkers on top of the cliff. I saw assault boats like ours take direct hits. The boats were zig-zagging to avoid being hit, which fouled up all the plans… The beach was covered with bodies, men with no legs, no arms – God, it was awful.'

Sergeant Harry Bare, 116th Regiment.
From *Bastable: Voices from D-Day*, 'Bloody Omaha'

awaiting armoured support. Nevertheless the Canadians continued to land, pass through the first assault lines and by the end of the day were well inland. A major problem remained to be dealt with on the morrow: 21st Panzer Division had made it as far as the sea at Luc-sur-Mer, between Juno and Sword.

The generous width of Sword Beach had been reduced to a mere strip by the extra-high tide and a great traffic jam built up as a result. On the low ridge inland there were strong bunkers and gun emplacements, each of which had to be overcome. Support fire from the Royal Navy was jeopardized by the death of the liaison officer; the infantry, later supported by tanks, had to take the positions one by one. The plan to strike inland as far as Caen could not be carried out. Lord Lovat's 6th Commando and Commandant Kieffer's 1st French Commando hurried forward and linked with the airborne troops to help consolidate the eastern flank.

By nightfall on 6 June the Allies were firmly established in Normandy, but they had not achieved all their objectives. The British front was cut in two by 21st Panzer and the Americans had a strong foothold inland of Utah Beach, an isolated outpost on the Point du Hoc and a position much smaller than desired at Omaha. On D-Day 75,215 British and Canadian troops and 57,500 Americans landed at a cost of 4300 British and Canadian and 6000 American casualties. They were there, ashore, and nothing the Germans would or could do was going to dislodge them.

VISITING THE D-DAY LANDING GROUNDS

The overall picture can best be understood by seeing the two major museums, the Memorial off the northern ring road around Caen and the Memorial Museum of the Battle of Normandy on the southern ring road around Bayeux.

The major sites all have museums and the visitor could spend days or weeks travelling from west to east calling at Ste-Mère-Église, Ste-Marie-du-Mont (Utah Beach), Vierville-sur-Mer and St-Laurent-sur-Mer (Omaha Beach), Arromanches, Ouistreham and Bénouville (Pegasus Bridge) and still have many more worthwhile exhibitions to see. To visualize the conflict in the terrain, a tour of the most impressive sights includes Pointe du Hoc, Omaha Beach (both for the walk up the path to the heights of the western cliff and for the view of, and from, the American cemetery at Colleville-St-Laurent), Arromanches (the cliffs to the east of the town reveal the remains of the Mulberry harbour) and the drive along the beaches to the east, which brings the visitor to the River Orne and to Pegasus Bridge.

There are at least eight specially marked tourist routes: Normandie Terre-Liberté. Blue and white pillars, bearing the logo of a seagull, indicate the sites that are detailed in the leaflet entitled *D–Day Landings and the Battle of Normandy* available in the principal tourist offices.

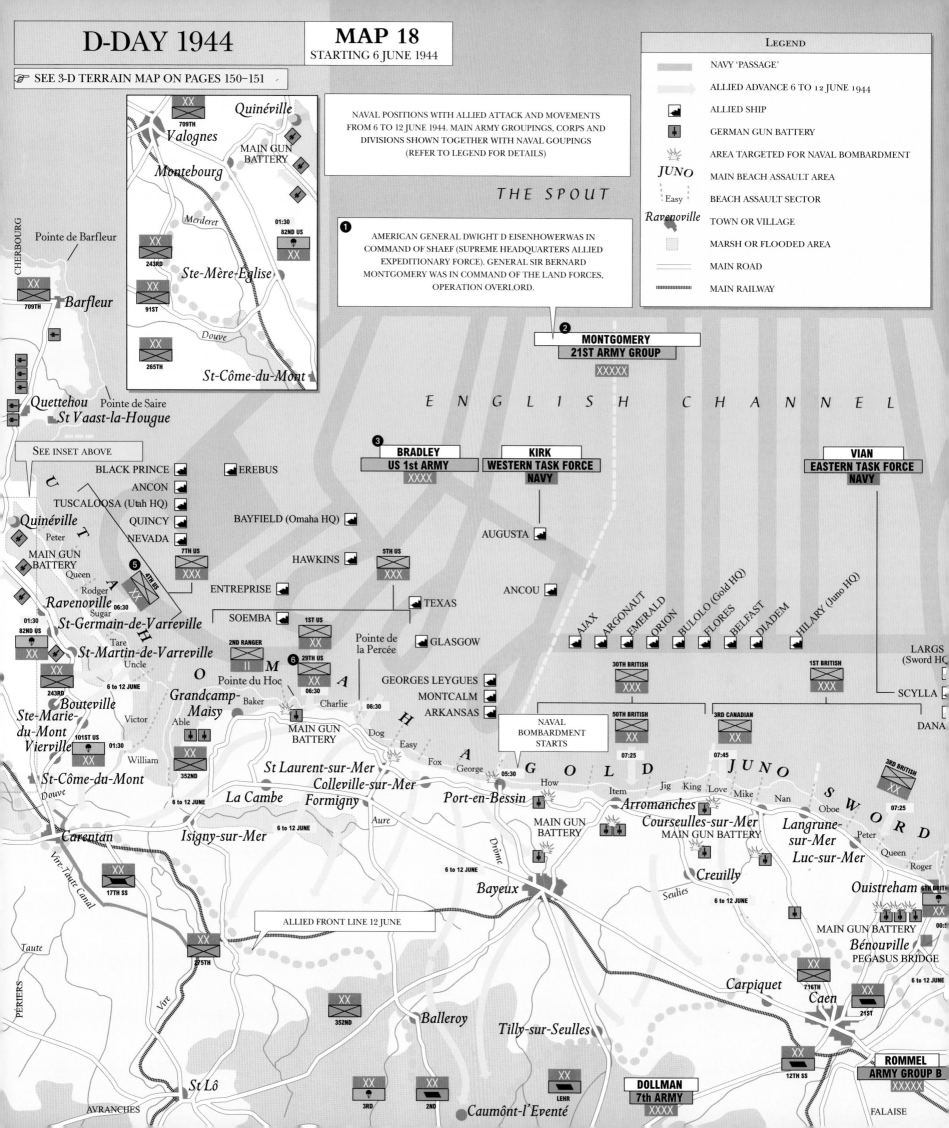

D-DAY 1944

MAP 18
STARTING 6 JUNE 1944

☞ SEE 3-D TERRAIN MAP ON PAGES 150–151

NAVAL POSITIONS WITH ALLIED ATTACK AND MOVEMENTS FROM 6 TO 12 JUNE 1944. MAIN ARMY GROUPINGS, CORPS AND DIVISIONS SHOWN TOGETHER WITH NAVAL GOUPINGS (REFER TO LEGEND FOR DETAILS)

LEGEND
- NAVY 'PASSAGE'
- ALLIED ADVANCE 6 TO 12 JUNE 1944
- ALLIED SHIP
- GERMAN GUN BATTERY
- AREA TARGETED FOR NAVAL BOMBARDMENT
- JUNO — MAIN BEACH ASSAULT AREA
- Easy — BEACH ASSAULT SECTOR
- Ravenoville — TOWN OR VILLAGE
- MARSH OR FLOODED AREA
- MAIN ROAD
- MAIN RAILWAY

① AMERICAN GENERAL DWIGHT D EISENHOWER WAS IN COMMAND OF SHAEF (SUPREME HEADQUARTERS ALLIED EXPEDITIONARY FORCE). GENERAL SIR BERNARD MONTGOMERY WAS IN COMMAND OF THE LAND FORCES, OPERATION OVERLORD.

② MONTGOMERY — 21ST ARMY GROUP — XXXXX

③ BRADLEY — US 1st ARMY — XXXX
KIRK — WESTERN TASK FORCE — NAVY
VIAN — EASTERN TASK FORCE — NAVY

NAVAL BOMBARDMENT STARTS

ALLIED FRONT LINE 12 JUNE

THE SPOUT

ENGLISH CHANNEL

UTAH — OMAHA — GOLD — JUNO — SWORD

DOLLMAN — 7th ARMY — XXXX
ROMMEL — ARMY GROUP B — XXXXX

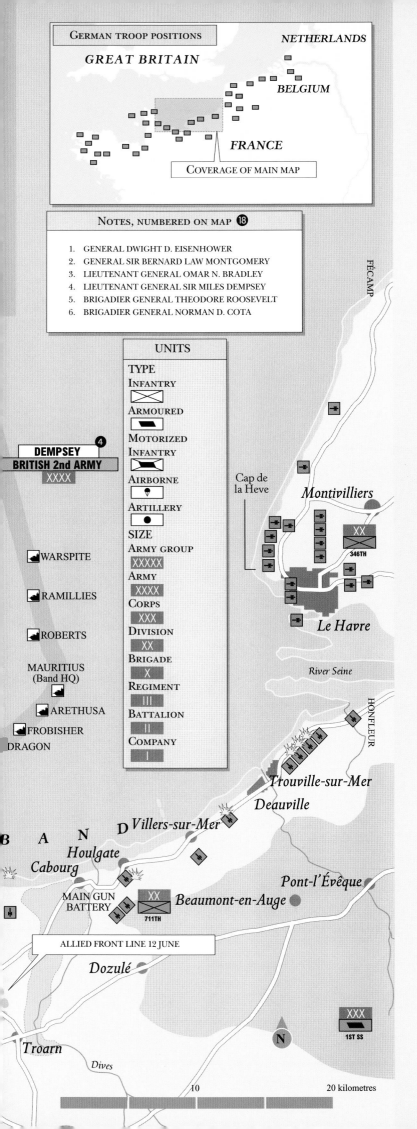

VISITORS' FACT FILE

- Mémorial, Caen. Tel: ++ 33 (0)2-31-06-06-52. www.memorial-caen.fr
- Musée Mémorial de la Bataille de Normandie, Bayeux. Tel: ++ 33 (0)2-31-51-46-90.
- US Airborne Museum, Ste-Mère-Église. Tel: ++33 (0)2-33-41-41-35.
- Musée du Débarquement Utah Beach, Ste-Marie-du-Mont. Tel: ++ 33 (0)2-33-71-53-35.
- Musée D.Day Omaha, Vierville-sur-Mer. Tel: ++ 33 (0)2-31-21-71-80.
- Omaha Mémorial Musée, 6 Juin, St-Laurent-sur-Mer. Tel: ++33 (0)2-31-21-97-44.
- Musée du Débarquement, Arromanches. Tel: ++ 33 (0)2-31-22-34-31. www.normandy1944.com
- Arromanches 360 (cinema). Tel: ++ 33 (0)2-31-22-30-30. www.arromanches360.com
- Musée du Mur de l'Atlantique, Ouistreham. Tel: ++ 33 (0)2-31-97-28-69.
- Musée du No 4 Commando, Ouistreham. Tel: ++ 33 (0)2-31-96-63-10.
- Mémorial Pegasus, Museum of the British Airborne Troops, Ranville-Bénouville. Tel: ++ 33 (0)2-31-78-19-44. www.normandy1944.com

D-DAY TIMELINE

6 December 1943

Eisenhower appointed Supreme Commander, Allied Expeditionary Force, for the invasion of France.

15 May 1944

Final planning conference for Operation Overlord. 5 June fixed for the invasion to start.

4 June

04:15 Landings delayed for 24 hours due to bad weather.

21:45 Eisenhower decides Overlord will begin on 6 June.

5 June

09:00 First landing craft leave Portsmouth area for France.

6 June

00:30 Parachute and glider troops, British 6th Airborne Division, land on eastern flank. Pegasus Bridge taken.

01:30 US 101st Airborne and 82nd Airborne divisions land to secure western flank.

03:00 Allied heavy and medium bombers attack German defences and naval bombardment begins.

04:30 US 82nd Airborne take Sainte-Mère-Église.

06:15 Second wave of air attacks.

06:30 American landings begin. Minimal resistance at Utah Beach.

07:25 British landings begin. Sword Beach proceeds according to plan.

07:50 Canadians land on Juno Beach, twenty minutes late.

10:00 All Juno Beach objectives taken.

11:00 American troops begin to move off Omaha Beach.

11:19 All Gold Beach objectives taken.

15:00 21st Panzer Division held by British 3rd Division, but elements reach Luc-sur-Mer; held by Canadians.

20:00 German 'Hillman' strongpoint, inland of Sword, finally taken.

7 June

00:00 Omaha bridgehead secured.

D-DAY 1944

OMAHA BEACH

Of all the invasion beaches selected for Operation Overlord, Omaha presented the greatest challenges for Allied troops. It was exposed to bad weather and cross-Channel swells, had a very wide tidal range and was backed by steep bluffs that made exit difficult. However, as the only significant stretch of beach between the British and Canadian beaches (Gold, Juno and Sword) and the wide expanse of Utah Beach further to the west, it had to be taken. The task was entrusted to General Clarence R. Huebner's 1st Infantry Division, the famed 'Big Red One', together with the 116th Regimental Combat Team of the 29th Division and two battalions of elite Army Rangers. The Rangers were given the task of destroying the German batteries at Pointe du Hoc, situated a few kilometres west of the main landing area. The illustration on these pages shows the western portion of Omaha beach at approximately 05:00 on 6 June.

The red lines indicate the positions reached by the middle of the day.

① Sea wall: Omaha beach was bounded by a sea wall about 3.5m (12ft) high. In places this had been damaged by bombardment from Allied naval ships offshore. Immediately below the sea wall was a strip of shingle beach. At 07:00, the tide was up to the shingle strip, creating a dangerously narrow lodgement on the exposed beach.

② Beach exits: Key objectives were the four narrow gullies leading up from the beach to the inland plateau. These are sometimes referred to as 'draws'. Control of the beach exits would allow a rapid build-up of Allied tanks and infantry once the beach was secured. American troops had begun to gain control of the exits by around 09:00.

③ Beach obstacles: all the landing beaches were studded with obstacles erected by the Germans to prevent amphibious landings. The obstacles consisted of heavy iron frames fitted with rollers, logs driven into the sand at an angle and log ramps. Most of these obstacles were mined, and were designed to wreck incoming craft. Naval engineers were assigned to disarm the mines, but many landing craft were lost as a result of hitting mined beach obstacles.

④ Landing craft: Specially designed for beach landings, the landing craft used on D-Day could carry up to 30 or 40 combat troops. Soldiers boarded the landing craft from large transport ships as much as 20km (12 miles) offshore. Due to bad weather earlier in the week, the journey to the beach was rough, and many suffered from seasickness. The heavily laden soldiers had to disembark into water that was often up to their shoulders. The size of landing craft in the illustration has been exaggerated.

⑤ Cliffs: at either end of Omaha's roughly 7km (4-mile) length were substantial cliffs, although the entire beach was characterized by substantial bluffs and height of land.

⑥ German defensive positions; trenches and firing positions were sited along the bluffs and high ground, with the strongest positions protecting the beach exits. The Germans were well dug in on the high ground and had built gun emplacements in the cliffs themselves, enfilading the beach.

⑦ Earth-and-hedge field boundaries of the bocage country (characterized by small fields, high hedgerows and sunken lanes).

⑧ Sectors: the beach was divided into eight sectors of 0.5km–1km (500–1000 yards) wide, with particular units assigned to land in each sector. Nevertheless, the landing was marked by great congestion on the beach, a problem compounded by the exceptionally high tide and strong German resistance. Sectors named as follows: (a) Fox Red; (b) Fox Green; (c) Easy Red; (d) Easy Green; (e) Dog Red; (f) Dog White; (g) Dog Green; (h) Charlie.

⑨ Vierville-sur-Mer: Troops from the 116th Regimental Combat Team, together with Army Rangers, reached the town around noon. However, by nightfall the area held by the Americans was still dangerously narrow and exposed to German counterattack.

⑩ Les Moulins

⑪ Position at noon

⑫ St Laurent-sur-Mer

⑬ Colleville-sur-Mer

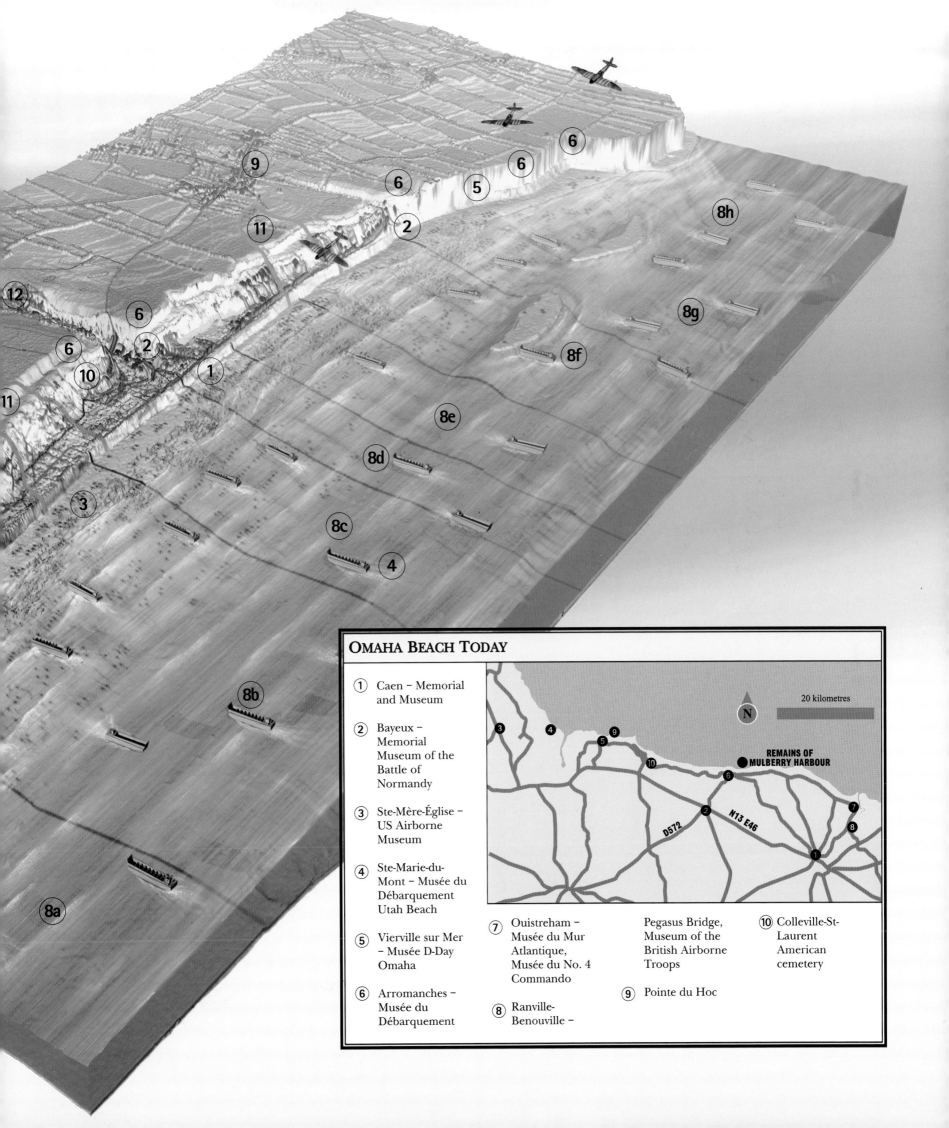

OMAHA BEACH TODAY

1. Caen – Memorial and Museum
2. Bayeux – Memorial Museum of the Battle of Normandy
3. Ste-Mère-Église – US Airborne Museum
4. Ste-Marie-du-Mont – Musée du Débarquement Utah Beach
5. Vierville sur Mer – Musée D-Day Omaha
6. Arromanches – Musée du Débarquement
7. Ouistreham – Musée du Mur Atlantique, Musée du No. 4 Commando
8. Ranville-Benouville –
   Pegasus Bridge, Museum of the British Airborne Troops
9. Pointe du Hoc
10. Colleville-St-Laurent American cemetery

REMAINS OF MULBERRY HARBOUR

20 kilometres

N

D572   N13 E46

ARNHEM 1944

By Martin Marix Evans

Paris was liberated on 25 August 1944 and on 1 September General Dwight D. Eisenhower's Supreme Headquarters Allied Expeditionary Forces (SHAEF) became the pinnacle of the three-group force. Reporting to him were Field Marshal Sir Bernard Law Montgomery (21st Army Group), Lieutenant General Omar N. Bradley (12th Army Group), both of whom had taken part in the Normandy invasion, and Lieutenant General Jacob Devers (6th Army Group) who had commanded the invasion of southern France on 15 August 1944. The Canadian 1st Army was fighting its way up the coast and took Antwerp on 4 September. However, that port was of no use to the Allies until the Germans had been cleared from the shores of the Scheldt Estuary. Supplies, therefore, were still being shipped onto the Normandy beaches and hauled across France and Belgium. Montgomery and Bradley vied for the

greater share of them, the former to push through the Netherlands, the latter to thrust east into Germany. The Germans had built a defensive line called the West Wall which petered out in the north to the east of Nijmegen, south of the Rhine and west of the Reichswald forest. Bradley proposed to smash through it, Montgomery to out-flank it. On 10 September Eisenhower approved Montgomery's strategy.

Operation Market Garden, as the undertaking was named, had two elements: the first was airborne, the second a land-based strike. XXX Corps, under Lieutenant General Brian Horrocks, would be used for Garden, the strike north from the Belgian border into the Netherlands as far as the IJsselmeer. It comprised the Guards Armoured Division and the 43rd and 50th Infantry Divisions and would be strongly supported from the air. XII and VIII Corps would be following up on the flanks.

Market was to be undertaken by 1st Airborne Corps of Lieutenant General Lewis H. Brereton's First Allied Airborne Army under the command of the British Lieutenant General F.A.M. 'Boy' Browning. The three divisions that made up his command were to secure the river and canal crossings and to guard against flank attacks by landings in the regions of Eindhoven, Nijmegen and Arnhem to make Horrocks' advance possible. Thus the vulnerable German front between the Rhine and the IJsselmeer would be

ABOVE *The bridge 'too far' immediately after the battle of Arnhem. The Germans have cleared the wreckage of the 9th Panzer's reconnaissance battalion to leave the highway passable. The blackened ruin of the defensive tower stands on the right of the bridge's approach ramp. Further to the right one of the houses occupied by the British stands roofless, one of many so damaged that they were demolished to leave the open space seen by visitors today.*

exposed to a shattering and terminal blow by 21st Army Group's 52nd (Lowland) Division. It was a daring plan designed to end the war in 1944.

1st Airborne Corps was made up of one British and two American divisions. 101st US Airborne was commanded by Major General Maxwell Taylor. They were tasked with securing the bridges over the Wilhelmina and Willems canals and the rivers Aa and Dommel after landing north of Eindhoven. 82nd US Airborne under Brigadier General James M. Gavin was to land south of Nijmegen between Grave and Groesbeek to take the crossings of the Maas and Waal rivers and the canal joining them as well as to screen the advance from a counterattack from the Reichswald. Both American formations had fought in Normandy. The British 1st Airborne under Major General R. E. Urquhart was to land north of the Rhine and west of Arnhem and then move swiftly to secure the road and railway bridges in the town.

The distance from the start-point of XXX Corps on the Meuse–Escaut Canal near Lommel to Arnhem is some 100km (60 miles). The land advance was planned to get to Eindhoven on the first day, Nijmegen on the second and Arnhem on the third. Operation Market Garden was to begin on 17 September. There was just one week to plan and organize it and put it into execution.

THE BATTLE FOR ARNHEM

The problems facing British 1st Airborne were many. Outstanding among them was that the terrain south of the Rhine was unsuitable for landings: it was polder (fenland) cut through with ditches for drainage and with raised roads. Anti-aircraft guns north of Arnhem were another danger, as were the woodlands on the higher ground north of the Rhine. Only to the west-northwest was there open space for parachutists and gliders. Further, there was a lack of air transport: the Corps would have to be flown in over three days. As for the enemy, 1 Parachute Brigade's intelligence summary of 13 September said, 'There is no direct evidence on which to base an estimate ...' That it was a training area for German troops was known, and there were reports of the presence of the 9th and 10th Panzer Divisions refitting nearby, but these were either ignored or discounted.

The morning fog of 17 September cleared by 09:00 and the first lift of 359 gliders took off at 09:45. At 12:40 the pathfinders, 21st Independent Parachute Company, dropped to mark out Landing Zone S (LZ-S) northwest of Wolfheze, and Drop Zone X (DZ-X) and LZ-Z to the southwest. At 13:00 the gliders, flown by the oft-forgotten men of the Glider Pilot Regiment, began to land, and an hour later paratroops were dropped. 1st Airlanding Brigade, under Brigadier P. H. W. Hicks, landed on LZ-S and was responsible for defending the landing and drop zones in anticipation of the later airlifts. 1st Parachute Brigade under Brigadier G. W. Lathbury

---

MAIN CHARACTERS FEATURED

GERMAN
Field Marshal Walter Model
General Wilhelm Bittrich
(II SS Panzer Korps)
General Friederich Kussin
Sturmbannführer Ludwig
Spindler (artillery
commander)
Sturmbannführer Krafft

ALLIED
General Dwight
D. Eisenhower (Supreme
Headquarters Allied
Expeditionary Forces –
SHAEF)
Field Marshal Sir Bernard Law
Montgomery (21st Army
Group)
Lieutenant General Omar N.
Bradley (12th Army Group)
Lieutenant General Jacob
Devers (6th Army Group)

Lieutenant General Brian
Horrocks (XXX Corps)
Lieutenant General Lewis
H. Brereton (First Allied
Airborne Army)
Lieutenant General F.A.M.
'Boy' Browning
(1st Airborne Corps)
Major General Maxwell
Taylor (101st US Airborne)
Brigadier General James M.
Gavin (82nd US Airborne)
Major General R. E. Urquhart
(British 1st Airborne)
Brigadier P. H. W. Hicks
(1st Airlanding Brigade)
Brigadier G. W. Lathbury
(1st Parachute Brigade)
Lieutenant Colonel John Frost
(2nd Battalion)
Major Freddie Gough (Recce
Squadron, 1st Parachute
Brigade)

Field Marshal Walter Model | *Field Marshal Sir Bernard Law Montgomery*

ABOVE *Men of 1st Battalion, the Border Regiment, man a 3-inch mortar in defence of the enclave between the Hartenstein Hotel and the river in Oosterbeek, where the British made their last stand. From 21 September they were under fire from Kampfgruppe Von Tettau on high ground to the west.*

touch with the action became unavailable as they dashed about by jeep visiting their units. Gough, for example, was sent for by Urquhart later that afternoon and, having pulled back from the encounter with 16th SS, discovered Urquhart was absent from the Hartenstein and chased after him.

Frost's men, setting off at 15:00, were held up for a while – not by the enemy, but by the welcome accorded them by the Dutch. The railway bridge was blown before they could get to it and the pontoon bridge between the two permanent structures was partially dismantled, so the southern bank of the river was denied to them. In spite of fire from the higher ground of Den Brink, 2nd Battalion pushed on in the growing darkness to the road bridge and secured the northern approach ramp and surrounding houses. They were joined by Gough's Squadron, which had missed Urquhart, and by part of the headquarters group of 1st Parachute Brigade. A defensive tower was set ablaze after 22:00 and a number of German trucks caught fire. As 18 September dawned some 740 men held the bridge. They destroyed 9th SS Panzer's Reconnaissance Battalion when it tried to come over from the south and repelled a tank attack from the east later in the day.

landed on DZ-X, while LZ-Z was the destination of General Urquhart and his staff, 1st Airborne Reconnaissance Squadron and various divisional troops, artillery and medical units. They were virtually unopposed and quickly assembled in good order, but unaware of the presence of a German battalion training in the area just to their east.

As 1st Parachute Brigade prepared to move off, Major Freddie Gough's Recce Squadron, attached to the 1st, was ordered to hurry along the northern side of the railway and head for the road bridge. They were stopped short east of Wolfheze (where the autobahn is today), where the training battalion had been hastily deployed by Sturmbannführer Krafft. The 3rd Battalion took Tiger route in the centre, heading along the Utrechtseweg towards Oosterbeek. On the left, 1st Battalion, on Leopard, moved towards the railway. Lieutenant Colonel John Frost's 2nd Battalion on the right set off by Lion to cross the higher, wooded ground of Westerbouwing before taking the riverside route. Leopard was blocked by Krafft's 16th SS Battalion and Tiger was partially covered by that unit as well. 1st Para were stopped and 3rd were delayed, only reaching the Hartenstein Hotel in Oosterbeek that evening. They had been engaged in a skirmish on the way, during which General Friederich Kussin was killed. The Hartenstein Hotel became headquarters. The British were severely hampered by the failure of their radio communications. Commanders attempting to remain in

GERMAN REACTION

The German reaction to the landings was swift. Field Marshal Walter Model, by chance, was in Oosterbeek on 17 September as was II SS Panzer Korps under General Wilhelm Bittrich. Model ordered Bittrich to send 10th SS Panzer to block a crossing at Nijmegen and use the elements of 9th Panzer that were there to deal with the British while the rest were recalled from Germany. The division's artillery commander, Sturmbannfürer Ludwig Spindler, was given the task of frustrating any British attempt to reinforce the troops at the road bridge, and he set up blocking lines running north to south just to the west of Arnhem and in the town, about 1000m west of the bridge. Against these lines the British failed.

On the afternoon of 18 September General Urquhart was advancing with 3rd Battalion when he, Lathbury and two staff officers were forced to take cover in houses near St Elisabeth's Hospital. Twelve hours passed before they could get back to HQ in Oosterbeek. Meanwhile Brigadier Hicks assumed command and sent the 2nd South Staffordshires into Arnhem together with the 11th Battalion of the newly landed 4th Parachute Brigade. The next day was the day XXX Corps, driving up from Belgium, had been due to reach them. While Frost held the bridge under ever-increasing pressure, no significant progress was made either north or south of the railway against 9th Panzer and the other German units. Urquhart was obliged to pull his men back towards Oosterbeek. Poor weather prevented effective air supply or reinforcement by the Polish Parachute Brigade. On 20 September Frost was wounded and had to hand over command at the bridge to Gough. It was clear to all that relief would not now reach them and the last of them surrendered the next morning.

Urquhart's only option now was to defend the Oosterbeek enclave until XXX Corps arrived from the south. The German attacks were intense; relieved only by a truce arranged to evacuate British wounded from the Schoonoord and the Vreewijk hotels on Utrechtseweg. British artillery close to the Rhine near the church held back German armour at a high cost.

To the south the 82nd US Airborne's 504th Regiment took the bridge at Nijmegen, but it was dusk before four tanks of the Grenadier Guards came across. They halted as ordered to hold the bridge. On 21 September the Irish Guards attempted to advance towards Arnhem, but were held all day by 10th Panzer's artillery. However, the guns of XXX corps, near Nijmegen, were now able to shell German positions around Oosterbeek. In spite of that support the 1st Border Regiment were driven off the hill at Westerbouwing by an ad hoc German formation, Kampfgruppe von Tettau, which attacked from the west. The arrival of the Poles at Driel, south of the Rhine, rendered little assistance since they lacked the means to cross the river in significant numbers.

Away to the south at Veghel on 22 September, 101st US Airborne had to fight hard to prevent the slender line from Belgium being cut by German attacks. While the British airborne troops stubbornly held out, and attempts were made to reinforce them, it became clear that survivors had to be evacuated. Orders to that effect reached Urquhart in the early hours of 25 September, just as the gallant attempt of the 4th Dorsets to assist him was failing. After dark that day, as XXX Corps's artillery pounded the enemy, and in steady rain, small groups of men streamed down to the riverside and were ferried away. A rearguard of 300 men remained with the wounded. Of some 11,000 men who had landed north of the river, 2120 were evacuated. The 1st British Airborne Division lost, north and south of the river, 1485 killed from a strength of 11,920 men (including the Polish Brigade which landed south of the Rhine). The territory gained, and retained, stretched almost 100km (60 miles) from Belgium, but heartbreakingly short of Arnhem. It become the start-point for the successful assault on Germany the following year.

VISITING 1ST AIRBORNE'S BATTLEGROUND

The best place to begin a visit is the Airborne Museum Hartenstein, set up in Urquhart's former headquarters in the Hartenstein Hotel, Oosterbeek. It contains a comprehensive collection of authentic equipment and offers the full story in maps, pictures and videos. A guidebook can be purchased to make a tour by car.

An excellent viewpoint can be enjoyed from the terrace of the Westerbouwing restaurant over the Oosterbeek enclave and the Driel ferry. It also gives a distant view of the road and railway bridges at Arnhem. The old church stands a short distance to the east.

In Arnhem itself the John Frost Bridge, as it is now called, is a rebuilt structure, the

ABOVE *Two hotels on the Utrechtseweg on the eastern side of the Oosterbeek perimeter were used as field dressing stations for the treatment of the wounded. By 20 September they were in the midst of the field of battle. Colonel G. M. Warrack negotiated a truce with General Bittrich and, while fighting was suspended, the walking and immobilized wounded passed into German care and captivity.*

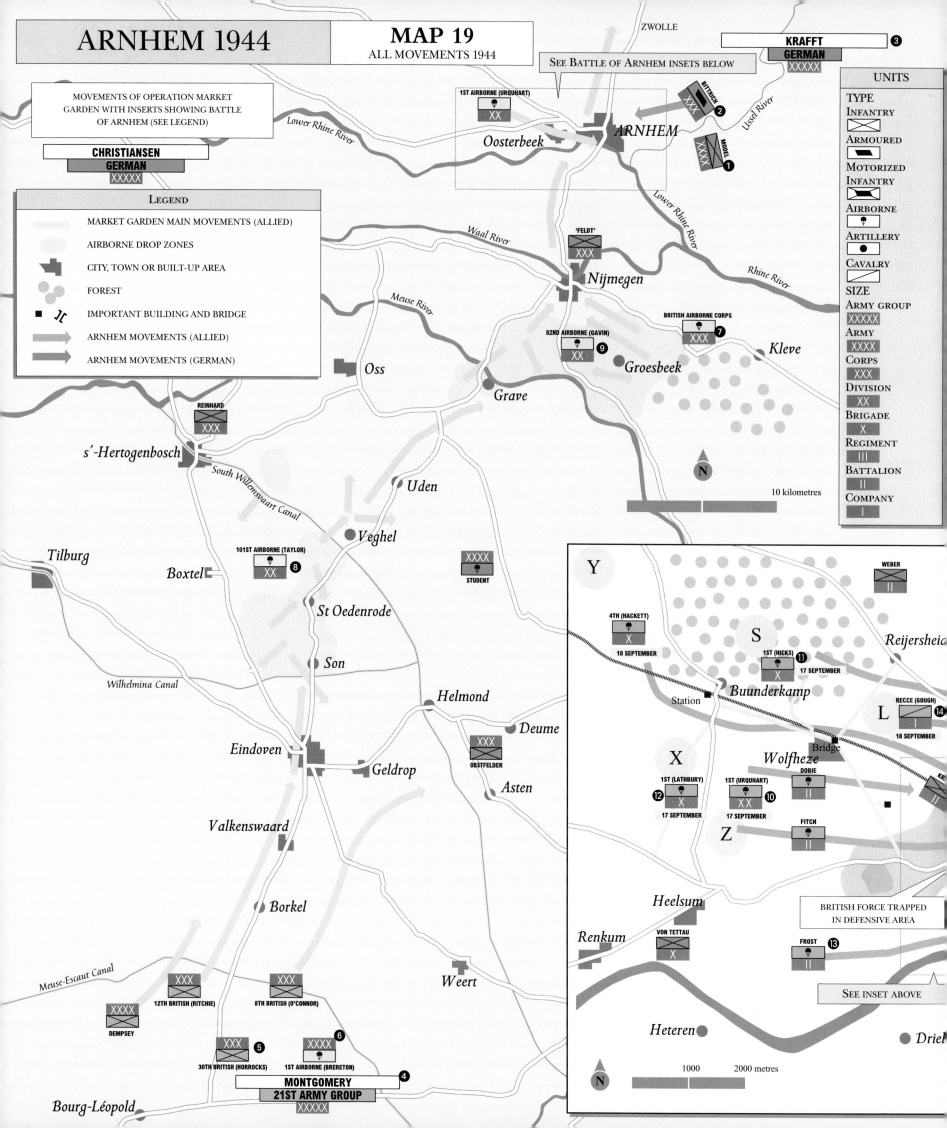

ARNHEM 1944

MAP 19
ALL MOVEMENTS 1944

SEE BATTLE OF ARNHEM INSETS BELOW

ZWOLLE

KRAFFT
GERMAN
XXXX ❸

BITTRICH
XXX ❷

1ST AIRBORNE (URQUHART)
XX

ARNHEM

MODEL
XXXX ❶

IJssel River

MOVEMENTS OF OPERATION MARKET
GARDEN WITH INSERTS SHOWING BATTLE
OF ARNHEM (SEE LEGEND)

Oosterbeek

Lower Rhine River

Lower Rhine River

CHRISTIANSEN
GERMAN
XXXX

Rhine River

Waal River

'FELDT'
XXX

LEGEND

	MARKET GARDEN MAIN MOVEMENTS (ALLIED)
	AIRBORNE DROP ZONES
	CITY, TOWN OR BUILT-UP AREA
	FOREST
◼ ⊓	IMPORTANT BUILDING AND BRIDGE
→	ARNHEM MOVEMENTS (ALLIED)
→	ARNHEM MOVEMENTS (GERMAN)

Nijmegen

Meuse River

BRITISH AIRBORNE CORPS
XXX ❼

82ND AIRBORNE (GAVIN)
XX ❾

Kleve

Oss

Groesbeek

Grave

UNITS

TYPE

INFANTRY	
ARMOURED	
MOTORIZED INFANTRY	
AIRBORNE	
ARTILLERY	
CAVALRY	

SIZE

ARMY GROUP	XXXX
ARMY	XXXX
CORPS	XXX
DIVISION	XX
BRIGADE	X
REGIMENT	
BATTALION	II
COMPANY	I

N

10 kilometres

Tilburg

REINHARD
XXX

s'-Hertogenbosch

South Willemsvaart Canal

Uden

Boxtel

101ST AIRBORNE (TAYLOR)
XX ❽

Veghel

STUDENT
XXXX

St Oedenrode

Son

Wilhelmina Canal

Helmond

Deurne

Eindoven

Geldrop

Asten

OBSTFELDER
XXX

Valkenswaard

Borkel

Heteren

Driel

Renkum

Heelsum

VON TETTAU
X

FROST ❸
II

**BRITISH FORCE TRAPPED
IN DEFENSIVE AREA**

SEE INSET ABOVE

Y

4TH (HACKETT)
X
18 SEPTEMBER

WEBER
II

S

Reijersheid

1ST (HICKS) ❶
X
17 SEPTEMBER

Station

Buunderkamp

L

RECCE (GOUGH) ❹
18 SEPTEMBER

X

1ST (LATHBURY) ❷
X
17 SEPTEMBER

1ST (URQUHART) ❿
XX
17 SEPTEMBER

DOBIE
II

Wolfheze

Bridge

KR

Z

FITCH
II

Meuse-Escaut Canal

12TH BRITISH (RITCHIE)
XXX

8TH BRITISH (O'CONNOR)
XXX

Weert

DEMPSEY
XXXX

30TH BRITISH (HORROCKS)
XXX ❺

1ST AIRBORNE (BRERETON)
XXX ❻

Bourg-Léopold

MONTGOMERY
21ST ARMY GROUP ❹
XXXX

1000   2000 metres

N

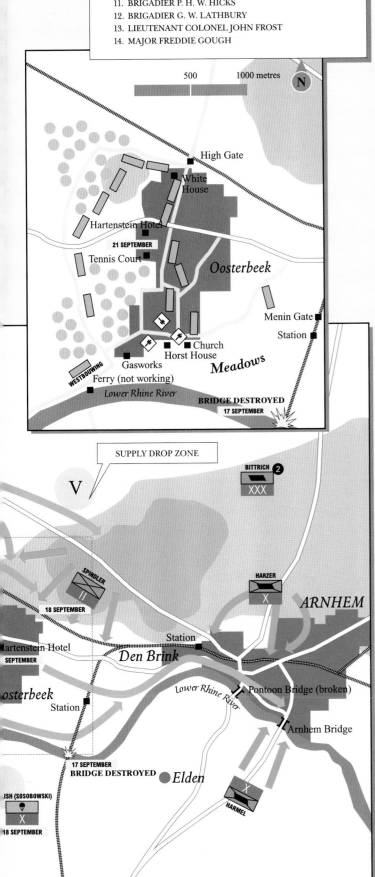

NOTES, NUMBERED ON MAP ⑲

GERMAN
1. FIELD MARSHAL WALTER MODEL
2. GENERAL WILHELM BITTRICH
3. STURMBANNFÜHRER KRAFFT

ALLIED
4. FIELD MARSHAL SIR BERNARD LAW MONTGOMERY
5. LIEUTENANT GENERAL BRIAN HORROCKS
6. LIEUTENANT GENERAL LEWIS H. BRERETON
7. LIEUTENANT GENERAL F.A.M. 'BOY' BROWNING
8. MAJOR GENERAL MAXWELL TAYLOR
9. BRIGADIER GENERAL JAMES M. GAVIN
10. MAJOR GENERAL R. E. URQUHART
11. BRIGADIER P. H. W. HICKS
12. BRIGADIER G. W. LATHBURY
13. LIEUTENANT COLONEL JOHN FROST
14. MAJOR FREDDIE GOUGH

one defended by Frost having been blown up by the Germans. An appreciation of the terrain can be had from the Eusebius Tower, Kerkplein. It is well worth visiting the environs of St Elisabeth hospital and the municipal museum, where the Germans stopped the British relieving force.

Further afield, a visit to the Nijmegen road bridge and, west of the bridge on the north bank of the river, the memorial to the Americans who took the crossing is informative and moving. Their gallantry can be seen as truly remarkable. Southeast of the town at Groesbeek, in the landing area of 82nd US Airborne, is another museum worth visiting and the energetic visitor can follow the action all the way through Eindhoven to the Belgian border.

VISITORS' FACT FILE

• Airborne Museum Hartenstein, Utrechtseweg, Oosterbeek.
  Tel: ++ 31 (0)26 333 77 10. www.airbornemuseum.com
• Liberation Museum, Wylerbaan, Groesbeek. Tel: ++ 31 (0)24 397 44 04.

ARNHEM TIMELINE

13 September

1 Parachute Brigade's intelligence summary states 'There is no direct evidence on which to base an estimate ...' (of enemy strength).

17 September

	Start of Operation Market Garden.
09:00	Morning fog clears.
09:45	The first lift of 359 gliders take off.
12:40	The pathfinders, 21st Independent Parachute Company, are dropped to mark out LZ-S northwest of Wolfheze, DZ-X and LZ-Z to the southwest.
13:00	The gliders began to land.
14:00	Paratroops are dropped; British radio failure.
15:00	Frost's men set off.
18:30	Railway bridge is blown before they get to it and the pontoon bridge between the two permanent structures is partially dismantled, denying them the southern bank of the river.
19:30	2nd Battalion secures the northern approach ramp of the road bridge, and surrounding houses. They are joined by Gough's Squadron and part of the headquarters group of 1st Parachute Brigade.
22:00	Defensive tower on the road bridge is set ablaze.

18 September

Dawn	Some 740 men hold the bridge. They destroy 9th SS Panzer's Reconnaissance Battalion and repel a tank attack from the east later in the day.

20 September

Frost is wounded and hands over command at the bridge to Gough; last defenders surrender the next morning.

21 September

Irish Guards attempt to advance towards Arnhem.

25 September

Orders given to evacuate survivors.

BATTLE OF THE BULGE 1944

By Jason Musteen

Following the D-Day landings at Normandy in June 1944, the Western Allies under Dwight Eisenhower advanced through France and Italy while Soviet troops toppled Nazi regimes in Eastern Europe. Although the Allies suffered a setback in Holland in September and absorbed horrendous casualties in the Hürtgen Forest in November, Adolf Hitler's 'thousand-year Reich' nevertheless appeared on the brink of collapse by the winter of 1944. Victory was all but secure; the Allies needed only to continue their drive to Berlin. However, the enemy always gets a vote and Hitler was planning an offensive of his own. He envisioned a surprise attack through the lightly defended Ardennes Forest of Luxembourg and Belgium in a narrow penetration that would cut through the Allied lines and separate Omar Bradley's American armies from Bernard Montgomery's British and Canadian armies. Hitler gambled that if he could reach the western edge of the Ardennes at the River Meuse, taking advantage of captured fuel along the way, his forces would be free to advance unimpeded to the sea. The goal was the port of Antwerp, where vast amounts of Allied supplies entered the

continent. Hitler reckoned such a manoeuvre could deny resources to the Allied armies and trap them on the continent, much as his attack in 1940 had done, and rupture what he considered a weak Anglo-American alliance.

However, the strategic situation in 1944 was nothing at all like it had been in 1940. Across the entire Western front, Hitler was facing veteran American, British and Canadian armies who had fought their way onto the continent. While Hitler's veterans remained in the lines, they were beaten. He had several new divisions in the west, but many of these were Volksgrenadier infantry divisions composed of young boys and old men. The eastern front, non-existent in 1940, also continued to consume the German army at a rate faster than it could be replenished as casualties increased daily. Moreover, British and American pilots owned the skies over Europe, and the Soviet army owned the oilfields of Romania, making Blitzkrieg impossible in 1944. The Luftwaffe was not even a shell of its former self; and to negate Allied air superiority, Hitler planned to launch his attack during the winter snows and fog of December 1944.

ABOVE *German infantry advance past burning American vehicles in Poteau, Belgium, during the Battle of the Bulge. The German attack caught the Americans completely by surprise, but fell far short of reaching Hitler's goal at Antwerp.*

RIGHT *Dozens of corpses litter a snowy field, the grim remnants of the Malmedy Massacre of 17 December 1944. SS troops murdered about 80 American prisoners of war near Malmedy, Belgium. The corpses were numbered to keep track of them during the investigation. January 1945 Baugnez, Belgium.*

THE BATTLE

At 05:30 on the morning of 16 December, Hitler began his last great offensive. Under the command of Field Marshal Walter Model, five Panzer divisions and twelve infantry divisions attacked across the West Wall defenses that protected Germany and into the Ardennes Forest. Calling it the 'ghost front', the Americans never expected a winter attack through the almost impassable Ardennes, and subsequently only five divisions were immediately facing the German attack. Those divisions were either composed of fresh recruits or had been sent to the Ardennes to recuperate after suffering devastating losses in the Hürtgen Forest a couple weeks earlier.

Although Hitler was counting on such light American resistance, he also knew that several rivers lay along his route of attack and, without the bridging equipment available to him in 1940, he would need to preserve the bridges intact. Therefore, the task of spearheading the attack fell to Lieutenant Colonel Joachim Peiper and his Kampfgruppe Peiper of the 1st SS Panzer Division, which Model expected to capture key bridges and fuel depots along the route of advance. Pouring through the Losheim Gap, Peiper's heavy Tiger and Panther tanks took advantage of the boundary between the US V and VIII Corps and dashed through relatively light resistance for 40km (25 miles). Most remembered for his execution of American prisoners outside Malmedy on the 17th, Peiper quickly outdistanced his communications and support before a single squad of American engineers, acting on initiative, stopped his advance at the bridge over the Amblève River at Trois Ponts.

Although Peiper's run continues to draw attention, it represented only a small portion of a much larger attack; three German armies stormed into the Ardennes defences on the 16th. Although initially surprised by General Josef 'Sepp' Dietrich's 6th SS Panzer Army, the US 2nd and 99th Infantry Divisions held the northern shoulder of the attack on the Elsenborn Ridge, the highest terrain feature in Belgium. In the south, the 4th Infantry Division held the opposite shoulder against General Erich Brandenberger's 7th Army. However,

MAIN CHARACTERS FEATURED

GERMAN
Field Marshal Walter Model (Army Group B)
General Josef 'Sepp' Dietrich (6th SS Panzer Army)
General Hasso von Manteuffel (5th Panzer Army)
General Erich Brandenberger (7th Army)
Lieutenant Colonel Joachim Peiper (1st SS Panzer Division)

ALLIED
General Dwight D. Eisenhower (Supreme Allied Commander)
General Omar Bradley (12th Army Group)

Lieutenant General Courtney Hodges (1st US Army)
Lieutenant General George S. Patton, Jr (3rd US Army)

Lieutenant General George S. Patton, Jr

in the centre, elements of General Hasso von Manteuffel's 5th Panzer Army overwhelmed parts of the 28th Infantry Division and almost immediately surrounded the 106th Infantry Division on the Schnee Eifel, a high ridge along the German–Belgian border. Two of the 106th's three regiments were completely isolated by the evening of the 17th when Eisenhower decided to release his only strategic reserve, the 82nd and 101st Airborne Divisions, to help stop the growing salient, or bulge, into his lines.

By 19 December, the isolated regiments of the 106th had surrendered en masse and the towns of St Vith and Bastogne were all but surrounded. As the 7th Armored Division tenuously held St Vith, the 101st precipitously arrived in Bastogne to assist the struggling defenders there. Although St Vith fell on 21 December and the Germans quickly succeeded in completely encircling Bastogne, the 101st stubbornly continued to hold its isolated position. When offered the chance to surrender on the 22nd, Brigadier General Anthony McAuliffe of the 101st responded famously with 'Nuts' and the paratroopers fought on.

Although the German advance in the centre had tremendous initial success, the Germans began to stall a week into the attack. After failing to seize the key bridges at Trois Ponts, Peiper had turned

north in search of another route before finally running out of fuel, tanks and time on the 19th at La Gleize, far short of his goal. After a futile attempt to salvage his mission, Peiper and a handful of his survivors abandoned their remaining tanks on the 23rd and withdrew to German lines on foot. About 40km (25 miles) beyond Bastogne, Manteuffel was checked at Celles, his greatest limit of advance, only 4km (2½ miles) short of the elusive Meuse. Hitler's 'supporting fog' also lifted on the 23rd, allowing the Allied air forces to drop crucial ammunition and medical supplies into Bastogne and to attack exposed German columns mired in the muddy, congested roads of the Ardennes. Still surrounded, the 101st repulsed one final German attack on Christmas Day before relief arrived. Eager to join the fight, George Patton, commanding the 3rd US Army to the south of the Ardennes, sped to relieve Bastogne as the weather cleared. Fighting through heavy German obstacles intended to block the way, Patton's 4th Armored Division raced the 250km (155 miles) to Bastogne, finally relieving the beleaguered paratroopers on the 26th.

Despite the surprise it had achieved, Hitler's ill-conceived operation was doomed from the beginning, and even if his generals had managed to reach Antwerp, the dire strategic situation

ABOVE *A massive German King Tiger tank passes soldiers of the 99th Infantry Division captured during the opening days of the Battle of the Bulge. A lack of fuel for these behemoths contributed to the ultimate German defeat.*

would hardly have improved for Germany on the eastern, southern or western fronts. Over the next month, the Americans advanced back over the terrain they had lost, erasing the bulge by 28 January. Hitler's last gamble had failed. Within weeks, the Allies crossed the Rhine into Germany for the final assault towards Berlin. Having spent his forces in the Ardennes, Hitler was unable to stem the tide in the west or to reposition troops in the east. His defences crumbled in the face of the new attacks, and on 7 May, after he had taken his own life, Hitler's Germany surrendered to the Allies.

TOURING THE BATTLEFIELD TODAY

Although towns like Bastogne and St Vith draw the most attention, the now pacific landscape of the Ardennes Forest of Germany, Belgium and Luxembourg are filled with sites of great interest to the traveller and historian. The Belgians and Luxembourgeois who live on the battlefields today

ABOVE *American soldiers on a rooftop in Beffe, Belgium, 1 January 1945. Much of the fighting took place in small villages such as this one.*

have not forgotten the war or Hitler's final attack, and seemingly every town in 'the bulge' has a monument to the defenders. These numerous battlefields can be easily toured today, especially since the European Union's borders are now completely open. There are many options available for the tourist who wants to see only key locations or for the enthusiast who wants to follow the entire campaign in detail.

For the full tour, a journey of at least four days is ideal, but it can take longer or shorter, depending on the amount of time spent on the battlefields and in museums. For a more focused, yet still detailed tour, it is possible to visit only the sites of the northern or southern shoulders at the locations of the earliest American resistance, to follow Kampfgruppe Peiper, or the route of the greatest German penetration through the Ardennes. Tours are available through the Belgian or Luxembourg tourist offices, or self-guided tours are possible by using a guide book such as *A Tour of the Bulge Battlefield*, by William Cavanaugh.

For the truncated tour, there are many battle sites and fine museums in several villages that take only a few hours to visit. As with any battlefield, some places should not be missed, including the positions of the 106th Infantry Division on the Schnee Eifel, the Elsenborn Ridge, Bastogne, St Vith and the Malmedy massacre site in Baugnez.

VISITORS' FACT FILE

- Association of Museums of the Battle of the Bulge: Association des Musées de la Bataille des Ardennes, 53 Route de Wiltz, B-6600 Bastogne. Tel 32 (0) 61 21 85 64. www.ambu.lu.
- Luxembourg Tourist Office: Luxembourg National Tourist Office, PO Box 1001, L-1010 Luxembourg. Tel 42 82 82 10. www.ont.lu.
- Diekirch–Musée National d'Histoire Militaire Diekirch, 10 Bamertal, L-9209 Diekirch. Tel (352) 80 89 08. ww.nat-military-museum.lu.
- Ettelbruck–General Patton Memorial Museum, 5 Rue Dr. Klein, L-9054 Ettelbruck. Tel (352) 81 03 22. www.luxembourg.co.uk/nmmh/patton.
- Wiltz–Musée de la Bataille des Ardennes, Château de Wiltz, L-9516 Wiltz. Tel (352) 26 95 00 32.
- Clervaux–Musée de la Bataille des Ardennes, Château de Clervaux, L-9712, Clervaux. Tel (352) 92 00 72.
- Perlé–385th Bomb Group Museum, Rue de l'Eglise, L-8826 Perlé. Tel (352) 23 64 94 65. www.385bg.com.
- Belgian Tourist Office: Office de Promotion du Tourisme Wallonie-Bruxelles, Rue Marché aux Herbes 63, B-1000 Bruxelles. Tel 00 32 (0) 2/504 03 90. www.belgium-tourism.net. www.wallonia-tourism.be.
- La Gleize–Historical Museum December 1944, 7 Rue de L'Eglise, B-4987 La Gleize. Tel 32 (0) 80 78 51 91. www.december44.com.

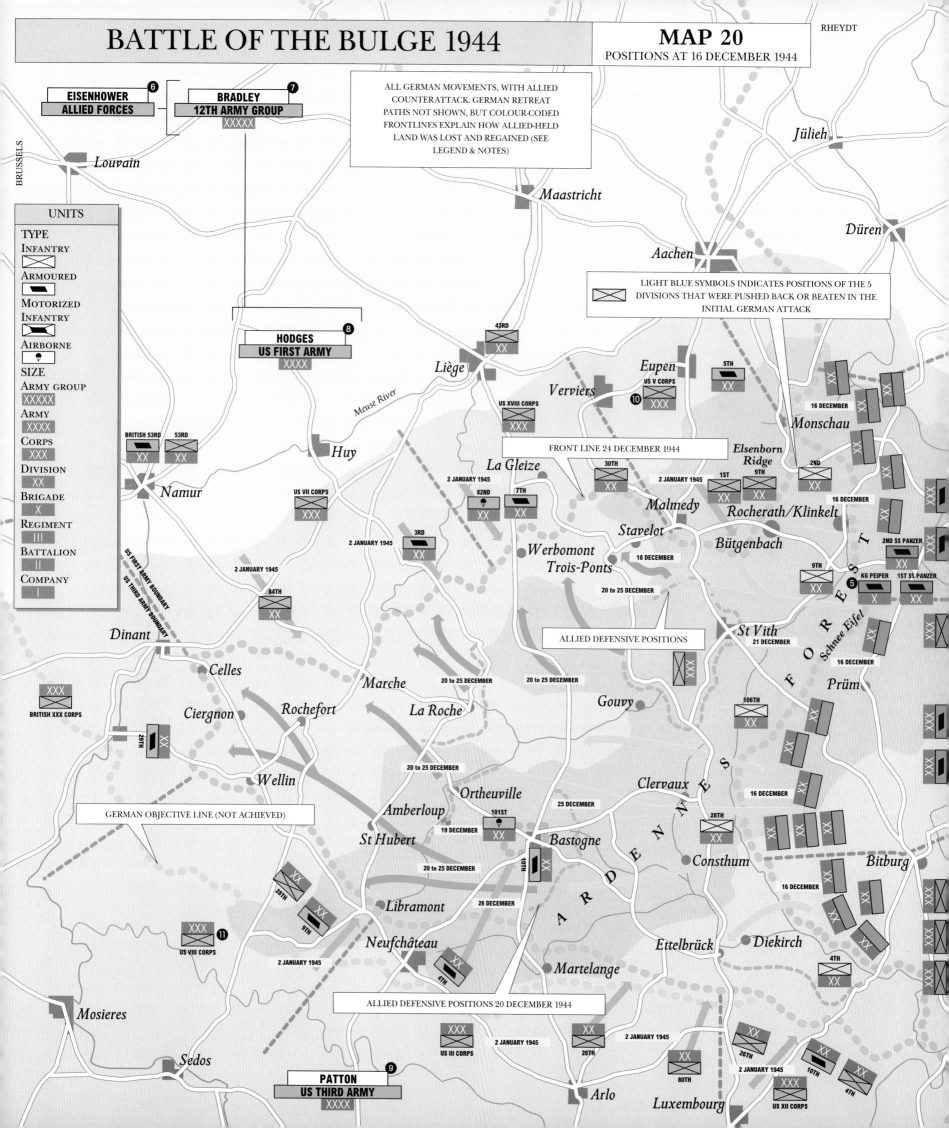

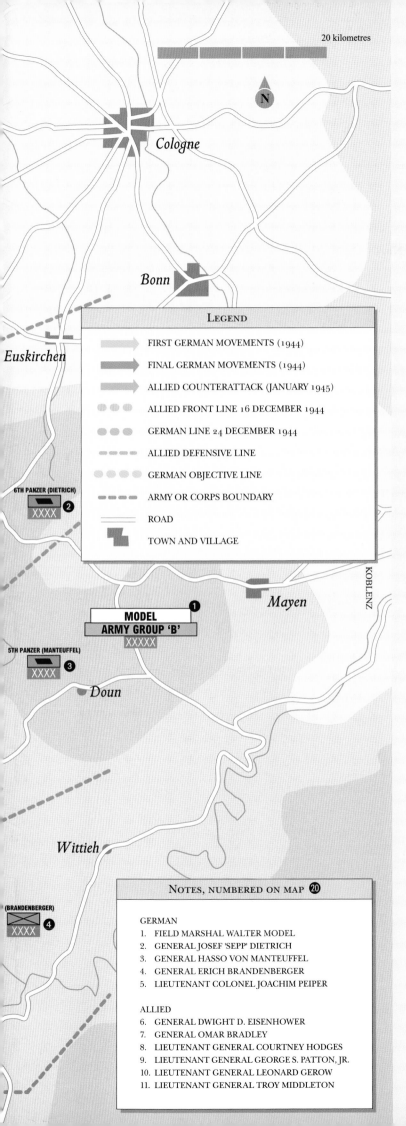

- La Roche-en-Ardenne–Musée de la Bataille des Ardennes, 5 Rue Châmont, B-6980 La Rocheen-Ardenne. Tel 32 (0) 84 41 17 25. www.batarden.be.
- Bastogne–American Memorial and Bastogne Historical Center, Colline du Mardasson, B-6600 Bastogne. Tel 32 (0) 61 21 14 13. www.bastognehistoricalcenter.be.
- Bastogne–Maison Mathelin, 1 Rue G. Delperdange, B-6600 Bastogne. Tel 32 (0) 61 21 17 58.
- Poteau-Ardennen Poteau '44 Museum, 22 Poteauerstrasse, B-4780 Poteau-St. Vith. Tel 32 (0) 80 217425. www.museum-poteau44.be.
- Camp Elsenborn–Truschbaum Museum, Camp Elsenborn, B-4750 Butgenbach. Tel 32 (0) 80 44 21 05. www.camp-elsenborn.be.

BATTLE OF THE BULGE TIMELINE

6 June D-Day – Allies land at Normandy.

16 September

  Hitler reveals the Ardennes plan to his generals.

17 September–4 October

  Allied failure in Operation Market Garden.

2 November–13 December

  Hürtgen Forest campaign.

16 December

  05:30 German offensive begins. American defences in the Losheim Gap are overwhelmed, but both 'shoulders' of the German attack stall early.

  Evening Eisenhower releases 7th and 10th US Armored divisions from reserve to halt German advance in the centre.

17 December

  Morning German 18th Volksgrenadier Division complete the encirclement of the US 106th Infantry Division.

  Afternoon Malmedy Massacre.

  Night Eisenhower releases the 82nd and 101st Airborne divisions from strategic reserve.

18 December

  11:45 Peiper is stopped at Trois Ponts.

19 December

  07:00 101st Airborne reaches Bastogne.

  16:30 8000 troops of the 106th Infantry Division surrender.

21 December

  St Vith falls.

22 December

  McAuliffe rejects German demand for surrender.

23 December

  Fog lifts, allowing aerial resupply of Bastogne. Remnants of Kampfgruppe Peiper retreat on foot.

25 December

  Final German attack on Bastogne repulsed. 2nd Panzer Division reaches Celles.

26 December

  US 4th Armored Division relieves Bastogne.

28 January 1945

  US troops retake all territory lost in the German attack – the 'bulge' is erased.

ABOUT THE AUTHORS

MICHAEL RAYNER is coordinator of the Battlefields Trust, a UK-based charity dedicated to the preservation, interpretation and presentation of battlefields. He has a lifelong interest in history, particularly military history, and has written on a range of military subjects, including *English Battlefields* (Tempus, 2004). He is currently Deputy Head at Langley School, Norfolk.

MARTIN MARIX EVANS has written more than 20 books on military history, ranging from the English Civil War to the Anglo-Boer Wars and the two World Wars. His work is informed by first-hand accounts, on-the-ground research of the fields of battle and his regard for visual evidence: maps, drawings and photographs.

CHRISTINA HOLSTEIN was originally trained as a lawyer, but her prime interest has always been military history. She is an acknowledged expert on the WWI battlefields of Verdun, the Argonne Forest and the St Mihiel Salient. In addition to writing, she leads tours of the battlefields for individuals and groups. Her first book was published in 2002.

COLONEL JOHN HUGHES-WILSON is President of the Guild of Battlefield Guides and one of Britain's leading commentators on intelligence and military history. He broadcasts for BBC television and presented the *What If?* series. His books include *The Puppet Masters, Military Intelligence Blunders* and *Blindfold and Alone.* He is an Archives Fellow of Churchill College Cambridge and the Royal United Services Institute, Whitehall. As an Infantry and Intelligence Corps officer, he saw active service in the Falkland Islands, Cyprus, Arabia and Northern Ireland as well as the political jungles of Whitehall and NATO.

DR CHRISTOPHER PUGSLEY, a former New Zealand infantry officer, is a Senior Lecturer in the Department of War Studies at RMA Sandhurst where he lectures on the evolution of warfare. He is the author of some 14 works and has twice been shortlisted for the Templer Gold Medal and Montana New Zealand Book Awards. His most recent book is *Operation Cobra* in the Battle Zone Normandy series.

ANTHONY HALL has edited books on military history for 15 years and has been a full-time writer on the subject for the last five. He has contributed extensively to histories of the American Civil War. He is the author of several books on D-Day, and has co-authored another on the history of body armour. He lives in Staffordshire, England.

DAVID RATTRAY has a BSc Honours degree in entomology and spent a period managing game reserves and working with wildlife in southern Africa. He and his wife built Fugitives' Drift Lodge in 1989, from where often distinguished guests set out to visit the battlefields of Isandlwana and Rorke's Drift. He is a Fellow of the Royal Geographical Society.

MAJOR JASON R. MUSTEEN is an active duty officer in the United States Army and has held various command and staff positions in armoured and armoured cavalry units. He holds MA and PhD degrees in history from Florida State University and is currently an assistant professor of military history at the United States Military Academy at West Point.

MAJOR JOSHUA MOON, PhD., teaches Military History at the United States Military Academy at West Point. Although his specialty is the Napoleonic period, he has led cadets and Army officers in several trips to Gettysburg and Antietam National Battlefields.

MICHAEL HANNON served in the Royal Artillery from 1950 to 1968. His natural interest in military history was enhanced while attending the Staff College, Camberley. He then worked for an international computer company until 1990. A third career began when he and his wife founded Grapeshot Tours, offering theme holidays 'in the footsteps of the Emperor Napoleon'.

BILL NASSON is Professor of History in the Department of Historical Studies at the University of Cape Town. He is the author of *Abraham's Esau's War* (Cambridge, 1991), *The South African War 1899-1902* (London, 1999) and *Britannia's Empire* (London, 2004). His current project is a history of South African participation in the First World War, to be published as *Springboks on the Somme.*

CHRISTOPHER L SCOTT was Head of Education for The Royal Armouries at the Tower of London. He is a trustee of The Battlefields Trust and The Guild of Battlefield Guides. He writes and lectures in military history, and was the editor of *Battlefield* and a re-enactment Lord General.

INDEX

PHOTOGRAPHIC CREDITS

Copyright © in photographs rests with the following photographers and/or their agents as listed below. Key to Locations: t = top; tl = top left; tr = top right; b = bottom; bl = bottom left; l = left; r = right; c = centre. (No abbreviation is given for pages with a single image, or pages on which all photographs are by the same photographer.)

AM=Airborne Museum; akgi=akg-images, akgi/LL=akg-images/Laurent Lecat; CdV/F/BM=Chateau de Versailles,France/www.bridgeman.co.uk – CdV/F/BM/G=Chateau de Versailles,France/www.bridgeman.co.uk/Giraudon – CdV/F/BM/L/G=Chateau de Versailles,France/www.bridgeman.co.uk/Lauros/Giraudon – PC/BM=Private Collection/www.bridgeman.co.uk – GMW/E/BM=Gurkha Museum,Winchester,England/ www.bridgeman.co.uk – NMGW/C/BM=National Museum & Gallery of Wales,Cardiff/www.bridgeman.co.uk – CdVF/BM=Chateau de Versailles,France/ www.bridgeman.co.uk – AH/WM/UK/BM=Apsley House/The Wellington Museum,London,UK/www.bridgeman.co.uk – L/P/F/BM/G=Louvre,Paris,France/www.bridgeman.co.uk/Giraudon – ANC/UK/BM=Army & Navy Club,London,UK/www.bridgeman.co.uk – DDG/P/USA/BM=David David Gallery,Philadelphia,PA,USA/www.bridgeman. co.uk; BMAL=The Bridgeman Art Library; BT= www.battletour.com; CH=Christina Holstein; FWW/GWW=First World War.com/The Great World War: A History edited by Frank A. Mumby; FWW/CPHWW=First World War.com/Collier's New Photographic History of the Worlds War (New York, 1918); G=Gallo Images/Gettyimages.com; GS!=Great Stock!; B/C=Bettmann/CORBIS; BM/C=Buddy Mays/CORBIS; C=CORBIS; HDC/C=Hulton-Deutsch Collection/CORBIS; MN/C=Michael Nicholson/CORBIS; MSt.MS/C = Michael St. Maur Sheil/CORBIS; NGC/C=National Gallery Collection/CORBIS; PV/C=Paul Velasco/CORBIS; RK/C=/Richard Klune/CORBIS; SA.M;E/C=Sally A. Morgan; Ecoscene/CORBIS; WK/C=Wolfgang Kaehler/CORBIS; IK=Ian Knight; IWM=Imperial War Museum; LMM=Liberty Memorial Museum; LoC/OS/TH=Library of Congress/O'Sullivan,Timothy H; LoC/BNPAG=Library of Congress/Brady National Photographic Art Gallery; LoC/BCWPG=Library of Congress/Brady Civil War Photograph Collection; LoC/GA=Library of Congress/Gardner, Alexander; LoC/VJ=Library of Congress/Vannerson, Julian; LoC/CWP=Library of Congress/Civil War Photographs; LoC/SWM=Library of Congress/Smith, William Morris; LoC/CWP=Library of Congress/Civil War Photographs; ME=Mary Evans; MJM=Major Joshua Moon; OM=Oorlogs Museum; PA=Photo Access

1		GS!/C	35	l	AH/WM/UK/BM	64	t	GS!/B/C	100		G	130		GS!/C
2-3		GS!/B/C	35	r	L/P/F/BM/G	64	b	MJM	101		GS!/HDC/C	131		GS!/B/C
4-5		GMW/E/BM	36		ANC/UK/BM	65		GS!/WK/C	102		LMM	132		GS!/C
6-7		NMGW/C/BM	37		PA	70-71		BMAL	103	l	FWW/GWW	133		GS!/B/C
8		GS!/DM/C	42-43		DDG/P/USA/BM	72		GS!/HDC/C	103	r	ME	138		GI
9		GS!/RK/C	44		LoC/OS/TH	74		IK	104		GI	139	l	akgi
10-11		PC/BM	46	l	GS!/C	75		GS!/HDC/C	105		GS!/WK/C	139	r	GS!/B/C
12		CdV/F/BM	46	r	LoC/BNPAG	76		IK	108		LMM	140		akgi
13		GS!/B/C	47		GS!/DM/C	77	t	GS!/PV/C	109	bl	FWW	141		GS!/B/C
14	l	GS!/MN/C	50		GS!/C	77	b	IK	109	r	FWW/CPHWW	144		GS!/C
14	r	G	52		GS!/C	78		IK	109	t	LMM	145	l	ME
15		GS!/B/C	53	l	GS!/C	79	t	G	110		GS!/MSt.MS/C	145	r	GS!/B/C
18		CdV/F/BM/L/G	53	c	LoC/BNPAG	79	b	IK	111		CH	146		GS!/C
19	l	akgi/LL	53	r	GS!/BM/C	84-85		akgi	114		GS!/MSt.MS/C	152		AM
19	r	ME	56	l	LoC/GA	86		GS!/HDC/C	115	l	FWW/CPHWW	153		GS!/B/C
20		ME	56	c	GS!/C	87		OM	115	r	IWM	154		IWM
22		akgi	56	r	LoC/GA	88	l	ME	116		IWM	155		AM
23		BT	57		LoC/GA	88	c	GS!/C	117		LMM	158		GS!/C
26		ME	58		PC/BM	88	r	GS!/HDC/C	122		GS!/MSt.MS/C	159	t	GS!/C
27	l	GS!/NGC/C	59	l	LoC/VJ	89		GS!/HDC/C	123	tl	GS!/C	159	b	GI
27	r	CdV/F/BM/G	59	r	LoC/CWP	92		GS!/HDC/C	123	tr	FWW/LVC	160		GS!/C
28		PC/BM	62		LoC/SWM	93		OM	123	b	LMM	161		GS!/C
30		ME	63	tl	LoC/BCWPG	94		akgi	124		GS!/B/C			
31		G	63	tr	LoC/BCWPG	95		G	125		GS!/SA.M;E/C			
34		AH/WM/UK/BM	63		LoC/GA	98-99		PC/BM	128-129		GS!/C			